A History of the Holocaust

From Ideology to Annihilation

Rita Steinhardt Botwinick

Florida Atlantic University

Prentice Hall
Upper Saddle River, New Jersey 07458

Library of Congress Cataloging-in-Publication Data

Botwinick, Rita S. (date.)
    A history of the Holocaust : from ideology to annihilation / Rita
Steinhardt Botwinick.
        p.   cm.
    Includes bibliographical references and index.
    ISBN 0-13-099292-5 (paper)
    1. Holocaust, Jewish (1939–1945)   I. Title.
    D804.3.B68   1995
940.53'18—dc20   95-43323
                                                           CIP

Editor in chief: Charlyce Jones Owen
Acquisition editor: Sally Constable
Editorial/production supervision, interior design,
    and electronic page makeup: Mary Araneo
Editorial assistant: Justin Belinski
Buyer: Nick Sklitsis
Cover concept: Alicia Botwinick
Cover designer: Bruce Kenselaar

 © 1996 by Prentice-Hall, Inc.
Simon & Schuster/A Viacom Company
Upper Saddle River, New Jersey 07458

Printed in the United States of America

10 9 8 7 6 5 4 3 2 1

ISBN 0-13-099292-5

PRENTICE-HALL INTERNATIONAL (UK) LIMITED, *London*
PRENTICE-HALL OF AUSTRALIA PTY. LIMITED, *Sydney*
PRENTICE-HALL CANADA INC., *Toronto*
PRENTICE-HALL HISPANOAMERICANA, S.A., *Mexico*
PRENTICE-HALL OF INDIA PRIVATE LIMITED, *New Delhi*
PRENTICE-HALL OF JAPAN, INC., *Tokyo*
SIMON & SCHUSTER ASIA PTE. LTD., *Singapore*
EDITORA PRENTICE-HALL DO BRASIL, LTDA., *Rio de Janeiro*

A History
of the Holocaust

For My Husband
The Man for All My Seasons

For My Husband
The Man for All My Seasons

Contents

Chapter 2
The World That Was Annihilated

Chapter 3
The Nazi Rise to Power

Chapter 4
Careers Built on Hate: Hitler and His Instruments

Chapter 5
Germany under the Nazis   86

Chapter 6
German Jewish Life to 1939   106

Chapter 7
Hitler's War   126

Chapter 8
From Ideology to Isolation

149

Chapter 9
The Genocide

172

Chapter 10
Resistance and Rescue

198

Obstruction in the U.S., 211   American Jewry, 213   The War Refugee
Board, 213   The Danes, 214   Setting the Scene, 215   The Plot, 215   The
Escape, 216   Accounting for the Danish Achievement, 217   Some
Concluding Thoughts, 217

Preface

This text is the product of two decades of teaching the history of the Holocaust, both at high school and university levels. It is intended to meet the need for a single volume on the topic and is based to a considerable extent on lecture notes developed over the years. Classroom experience dictated the dimensions of the book. Its content is based not on what students are supposed to have learned before they enter this class, but what they apparently have not learned. For example, Holocaust study cannot be grasped without some knowledge of the dynamics of prejudice, or of propaganda, or of the events of World War II. Many of the questions that arose in class discussions provided insight into specific insufficiencies or difficulties experienced by the students. In the same manner, areas of particular interest were also revealed. Whenever possible, these indications were incorporated into the course material. In the jargon of the day, this is a consumer-friendly book.

This history of the Holocaust does not purport to contain everything important on the subject. It is a throughway, paved for fast travel, with a beginning (causes), a middle (events), and an end (results). Many specifics of the panorama remain hidden. Users of the book are expected to design their own incursions for a closer view. The enormous amount of material on the Holocaust permits a wide variety of individual or small-group research into the human and historic facets of the Holocaust.

It is precisely the wealth of Holocaust documents, the great body of scholarly investigation, the remarkable number of personal memoirs, and the quality and quantity of literature on the Holocaust which persuaded the author to refrain from adding such material to the text. It is presumed that minimally, the course requirements will include readings from several primary sources and selections from the literary and personal outpourings in print. At the end of the book, the reader will find a selected annotated bibliography to aid in the choice of additional reading.

Finally, a word on terminology. A commonly used description of the murder of six million Jews during the twelve years of Nazi control of Germany is *extermination*. This, the author believes, carries the unfortunate connotation of killing vermin and unwanted pests and should not be used to describe the mass murder of innocent men, women, and children. Not everyone agrees that *Holocaust* adequately designates the event; the word, derived from the Greek, *wholly burnt*, gives a supernatural connotation to a man-made tragedy. Also, the media has trivialized the expression by overuse. No single word, however, would be adequate to describe the Nazi assault on the Jews of Europe. For lack of a better word, this text will refer to the Jewish genocide as the Holocaust.

Dear Student

You have elected to study the history of the Holocaust. The subject matter you will investigate will make some extraordinary demands of you. You may encounter difficulties in dealing with the facts. The events, even related in the sparest terms, will pull you into a world of such savagery, you may doubt their truth. But facts cannot be altered to ease our offended sensibilities. This text deals only with material exhaustively researched and confirmed by responsible scholars.

The intellectual mastery of the material might well be less exacting and less distressing than its emotional impact. The murder of six million, men, women, and children within four years cannot help but arouse your compassion and your abhorrence. You will become angry, sometimes depressed, and occasionally, much too rarely, experience a moment of elation. The students who have preceded you, most often used *disturbing* as the word which best described their reaction to this study.

From early childhood on, we are taught that problems have solutions. The investigation of the Holocaust, however, raises more questions than it answers. It is frustrating indeed, to have a wealth of data which nonetheless do not add up to a credible explanation. For example, we know a great deal about the political, social, and economic activities of Germany in the 1930s and 1940s, yet we cannot explain how it was possible that Germans, renowned for their culture, perpetrated the greatest crime in history. We have a profusion of information pertaining to the wartime conduct of the Allies but we are left troubled and dissatisfied with their replies when we ask: Why did Western nations do so little and so very late to save the victims? Nor can we gain any comfort from the response of the Christian churches when we inquire: Where was the spirit of Christ when you stood by as the innocent were killed in unprecedented numbers? And perhaps most disquieting of all is the search for the power and the mercy of God during the Holocaust. Is it enough to say that His ways are mysterious and beyond human comprehension?

As the history of the Holocaust is rigorous work for the students, so it is for the instructor. But the rewards are commensurate to the effort. No other teaching assignment results as frequently in the highest accolade an educator can receive: Students who declare that their newly acquired knowledge has made a difference in their thinking and behavior because henceforth it will be impossible for them to ignore or turn away from the suffering of others.

Best wishes,

R.S.B.

A History
of the Holocaust

Introduction

No longer is it necessary to mount an elaborate defense for the teaching of Holocaust history. The great number of secondary schools and college courses on the topic give ample evidence that educators see the annihilation of six million Jews by the National Socialist regime of Germany as an event which must be understood if we hope to make sense of the forces shaping the post–World War II world. As this century closes, it is evident that the right to destroy unwanted segments of the population is still claimed as a valid policy by existing governments. The Kurds, the Laotians, the Vietnamese, and the Croats are among those who can testify to the continued inhumanity of man to his fellow man. The dilemma remains: How can we foster such revulsion against policies of genocide so that no authority could implement them? In the arsenal to fight future destruction of so-called undesirables, education, slow, tedious, and undramatic, remains the primary weapon.

The Holocaust is more then a Jewish tragedy, it is a human disaster of unprecedented proportions. It represents a watershed which diverted Western history into uncharted channels. Mass murder by lawful decree reached extraordinary dimensions when organizational skills and technical expertise combined in the service of irrationality. Concepts of civilization held dear by many generations were undermined and/or shattered. The terrible waste of life and property of World War I had begun the process of questioning the rule of reason; the Holocaust removed all doubt. Such cherished ideals as rationalism and progress as the certain basis for societal conduct were swept away. Intellect and goodwill accounted for nothing in the Nazi era. Enlightened self-interest became but another discarded concept. The road leading to the man-made hell of Auschwitz was filled with the rubble of logic and Christian mercy.

The Holocaust raised profound questions for the religious communities. Where was God? To that cry, there is no answer. But what of the institutions built around religious faith, the rich and powerful churches? They failed the challenge to practice what they preached. The distance between the promise of Christianity and its performance has always been great, but the Holocaust revealed the enormity of the gulf. Love for mankind, and for children in particular, is the essence of Christ's teaching. Where were the churches when over a million Jewish children were killed? The fact that even after the disclosure of the death camps the major denominations carried on "business as usual" constitutes a serious indictment of Christian leadership. Only now, and only rarely, do church congregations hear sermons on the meaning of the Holocaust. The lesson still unlearned at the very core of the Judeo-Christian tradition is contained so succinctly in the words uttered by Cain, "Am I my brother's keeper?"

The uniqueness of the Holocaust is well established. Although the annals of history are replete with suffering and even genocide of other minorities, the Holocaust stands alone in its utter senselessness. Excluding the carnage inflicted in the heat of battle or during a civil disorder, when governments waged war against their own citizens, they did so in order to achieve some desired end. The destruction of the Jews, however, was itself the sought-after goal. The factories of death did not promote national synthesis or religious unity. They did not enrich the state nor advance its borders. They did nothing to promote public security. The gas chambers were not installed to effect the submission of a rebellious segment of the population. Rather than enhancing the economy, the Holocaust deprived Germany of hands and minds desperately needed in the conduct of the war. The belief that the killing of the Jews would provide the nation with the vaunted Aryan racial purity and master race superiority was never more than a fantasy. One look at Hitler and his most prominent henchmen makes a mockery of Goebbels's own propaganda. We cannot know how many of the killers actually believed in the concept of German Aryan superiority, but we do know that every German schoolchild was taught the *Voelkerwanderung,* the centuries-long trek of Goths, Vandals, Huns, et al., across the center of Europe. The preservation of ethnic purity on the crossroads of such vast population movements is clearly mythical.

The scale of Holocaust killings within the brief time of a mere four years, is another aspect which makes Holocaust history unique. Concentration camp commanders reported to their superiors with pride that they fulfilled or exceeded their death quotas. The chilling cruelty and efficiency of the mass murders are sometimes called a return to savagery. But that is inaccurate. The man in the SS uniform who wanted to impress Himmler with his effectiveness was not a savage, he was an official of an established authority. He did not run amok with a knife between his teeth, he sat in his office and issued orders. He may or may not have felt any emotion about his task. Certainly he did not view himself as a criminal. The murders committed within his sight and sound were carried out by a complex machinery involving many government agencies, cooperation from German industry and technology, and the apparent acquiescence of considerable segments of society. The impersonal nature of modern warfare had reached inside the barbed wire surrounding the ghettos and the camps.

The number of civilians murdered by the Nazis, six million Jews and five million Gentiles, has no known equal. The human imagination cannot envision so many corpses. The unlimited power of a twentieth-century dictatorship was unleashed to expedite the killings. The scope of the operation required total commitment to the task. Scientific data emanating from laboratories had to be applied to resourceful innovation on the sites of execution. Considerable organizational skill was required to keep the flow of victims coming into the killing centers. Disposing of so many thousands of bodies every day was a task which caused camp commanders moments of despair. The administratiors of German medicine and justice had to become tools of perversion. From the Nazi point of view, the business of mass murder was successfully carried out. When Allied armies closed in on a defeated Germany, Hitler consoled himself that at least he had won his war against the Jews.

Great historical events are generally subject to divergent points of view. Issues are rarely clear-cut; differences of interpretation are expounded, defended, and attacked. But the Holocaust does not lend itself to a debate on pros and cons. There is no justification, no defense, no rejoinder, there is only sorrow and guilt. Except for a small lunatic fringe which refuses to deal with facts, the world acknowledges that the Holocaust happened and that it stands as a landmark of man's faculty for evil. The amount of evidence is staggering. This would be true even if only German sources were available. The intent and execution of the so-called "final solution of the Jewish question" simply cannot be argued. German governments since the fall of the Third Reich have acknowledged the culpability of their predecessors and have attempted to indemnify Holocaust survivors.

Although there can be no question concerning the reality of the Holocaust, a number of specific issues have given rise to conflicting points of view. Several such questions are treated in this text. The author offers no conclusions, but it is hoped contrasting assessments will stimulate discussion and research. Among the controversial topics are the following:

1. Was the Holocaust the inevitable final step of centuries of anti-Semitism, a pogrom of unprecedented magnitude, or was Hitler's persecution a distinctly different assault?
2. The Intentionalists and the Functionalists debate whether the destruction of the Jews had been Hitler's plan from the inception of his ideology or whether the death camps evolved as an outgrowth of events not originally foreseen by the Nazis.
3. Did the victims go to their deaths like the proverbial sheep to the slaughter or was there significant Jewish resistance to the implementation of the Final Solution?
4. Was Germany under the Nazi regime a goose-stepping, Hitler-*heil*ing monolith of obedience or was support for the dictatorship less widespread than generally believed?
5. What were the reasons for Hitler's assault against the Jews? Was he motivated by desire for their alleged wealth? Fear of their supposed power? Or were the reasons for his hatred psychological rather than political in nature?
6. What and when did the world learn of the Holocaust? What actions resulted from such knowledge? Could earlier intervention have averted the magnitude of the disaster?
7. How should the operation of the *Judenraete* be evaluated? Did work of these

councils of elders, who carried out the day-by-day administration of the ghettos, help or hinder the SS in the commission of their assignments?

8. How was it possible for some individuals, usually designated as the Righteous Gentiles, to remain true to their ethical standards? Though small in numbers, their courage and integrity testify that even in the midst of evil, there was goodness. What inner forces compelled them to risk their own lives to save others?

This book is a history text. It is a narrative that delineates what happened, where, how and when, to whom and by whom. The essentially philosophical *why* remains an enigma. Holocaust study is humbling; it raises as many questions as it answers. Nevertheless, or perhaps because it teaches without answering the ethical dilemma it poses, the Holocaust provides a vehicle for true learning. Information is not enough. Only when attitudes are changed and behavior is altered does education happen. The Holocaust reminds us that civilization is but a thin veneer, that political apathy is very dangerous, that prejudice is a cancer that can infect and destroy an entire national body, that persuasive powers, even charisma, are no substitute for character, that there are no quick fixes for serious problems, that to mind one's own business when others are oppressed is to participate in that injustice, and that each of us has to bear a responsibility that *"never again"* becomes the watchword for the protection of the powerless everywhere.

Chapter 1

The Nature of Prejudice and the Historic Roots of Anti-Semitism

The Holocaust, that is, the destruction of the lives of two-thirds of the Jews living in Europe, is history's most dreadful instance of mass murder at the direction of a legally constituted government. Hitler had achieved power lawfully and his party platform clearly defined its anti-Jewish prejudice. The Holocaust was the fruition of a national policy based on a hatred so deadly that it judged an entire people to be unworthy of life.

In recent decades, it has become socially acceptable to admit to prejudice. "Everybody doesn't like somebody," demonstrates an attitude of tolerance toward intolerance. Perhaps, if the suffering which results from prejudice were better understood, such indulgence for a basically destructive emotion would fade.

SOME DYNAMICS OF PREJUDICE

Prejudice may be defined as a stereotyped negative attitude toward a person or group which is unrelated to factual information. It is a learned reaction, not an instinct. Most often it is acquired at such a young age that the adult cannot recall its origin. Investigations by psychologists and sociologists confirm that dislike of a particular people generally predates school age. Thus, prejudice is instilled before the child is capable of independent reasoning. The capacity to make critical judgments usually begins at eight years old; before that age, children accept without question the values and mores of those in authority, usually mothers and fathers. It is not necessary for parents to verbalize their own prejudices, children will absorb them indirectly from their environment. Obviously, parental praise for conforming to acceptable attitudes or punishment for opposing them, will very effectively reinforce prejudice. The tone of voice, the dismissing gesture of the hand have a language of their own which children understand very well.

The bias accepted during early childhood is difficult to change even in the face of contrary information. We tend to cling to our heritage even when certain aspects of it are harmful to ourselves and others. To hold a view which does not reflect the echoes of home seems a denial, almost a rejection of one's family. It is not true that prejudices result from a disagreeable or frightening personal experience although such an experience may confirm an existing negative disposition. If all unpleasant encounters were to create prejudice, all of us would be ill disposed toward the rest of the world.

PERSONALITY AND PREJUDICE

People who are exposed to similar attitudes during childhood, however, do not always or necessarily develop similar biases. The environment is not the only determining factor in the creation of a prejudiced person. Individual personality differences play an important role in the willingness to accept or reject the social inheritance of one's culture.

Research in the field has ascertained that those possessing authoritarian personalities are particularly predisposed toward denying equality to selected ethnic groups, usually minorities. Such individuals exhibit a strong need to act in conformity with conventional values; their thinking is marked by inflexibility, and they are preoccupied with concerns regarding status. Authoritarian personalities are obedient to a fault toward strong authority figures and uncritically subservient to those in command. Ideals of law and order rank high among their priorities. Usually the attitude toward groups deemed to be inferior is one of disdain, dislike, even hatred. Psychiatrists hold that aggressive emotions, which remain pent up in dealings with dominant members of society, are then released in offensive behavior toward weaker groups or individuals. Harm done to the weak is viewed as well deserved as expressed in "they had it coming."

The origins of the authoritarian personality are believed to arise in childhood. An upbringing that emphasizes obedience in a household wherein children may be seen but not heard creates traits of apparent acquiescence and buried resentments. These characteristics are retained in adulthood. A convenient target for the hidden antagonism is the ethnic minority. Since some biases against particular racial and/or religious groups are already well entrenched in most cultures, even in our day, prejudice continues to exist.

Bigots look for the company of other bigots. Their frustration seeks redress by depreciating others. They are followers rather than leaders and seek the approval of their peers. Fellow bigots, expressing similar feelings, legitimize this prejudice. In fact, when intolerance takes on the aura of communal acceptance, it offers comfort and cohesion to a group. Thus, it is possible to speak of institutionalized prejudice which is characterized by hostility by consensus. "Everybody hates. . . ." The bond of hatred is as strong as the bond of love.

Prejudiced people avoid examining their intolerance by stereotyping. Their victims are invested with flaws that then form a negative picture in their minds. Facts are of little importance, while oversimplification is typical. For example, if their bias is directed against Jews, often the single characteristic used to taint all Jews may be their supposed avarice. Any positive traits of the Jews are ignored or denied. In the event that Jews show themselves to be charitable, a rationalization is offered to explain the "exception to the rule." If presented with statistics proving that Jews as a group donate more money to the needy than other groups, the information is likely to be judged erroneous or suspect.

ECONOMICS AND INTOLERANCE

Though ever-present, prejudice may vary considerably in its outward manifestations. One is tempted to compare its fluctuations with those of the stock market. When the economy is strong and expectations high, bias remains tacit and relatively subdued. Scapegoating, close kin of stereotyping, is concealed. But when economic hardships reappear, so will overt prejudice. Those with authoritarian personalities find it almost impossible to accept any blame for their own failures or reverses. They need to alleviate their disappointments, whatever their true origin, by placing the guilt on the targeted minority. The greater the frustration, the more intense the culpability of the hated group. During periods of severe suffering, it is possible to inflame prejudice into violence. If governmental and/or religious leaders countenance or encourage the population to hold a minority responsible for their ills, then passion is given free rein and bloodshed and plunder result. The pogroms perpetrated against generations of Russian Jews illustrate the point rather too well.

When prejudice progresses into brutality, resulting atrocities are nearly always committed by groups of people. The sense of solidarity gives license to individuals to commit criminal acts they would never perform alone. Even after the exhilaration of action has worn off, guilt is so diffused among the perpetrators that it invokes justification rather than self-condemnation. The outrages committed by the Ku Klux Klan after the Civil War are a familiar example of criminality by consent. Far from viewing themselves as arsonists and murderers, Klan members wrapped themselves in the flag of Southern patriotism. Theirs was a "crusade," begun in an era of great suffering in the South. History, unhappily, is replete with examples of prejudice degenerating into inhumanity.

RACISM

Prejudice wears many masks. Most familiar to Americans is the scourge of racism. Until the second half of this century, the myth of Negro inferiority was given official sanction. The struggle to right that wrong has been long and painful and continues to the present day. Racism was also a basis for the dark chapter of American relations with the Native Americans as the destructive policy of subjugation and decimation was incited, legalized, and enforced by the government. Cloaked as patriotism, the crimes committed by governments are always most difficult to face and eradicate. Racism usually has economic components; the free or cheap labor of blacks made cotton king. The vast lands of the Amerinds stood in the way of the vaunted manifest destiny of the nation. In the case of European Jews, pogroms were invariably accompanied by looting. Expediently, greed drowned out the voice of conscience. Whether racism is made more palatable when camouflaged as a religious obligation, as a political necessity, or as an economic essential, its appeal persists.

THE COSTS

How many potential contributions to the welfare of mankind were never realized because prejudice closed the doors to potential achievements? We will never know how much beauty, how much talent in art, music, literature, science, statesmanship, and industry are squandered.

Social scientists have studied the reactions of both the victim and the victimizers of negative stereotyping. Both pay a dear price. The oppressor does not remain untainted by his power. In order to hate blindly, it is necessary to become blind. The act of prejudging another person on the basis of inherited misinformation demands the suspension of independent thought and much freedom of action. Bigots must stifle the impulses of compassion for those who suffer at their hands. In order to affirm and reaffirm the illusion of their superiority, they must play elaborate games of self-deception. They will search for distorted religious and ethnic confirmation from any source to rationalize or sanctify their bias. That still, small voice that whispers to them in the quiet hours must be silenced. The greater the injustice of their conduct, the greater the amount of psychic energy required to maintain the facade of their superiority.

The victims of prejudice are, of course, deeply affected. They may lose more than personal freedom; they may lose their sense of wholeness, the self-respect that is so vital to human well-being. Actually or seemingly powerless, they may accept society's rejection as justified. The resulting self-depreciation will aggravate their doubts. A sense of worthlessness coupled with hopelessness will weaken any efforts to bring about change. The need to fit in, to be identified with the majority seems an almost universal human trait. The herd instinct, especially strong during teenage years, exerts a life-long influence. When the dominant element in society excludes a minority, individuals often react by questioning, even denying, the values of their own culture. For example, lightness of skin may be valued higher than darkness; aquiline noses are straightened and names changed to echo those of the majority; Jews convert to Christianity for nonreligious reasons; tradition is abandoned as ill-suited to the main currents in society. In the process, pride in one's heritage, so essential in a well-adjusted personality, is traded for the plastic image of conformity.

Oppressed people respond in a variety of ways to their condition. They may withdraw from contact with the majority. Why chance the possibility of pain and rejection? So, they stay within their own circle and create islands of self-contained neighborhoods. Communication with the world outside is restricted to economic dealings; children are protected as long as possible from realizing the hostility they will encounter outside the ghetto. Residents of the community insulate and culturally separate themselves from the larger environment. Often they resent and reject any proposal leading toward acculturation, speak their own dialect, exaggerate their differences by wearing unconventional clothing, or by having unusual hairstyles. Although these reactions are understandable, they obviously widen the gulf between peoples.

It requires no imagination to recognize that a common reply to prejudice is prejudice. Hate begets hate and the gulf of misunderstanding deepens. Generalized accusations are thrown into the air to further poison the atmosphere. "All white people are racist," "all Christians believe that Jews killed their Lord," "all men want to dominate women," "all Arabs are double-dealing," and so on. Stereotyping and scapegoating are handed down from one generation to the next as if these were worthy gifts.

DEFENSIVE TECHNIQUES OF SURVIVAL UNDER SLAVERY

The history of slavery in the United States and the degradation of the Jews of Europe during the Middle Ages and early modern era present a case for interesting comparison and contrast. Both groups were denied the opportunity to enter the mainstream of society. Both were exploited and denied legal, social, political, or economic equality. Both experienced physical insecurity and psychological debasement. Both were regarded as separate but not equal. Both developed techniques of survival which involved creating a dual personality; one for the world within and another for the world outside.

The slave showed his master a protective and deceptive face of obedience. Bitter experience had taught him the futility of expressing either his rage or his despondency. So, his overseer saw humility, the bowed head, and shuffling feet. Beneath the surface were dreams, sometimes actual plans of revenge, conspiracy and revolt. One mode of expressing defiance was to deny the master the fruits of his labor by working as little and as slowly as possible. Thus was born the myth of ineptitude and sloth; the portrait of the lazy, stupid Negro was the price paid for this tactic. Some slaves resisted their masters by means of sabotage, escape to free territories, and even self-mutilation. When hopelessness became overwhelming, suicide became the final epithet that expressed the anguish of captivity.

Slaves were not permitted into the schoolroom and thus were denied the consolation of education. Christianity and its promise of heavenly redemption provided solace for many of the oppressed. Prayer and song fused into expressions of hope and liberation in the next world. Perhaps the most devastating characteristic of American slavery was its denial of the right to a stable family life. Children did not belong to their mothers, they belonged to their masters. The role of the father was minimal and the owner, not the father, was responsible for providing the young with the necessities for survival. The heritage of the single-parent household, headed by the mother, is a familiar phenomenon. In this respect, the Jewish experience presents a sharp contrast.

ORIGINS OF ANTI-SEMITISM

Anti-Semitism is a modern word for an ancient malignancy. One could begin to trace its history at various points, for example, from the date of the final destruction of Jewish national life in 70 C.E. The Diaspora, that is, the scattering of Jews throughout the world, began after the Romans grew impatient with the rebellious Hebrews. What a strange and stubborn people were these Judeans. Their monotheism would not permit them to conform to the customary worship of the Roman emperors. They would die, even at their own hands, rather than break the commandments of their God. A jealous God, who would not take his place amid the pagan pantheon. The moral demands of that nameless, invisible, all-powerful, all-knowing God were onerous indeed. He commanded his people to adhere to ethical standards no other god required. Sacrifices and festivals in his honor did not suffice; this deity invaded the daily life, the very thoughts of his worshippers. Jewish rituals, such as circumcision and food taboos, although burdensome and isolating, did not diminish the zealous attachment of the Jews to their God and his law. Few conquests under Roman dominion were as troublesome. After decades of seething unrest, the Roman legions in 79 C.E. destroyed the center of Jewish life in Palestine. Most of the population was dispersed, the Diaspora had begun.

Unlike many other ancient civilizations, the Jews maintained their religion and their culture despite the loss of their national entity. Not until 1948, when the state of Israel was reestablished, did they regain their homeland. For nearly two thousand years, they lived as strangers in other people's lands.

The dominance of ancient Rome in the Middle East was replaced by that of Arab peoples. After the founding of Islam by Mohammed in 622, his followers swept across the Arabian Peninsula, fusing warring tribes into a religious nation. The wave of conquests extended to include the eastern regions previously under the sway of the now-disintegrated Roman Empire. It is interesting to note in view of the present Arab-Israeli conflict that Islam did not force the subjugated peoples into conversion. The Jews of the Middle East lived in general peace and harmony under their Islamic masters. When, in the eighth century, the Moslems advanced into Iberia, large numbers of Jews settled in Spain. The Golden Age of Jewish culture was celebrated during the Moslem domination of Spain. Jewish achievements in the areas of literature, science, philosophy, and religion remain monuments to an age of greatness realized by virtue of the bygone spirit of Islamic tolerance.

CHRISTIANITY AND THE JEWS

The emergence of Christianity as the primary faith of Europe marks the most important cultural revolution of the West. For the Jews, this was a disaster. As United States citizens, we accept the fact that it is possible for people of different faiths to live side by side. This concept, however, is a recent and wonderful New World innovation.

The European record reveals an appalling history of mankind's inhumanity to the men and women who pray in different houses of worship. In the name of the Prince of Peace, religious persecutions and wars of atrocious cruelty were carried out. All major Christian denominations, however, were united in their animosity toward Jews.

For nearly two thousand years, Jews stood outside the Christian world. They were outcasts because they denied that Jesus was the messianic son of God. Jewish devotion to the faith of their ancestors was construed as a challenge and an insult to Christianity. The conversion of the Jews was, and to some degree remains, an abiding missionary objective. Although the stream of modern anti-Semitism is fed by national and racial tributaries, religious motivation provides the strongest and deepest current.

JEWISH ROOTS OF CHRISTIANITY

The historic Jesus, as opposed to Jesus as the object of religious veneration, is shrouded in mystery. He wrote nothing at all. Later descriptions of his life were more concerned with his message than with his biography. We know that he was born in the year 7 B.C.E. during the reign of the Roman client King Herod. The meager material available acknowledges the fact that Jesus was born a Jew, that he was baptized in a public ceremony by an Essene preacher named John. The Dead Sea Scrolls, found in a cave near the Dead Sea in 1947, gave researchers a more detailed picture of the life and times of John and Jesus. The Essenes were one of several Jewish sects which arose in response to the challenges of Greco-Roman civilization. Its members lived ascetic, pious lives in communities isolated from the world. John exhorted all who would listen that the coming of a Messiah was imminent. God's promise of a heavenly kingdom on earth, which had been prophesied earlier by Isiah, would soon be fulfilled. In preparation for that day, all sinners must repent. The contrite and penitent congregation then took part in a ritual of washing away past transgressions in the river Jordan. Among those thus baptized was Jesus.

Jesus began his work as a teacher when he was thirty. The best summary of his ministry is contained in his Sermon on the Mount: God's blessing has nothing to do with earthly wealth and power; the meek, the children, the peacemakers, those who live in purity and act justly will receive mercy from the heavenly father. He stressed God's love and spoke of the power of faith. His teachings urged men and women to obey the law and to share their worldly goods. The empty rituals which had replaced the core of Jewish ethics were an abomination to Jesus who preached that spiritual, not material, values secured eternal life. He lived during a sterile time in Jewish life when zealots, moderates, and conservative factions bickered endlessly with each other and with their Roman overlords. According to Jesus, the promise of salvation, that is, life after death, was open to all who lived righteously. His insistence that neither social standing nor worldly success won any merit before the throne of God offended the established power structure of the day.

Jesus' ministry probably lasted only one year, three at most, and the influence he exerted in that brief time leaves us in awe. Because Jesus referred to himself as the Son of Man, as the Son of God, and as King, it is impossible to reconstruct how he viewed his role. The fact that he urged his followers to observe certain practices, now called sacraments, might imply that perhaps Jesus wanted more than to merely reform the Jewish faith. However, the institution of Christianity was not his work. The church was founded by his disciples after his death.

Jesus lived and died a Jew. In his own words, he had not come to destroy the law, but to fulfill it. He acknowledged that he was indeed the long-awaited Messiah and journeyed to the capital of Jerusalem to make a public pronouncement. There he denounced the leaders of the community for their hypocrisy and their materialism. The crowds following him probably grew in size and anger. The priests, who were responsible to the Romans for keeping the peace, feared that a rebellion was in the making. In that event, the Roman legions would descend upon the population and a general slaughter would ensue.

LEGACY OF THE CRUCIFIXION

The crucifixion of Jesus plays an important role in the history of anti-Semitism. Few events have caused as much controversy and misrepresentation. It is generally accepted that Jesus was arrested on the night of the last supper, the Seder meal he shared with his closest disciples. It is also believed that Judas of Kerioth betrayed him and that the Sanhedrin, the Jewish court, indicted him and turned him over to the Romans for punishment. Accounts of the trial relate that when questioned Jesus replied that yes, he was the Messiah. This assertion confirmed the threat he allegedly posed to the tranquillity of the city. Since the Sanhedrin had no jurisdiction over capital offenses, as were blasphemy and messianic claims, the prisoner was probably turned over to the Roman procurator, Pontius Pilate. The biblical account of Pilate's reluctance to condemn Jesus was written almost a century later and may or may not be correct. We do know that the Romans used crucifixion, an agonizing death, routinely for political offenders.

The Romans, who had a great deal of experience in dealing with revolts, and the priests, who had encountered numerous messianic claims, surely believed that with the death of the Nazarene, his influence would fade away. After all, these so-called Christians (translated "followers of the messiah") were a mere splinter group in the total body of Judaism. Its early congregants were Jews, observant of the law but differing from the majority in their conviction that Jesus was indeed the Messiah. The teachers of this small sect, led by the apostle Peter, lived according to the principles of brotherly love and shared their possessions. The only rituals they observed which were not part of established Judaism were baptism and the Lord's Supper. The most revolutionary doctrine concerned their certainty that Jesus had ascended to heaven after three days in his tomb and that he would return once again to earth to establish his kingdom.

THE NEW FAITH ESTABLISHED

The beginning of the amazing transformation of Christianity from a gentle brotherhood to a triumphant, worldwide church was largely the work of a Roman citizen named Saul of Tarsus, Paul of the New Testament. An observant Jew until his maturity, he experienced a vision which changed his life. He became, in fact, the founder of the church by detaching the Christian sect from the parent faith. Paul made the far-reaching decision that the Gentiles, that is, the pagan world, should be converted to the faith of Jesus. The church would be *catholica*, that is, "universal." No longer was Jesus the king of the Jews, but the king of the entire spiritual cosmos. Paul's missionary zeal took him through much of the Roman world and his success was extraordinary. In the process of that expansion, the simple faith of Jesus was elaborated and given doctrinal foundations. He developed the dogma of grace, that special gift whereby God reclaims sinners. All mankind is sinful, ever since Adam and Eve disobeyed God in the Garden of Eden, but God is merciful and through the martyrdom of Jesus, redemption is possible. Death can be defeated. Those who share faith in Jesus will receive everlasting blessedness in the world entered after death.

Paul preached equality to the downtrodden, humility to the powerful. He viewed the faith of his fathers as preparatory to Christianity; Jesus was sent to keep God's promise. But, according to Paul, the carpenter from Bethlehem was not an ordinary human being, nor was he merely a great prophet; He was God's own beloved son. Paul ordained that circumcision was no longer required of converts. Dietary restrictions were removed. The concept of the Messiah of the Old Testament was revised. In the Jewish tradition the redeemer would bring into existence an earthly realm of peace and plenty; the Pauline view elaborated on the heavenly kingdom to reward the just. And thus the distance between Jews and Christians widened. It became impossible for converts to be both Jews and Christians at the same time. Most of the inhabitants of Palestine were won over to the new religion. The final rupture in the threat connecting the old and the new faiths took place when Paul, toward the end of his life, broke with Judaism. From the foundations he had constructed, other fathers of the church would erect a mighty edifice.

THE EARLY CHURCH

In the centuries following the crucifixion of Jesus, the Christian church spread across the Roman Empire and beyond. It evolved from a small band of persecuted martyrs to a privileged position. When Roman authority collapsed in the fourth century, the Christian church prevented the complete breakdown of civilization. As the influential Roman bishops assumed leadership on questions of orthodoxy, the papacy developed. Ultimately, Popes assumed preeminence in all religious, legal, economic, and organizational affairs of the church.

The simple exhortation of Jesus to love one another was superseded by an elaborate theology, dogma, liturgy, and a comprehensive body of law. The decrees of the church were obeyed by paupers and kings, its spiritual promise valued beyond earthly honors, its wealth greater than that of emperors. In a world where ordinary people spent their brief lives in ignorance, toil, fear, and warfare, the medieval church offered solace and stability. In an age that forgot how to read and write, where the legal system had disappeared, the Christian church stepped in to fill the void. The human need for beauty was realized by the building of magnificent cathedrals which often became focal points for the revival of towns. Monks, nuns, and priests provided hospitals, schools, and charity. The power of excommunication brought sinners to conformity, be they emperors or beggars. Not until the sixteenth century, when monarchies challenged the economic and political power of the church, was it possible to rival its authority.

The church was often challenged by heresies, doctrines which were declared unsound and unacceptable by the orthodox hierarchy. The bloody chapters of religious persecutions within the faith need not be examined here. It is sufficient to be aware of the consummate determination of the church to root out doctrinal opposition. Disobedience to a specific article of faith was (and is) a grievous sin. Tolerance, as we interpret that concept today, was not viewed as benign, not even acceptable, because diversity in religious thought was seen as destructive. When one considers the ferocity expended in the persecution of heretics, the dilemma of the Jews living in the Christian world becomes self-evident.

MEDIEVAL CHRISTIANITY AND THE JEWS

The history of the Jews in Europe during the Middle Ages is a blot upon Western civilization. During the Age of Faith, the church was suzerain over man's life from conception to beyond the grave. Every political, economic, and social activity was measured against the yardstick of religious conformity. Faith had hardened into the absolute conviction that Christianity, as interpreted by its hierarchy, was the truth, the only truth. No compromise was possible. Those, like the Jews, who insisted on clinging to the error of their ways, were condemned to live in degradation. Their very misery was then exploited as a sign of God's punishment for their rejection of Christ. Isolation, economic ruin, false accusations, extortion, expulsion, and murder were mechanisms employed in the attempt to eradicate the faith which once had been practiced by Jesus. From the Crusades, which began at the close of the tenth century, until the Age of Enlightenment in the 1700s, hatred for Jews was a common denominator within the diversity of European culture. Although the waves of persecution varied in time and place, they were always threatening and sometimes crested into orgies of destruction.

The Crusades were a watershed event in Jewish history. With the exception of the Iberian Peninsula, the religious fervor which aroused hundreds of thousands of Christians from every walk of life to fight for their faith was a calamity for non-Christians. The movement, lasting nearly two hundred years, combined religious and martial zeal. The original motivation, to free the Holy Land from the occupation of the Islamic Turks, was adulterated by the expectation of material benefits, such as wealth, land, trade, and freedom from serfdom. The cry, "God wills it" commanded the faithful to join the war against the infidels. But why wait to fight the non-believer in Jerusalem; there were Jews close at hand. Moslem or Jew, it made no difference. Salvation was believed to be the reward for slaying either. And killing Jews had the advantage of gaining their possessions right here, right now. As the disorganized bands of the first Crusade pillaged their way across Europe, mobs attacked the Jewish communities wherever they found them. Even when church leaders tried to restore order, they could not be stayed. The events in the German city of Worms serves as a case in point.

About eight hundred Jews had been granted refuge in the Episcopal palace of that city. Those Jews who had remained in their homes were butchered, stripped of their clothing, and left naked in the streets. Many corpses had been mutilated. The bishop protested but was unable to exercise any control. The rioters then attacked the palace. In two days they overcame its defenders and proceeded to murder all but a few of the surviving Jews of Worms. Many committed suicide before the killers could reach them; a handful were spared because they consented to be baptized. The cities of Speyer, Mainz, and Cologne fell victim to similar mania.

PERSECUTIONS CONTINUE

Long after the Crusades had disintegrated into movements fueled by avarice and the Moslems had retaken the Crusader enclaves, the hatred for the Jews persisted. The term *accursed race* became interchangeable with Jew. From the eleventh to the eighteenth centuries, Jewish history in Christian lands is one of affliction interspersed with periods of violence. The kings of France, England, and later Spain, as well as various German and Italian princes, ordered their expulsion. Always they left as paupers. Sometimes they were permitted to return upon payment. German rulers contrived a new indignity— their Jews were designated as chattel—possessions of the monarch who could sell their services and their future taxes. Conversion granted release from the bitterness of Jewish life. It was offered again and again, a simple ceremony that would gain the Jews acceptance and greater security. Against all reasonable persuasion, few Jews left their faith. The stronger the push toward the baptismal font, the greater the unwillingness of the Jews to accept Christianity.

There were voices raised imploring the Christian world to show mercy and sanity, even from within the Christian hierarchy, but these were whispers drowned by the shouts of the many. The Jews had evolved into all-encompassing scapegoats. They surpassed all others, such as devils and witches, in their culpability for every ill besetting mankind. The church had burdened them with deicide and Easter week was a period of particularly brutal Jew baiting. When Christians blamed the Hebrews for the crucifixion, all generations for all time were condemned to share the guilt. Thus all atrocities were thinkable and doable. Among the most notorious accusations were the following:

> Jews were infidels, that is pagans.
>
> Jews required Christian blood to prepare their Passover Matzos; the mysterious death or disappearance of a Gentile child served as "proof" of a ritual murder.
>
> Jews desecrated the host (wafer used during mass) by piercing it with sharp instruments, in that way reenacting the killing of Jesus.
>
> Jews were Satan's allies and assistants.
>
> Jews poisoned wells.
>
> Jews caused the Black Death which annihilated one-fourth or more of the population of Europe.
>
> God hated the Jews as was evident by their miserable state.

PROHIBITIONS AND PROSCRIPTIONS

The certainty that Jews were an abomination was translated into decrees designed to prevent contact between the Christian majority and the infectious Jewish minority. Church councils, Popes, temporal rulers large and small competed in enacting orders designed to disconnect Jews from Gentiles. Within their own communities, the Jews could work as they pleased, but commerce with the world beyond was severely restricted. A partial list includes these regulations:

> Jews were prohibited from joining guilds, thus making it impossible for them to engage in nearly all business and manufacturing activities.
>
> Jews could not practice medicine or law.
>
> Jews could not own land.
>
> Jews could not hold public office.
>
> Jews could not leave their homes during Easter week.
>
> Jews were forced to wear distinctive badges or hats in public to alert any unsuspecting Christians.
>
> Jews could not intermarry with Christians.

The most restrictive laws concerned the separation of housing, the ghetto. By forcing Jews to live in their own always crowded and miserable quarters, their isolation was assured. Whether walled in or barricaded by fences, they lost contact with events outside their narrow world. There were a handful of exceptions who might be exempt from ghetto life: Jews who achieved prominence in import-export trade, in banking, or as special "court Jews" in service for a ruler. Their unique circumstances did not diminish the general poverty of the ghetto dwellers. Despised and segregated, degraded and fearful, the once-proud people of the Bible reacted to their plight with both negative and positive responses.

EARLY GHETTOS

Within the confines of their ghettos, they sought solace in their faith, their rituals, their prayers, and their holy books. During the long years of isolation and ostracism, they delved into the mysticism of the kabbalah, followed false messiahs, and quibbled endlessly over minutia in the interpretation of holy texts. In the process, they became alienated from nature, from sports, from play. Children were taught to avoid confrontations, especially with non-Jews. Eastern Jews spoke and wrote in their own language, a mixture of obsolete German and Hebrew that was called Yiddish. The descendants of the Spanish expulsion developed Ladino, a jargon of Spanish and Hebrew. In the presence of Christians, they were humble, compliant, and often obsequious. These mannerisms tended to aggravate existing prejudices.

The ghetto also engendered more positive responses. The Jews developed a deep sense of community, a bond forged of shared suffering. Life was centered around the synagogue. Religious, communal, and personal life overlapped. In a world of illiteracy, most male Jews could read and write. The most valued leader of ghetto society was its religious sage and pious teacher. The family was the source and center of joy and pride. Any inroads from the world outside were guarded jealously. A child who married a Christian was mourned as dead; his or her name was extinguished forever from the community. Tradition hardened into a hidebound and stifling precision which was dictatorial even in such matters as clothing and the shape of beards. The world beyond the ghetto was viewed with suspicion and superstition. Hatred was repaid in kind.

It is estimated that toward the close of the Middle Ages there were three million Jews in the world. Nearly all lived in designated quarters in villages and towns. If local law permitted, they eked out their livelihoods in such trades as peddling, money-lending, innkeeping, or tailoring. Often, restrictive laws were not enforced, giving the Jews moments of economic revival. Not every ruler who exercised dominion over the Jews held them in contempt, and pockets of liberality survived even during the worst of times. Holland was such a haven, welcoming or at least accepting many of the Jews expelled from Christian Spain in 1492.

The medieval social order was rigidly fixed. It consisted of the nobility, serfs, the clergy, and a small middle class which provided necessary goods and services. But Jews did not fit into the established categories. It was necessary to accord them their own classification which varied from place to place. Usually, the lord or king in control of their communities considered them as personal wards. He could grant his Jews the right to remain or expel them from his realm. He could treat them with moderation or harshness as he saw fit. His main interest concerned the taxes collected from the ghetto population by its own governing body. Within its walls, the Jews were autonomous. They elected their own leaders, established schools, held trials, made laws, and administered the welfare system. Ghettos were places of squalor and overcrowding, often with a scant water supply. To the Gentiles, they represented an alien and evil world. In actuality, the vast majority of Christians never saw a Jew. If they did, his bedraggled appearance was likely to confirm the dehumanizing prejudices which had been instilled so early and so thoroughly.

JEWISH SURVIVAL

While their pariah status was justified as "God's will," the Jews as a people were permitted to survive. The church did not advocate their physical destruction. According to the New Testament, the Second Coming of Christ will be preceded by the conversion of the Jews and their in-gathering in the Holy Land. General acceptance of that doctrine hung as a double-edged sword over the ghettos; the Jews could live in wretchedness so that baptism would have the greatest possible appeal.

THE REFORMATION

The Middle Ages seemed stagnant, but actually, slow and uneven change was taking place. The Renaissance, that surge of renewed intellectual activity, was fueled by the spirit of inquiry. All things were open to question. An obvious sphere for conflict and confrontation was the church. The uses and abuses of its temporal and spiritual power had long disturbed men of courage and vision. Their pleas and warnings went unheeded. The church labeled them heretics, excommunicated them, and condemned them to die at the stake. Not until Martin Luther did a reformer succeed in defying the Catholic church. In the process, he destroyed the unity of Western Christendom. The legacy of that revolt is pertinent to our commentary on Jewish life.

Luther came from within the church. He was an Augustinian monk and professor of theology at the University of Wittenberg. His personal crisis of conscience led him to protest the church's solicitation of money known as indulgences. He opposed the practice because it led to the belief that donations could serve as a substitute for penance and thus shorten or ease the suffering of the soul in purgatory. His first act of protest was modest enough, ninety-five theses detailing his objection to indulgences. The complaint was written in Latin, hardly a cry of revolt to incite the masses. He nailed the text on the church door at Wittenberg in 1517 and hoped it might lead to a debate within the church. His aim was simply to stop indulgences because their sale made false promises to sinners. But economic and political abuses of the church had readied great numbers of the faithful to confront a wide range of religious practices. Common folk and princes, the elector of Saxony prominent among the latter, united in a spiritual opposition which had economic and political bases as well. Rulers begrudged the great wealth flowing from their countries to Rome. A developing national consciousness resented papal interference in political issues. As pressure mounted for and against Luther, the rift between his doctrines and the established tradition widened. A man of great personal courage, Luther stood by his convictions. Unlike some of his predecessors who died at the stake, his excommunication did not prelude a fiery death. Instead, his supporters multiplied. The split grew into a chasm that could not be crossed.

The establishment of Lutheran churches in northern Germany was followed by other religious revolts. Once the principle was fixed that individuals, not the dictates of the Popes, may interpret the Bible, a bewildering number of sects evolved. The meaning of every phrase, every word of the holy texts was weighed and measured. Differences in interpretations became the basis for the founding of many denominations, each claiming to be in sole possession of the truth.

LUTHER AND THE JEWS

In his relationship with Jews there are two Luthers. The early idealist believed that the long-sought conversion of the Jews was imminent. The Renaissance with its cosmopolitan humanistic views had ushered in a period of relief from the most severe oppression for some Jews. But even as the scholars studied the Gospels with renewed vigor, often leaning upon the Jewish erudition of the Old Testament, the pressure to convert the Jews intensified. Luther understood the Jewish origins of Christianity and had rebuked the Catholic hierarchy for its shameful treatment of the Jews. His pamphlet *Jesus was Born a Jew*, published seven times in one year, reminded Germans of the debt the Christian world owed the Hebrew people. He fully expected that his antipapal position, his admonition that Jews be treated with kindness, would result in massive conversions. When it became clear that the Jews refused to give up their faith even for his revised edition of Christianity, Luther became violently anti-Jewish. Some of his tirades could be mistaken for Nazi propaganda. His later pamphlet, *Concerning the Jews and their Lies,* repeated the worst stereotyped vilification. He urged civil authorities to raze the synagogues, confiscate Jewish property, and drive that obstinate people from the land. Unhappily, it is the second message that took hold.

AGE OF REASON USHERS IN CHANGES

The winds of change blew gingerly indeed over the Jewish communities in Europe. Here and there doors were cracked open to allow them the opportunity to thrive. Poland had been such a haven, Holland too, and England under Cromwell. Generally, the greater acceptance of Jews, though not on a status of equality with Christians, was in keeping with the growing rationalism of the educated classes. Monarchs were eager to encourage the new materialism of the seventeenth and eighteenth centuries. The accumulation of wealth promised power and Jews could be helpful in creating wealth through trade and industry. Guilds and their restrictions were losing their hold on the manufacture of nearly everything, thus opening opportunities for outsiders. The irrationality of keeping the Jews in degradation and then cursing them for their degraded position was blatantly unjust and some clarion voices were raised in defense of brotherly love. Among the most influential was Gotthold Ephraim Lessing, the German dramatist whose *Nathan der Weise* made a valiant appeal for tolerance. A Prussian counselor named Christian Wilhelm von Dohm wrote extensively in support of political, economic, and educational equality. Several of the French philosophers, notably Montesquieu and Mirabeau, vehemently decried the inhumanity of the archaic Christian posture concerning the Jews.

The masses, as always, found the attacks on their cherished prejudices intolerable. The Age of Enlightenment shed little light below the level of the salons frequented by the intellectuals. Even so, the forces impelling a reshaping of society were irrevocable. The middle class would no longer be denied its rightful place. In the great upheaval of the French Revolution the vestiges of feudalism were eradicated, absolute monarchy was shattered, and outdated class distinctions were demolished. The storm sweeping away so many inequities of the past turned out to be a windfall for the Jews.

THE FRENCH REVOLUTION

The changes wrought by the French Revolution stirred the entire continent. Despite the excesses of the Reign of Terror and the short-lived Republic, the principle of *Egalite* took root; not social equality, that is a fantasy at best, but equality before the law. For the first time in Western European history, the privilege of citizenship was granted to all regardless of religion. In the wars that followed the execution of Louis XVI, victorious French troops exported the ideals of the *Declaration of the Rights of Man* far beyond France. Holland was the second nation to tear down the restrictions under which large numbers of their comparatively prosperous Jews lived.

The phenomenal career of Napoleon Bonaparte extended the French influence across the German states. In his personal attitude toward the Jews, Napoleon vacillated between his desire to integrate them into French life and his acceptance of the well-worn allegation that Jews were incapable of patriotism. In total, his influence was salutary for the Jews. He went so far as to summon an assembly of Jewish notables in order to assure them of his willingness to lift them from their distress in return for their loyalty. Wherever French guns boomed during the Napoleonic Wars, ghetto walls fell; wherever members of Napoleon's family assumed the thrones vacated by fleeing rulers, Jews emerged from centuries of humiliation. There were instances of popular participation in the spirit of enlightenment as in the city of Bonn where the Christian citizenry broke down the ghetto walls and jubilantly linked arms with the Jews. No matter, after Waterloo many of the liberties were rescinded by the restored, so-called legitimate monarchies.

THE AGE OF REACTION

When Napoleon was exiled, so were many of the changes he had forced upon Europe. The victors met at Vienna in 1814 and tried to undo the novel concept that people are citizens, not subjects. The Age of Reaction attempted, and temporarily succeeded, in reversing the advances toward a more liberal society. Many of the old restrictions

were reestablished by kings who assumed that whatever they did, they were fulfilling God's grand design. Reactionary autocrats supported one another as they muzzled every vestige of freedom of expression. Between 1815 and 1848, liberal ideas were anathema and Prince Metternich's firemen were quick to extinguish the flames of freedom wherever in Europe they might flare up. For most of the Jews, the Age of Reaction reinstituted the medieval darkness of isolation and confinement, of ghettos and indignity, and of injustice and humiliation. From the Balkans across the German lands to the Spanish shores, the specter of misery reappeared in the narrow *Judenstrassen* ("Jew streets") of Europe.

But bayonets could not long hold back the impetus for change. The fear of the conservatives was justified; there was political ferment in the air. Inequalities accepted for hundreds of years were no longer borne in silence. The French Revolution had spread the message that the present need not define the future. The revolutionary spirit, long simmering beneath the surface, broke through. The German and Italian people, denied an independent national existence by the powerful Austrian hegemony, exploded into revolutions. Wherever suppression had become intolerable, from Spain to Poland, revolts shook the old order. Nationalistic enthusiasm combined with hopes for liberal constitutional governments. Patriotism was translated into rebellion in 1830 and, on an even wider scale, in 1848. Only England was spared. British governments, through evolutionary legislation, had permitted power to shift from the aristocracy to the middle class. By the middle of the century the full rights of citizenship were inherent privileges of all Englishmen, regardless of their denominational affiliation.

INDUSTRIALIZATION

The mid-century uprisings on the Continent met with partial success. Even repressive rulers such as the Prussian king and Austrian emperor, though able to regain control, could not resist the spirit of change for long. Another revolution, not political, but of the means of production, meshed with the political ideals of the age. The economic upheavals of the Industrial Revolution changed what people did and what people thought. The rising middle class derived its power from wealth, not nobility of birth, and economic strength became the lever for social and political changes. Fledgling capitalist systems needed men of ability in the boardrooms and the factory. The religion of either the financial director or the operator of a new machine was irrelevant. If the Jews were willing and able to promote the industrial development of the nation then they deserved political equality. Had not certain privileged Jews, such as the House of Rothschild, proven that they possessed great business acumen? The admirers of the Rothschilds and their peers created a new myth (based on the exception rather than the rule), namely that Jews were born with the ability to make money. The facts of the matter are that the age of the machine, of the investor, of improved quantity and quality of goods opened the door of opportunity to a wide range of underprivileged classes. Among these were the Jews, for so many centuries shut in behind the emotional and physical walls of oppression. Upon their liberation, Jews streamed into the main currents of whatever nation they called home. With the rest of the citizenry, they helped to lay the foundations for the glories and pitfalls of the industrial age.

THE TWENTIETH CENTURY

As the nineteenth century ended, western and central European Jews were found among factory owners and workers, teachers and shopkeepers, artists and inventors. Some grew rich, others achieved middle-class status, while many struggled to escape their hand-to-mouth existence. Politically, their affiliations ran the gamut from the radical left to the moderate center to the conservative right. When public schools admitted Jewish children, the youngsters quickly adopted the vernacular, dressed and behaved according to the dominant cultures, and imitated the patriotic fervor of their contemporaries. The process of assimilation was underway. Complete acculturation, however, was never achieved. Only if Jews gave up their faith could they hope to "belong," and even then, converts found that many social obstacles were still in place. Among the Jews, differences arose concerning the desirability of abandoning their separate and insular lives. Traditionalists opposed any cultural blending for fear of diluting the religious covenant. The split over how much or how little of the heritage could or should be forfeited split the Jewish people into Orthodox, Conservative, and Reform Judaism. The great majority in all three denominations remained within the faith although conversions and intermarriage became more common among the young.

The Renaissance and the Reformation, the emergence of the middle class, and the Industrial Age were movements whose influence stopped along the east German boundary. In Poland and Russia, the development of a modern economic system was delayed, perhaps by a hundred years. We have not yet dealt with the problems of Jewish survival in the Slavic states during the modern era even though the greatest numbers of Jews lived there. The population of these nations suffered immense losses during the Holocaust. As a result, an entire culture disappeared. By the middle of this century a unique civilization had been destroyed, a topic that will be discussed more fully in the next chapter.

It would seem that the practice of anti-Jewish prejudice in central and western Europe should have ended when it became clear that industrialism had no religion and that progress required the energies and abilities of all. Concern over the welfare of the soul after death had given way to goals of an earthly heaven of justice and plenty. Increasingly, Jews entered the political and economic fabric of Western society. Yes, there were pamphlets and speeches claiming that the Jews could never give up their evil habits, but such denunciations found few echoes. The wrenching Dreyfus trial in France was viewed by many as the final gasp of a briefly revived anti-Semitism. Continued Jew baiting in Russia and Poland was deemed clear evidence of the cultural retardation of the benighted Slavic states. For Western Europe, assimilation seemed the key to an ancient enigma.

THE NEW ANTI-SEMITISM

Appearances, however, were deceiving. The roots of prejudice were still intact beneath the surface. Different circumstances demanded different modes of venting familiar hatred. The new face of the old aversion was less crude, less obvious, yet was as emotionally charged and as antiintellectual as the old religious bias. Modern anti-Semitism (the term was introduced in Germany by Wilhelm Marr in 1873) emanated from two related sources: nationalism and racism. The advocates of the former claimed that Jews are forever aliens who cannot share the national ethos; the advocates of the latter asserted that innate racial differences prevent Jews from assimilating with the superior cultures of the host countries. Although several aspects of twentieth-century discrimination were new, the old religious bias fed this new strain of an old virus.

The forces of nationalism, stirred up since the Napoleonic Wars, had moved from rhetoric to action. The unifications of Germany and Italy and the expulsion of the Turks from nearly all European lands had been inspired by the passion for independence and self-determination. Pride in one's national heritage swelled everywhere and in many regions a competitive destructive chauvinism developed. In Germany, sentimentality merged with patriotism to create a mystical concept of Germanness. To be German, truly German, was not a mere matter of citizenship, it was based on an obscure sense of commonalty. Germanic blood and the German soil created an ethos that could not be acquired. Only birth could infuse that *Voelkisch* spirit. Clearly, Jews could only pretend to be German. Their creativity and contributions in science, philosophy, literature, art, and music notwithstanding, they were forever alien.

Thus, German nationalism was burdened with a romantic quixotic aspect from the outset. Johann Gottlieb Fichte was its founder who, in 1807, proclaimed the German ethos to be the seedbed for human perfection. His aim was the unification of the many small German states into a single nation. The fact that Fichte argued against Jewish emancipation gave ammunition to several generations of anti-Semitic politicians. The composer Richard Wagner wrote with a poison pen when he tirelessly and obsessively denounced the Jews. His revulsion seemed to stem from a conviction that German culture was "Judaized," that is, corrupted by Jews. His operas gloried in the Teutonic past, particularly its paganism. The notion that the German essence, sometimes described as its innermost or *Voelkisch* nature, went beyond the commonalty of language, and heritage was reinforced by other German nationalists. Friedrich Ludwig Jahn (1778–1852) favored the natural, simple German peasant over the educated civilized man who was disconnected from the soil. Georg Wilhelm Friedrich Hegel, founder of the philosophy of dialectics, taught at the University of Berlin during the first quarter of the nineteenth century. He glorified the state and asserted that heroes function outside the norm of history even as they trample on ordinary mortals. A similar note was struck by Heinrich Treitschke who persuaded innumerable Germans that unquestioning homage to the state was the ultimate expression of love and duty. Friedrich Nietzsche, whose works were later shamelessly misrepresented by the Nazis, formulated theories concerning super-

A column of victims moving toward the gas chambers in Auschwitz. (Public domain.)

human individuals who stood high above slavish parliaments and democratic disputations. Clearly, a broad stripe of antiintellectual and antidemocratic sentiment was woven into the German fabric.

ANTI-JEWISH RACISM

German nationalists, whose writings appear rather muddled and self-serving, had laid the groundwork for anti-Jewish prejudice. How deeply did their ideas affect and infect the ordinary German citizen? Certainly liberalism did not vanish but the rational concept of the equality of all men ran counter to the irrationality of the idealized and idolized state. Obedience to that state was tantamount to obedience to a higher spiritual power. From the unification of Germany in 1871 to the rise of the Nazis to power in 1933, the forces of modernism, that is, progress through material advancement, would be challenged time and again by advocates of a return to the past. It is not surprising that the barometer of anti-Semitism rose and fell in tandem with political and economic tensions. Jews, who could never belong to the world of German blood and soil, were held responsible for socialism, for capitalism, for stock market failures, and for labor strikes. Politicians from the ultra-conservative right could always count on considerable public approbation when they targeted the Jews for the painful economic dislocations which are part and parcel of industrialization. Anti-Semitism had become a cohesive political issue. The foes of democracy and reform had discovered the vote-getting appeal of rationalization over rationalism.

In the center of Nazi policy stood hatred of Jews. Hitler could call upon the past for instruction. He merely intensified and broadened the attack; history supplied the essential components. Every crudity of Nazi misrepresentation had antecedents. For example, had not Theodor Fritsch, in his *Handbook of Anti-Semitism,* asserted in the 1880s that Jesus was not a Jew but was of Aryan descent? Jews as a species were intrinsically vicious and irredeemable. If Germans valued their own survival, they must destroy the accursed race.

The division of peoples into races—black, white, yellow—originated as a system of classification unrelated to any value judgments. Race became racism when innate characteristics were assigned by pseudo-scientists to biological attributes. The fact that science does not recognize the existence of either a German or a Semitic race was nullified and a new nationally correct biology was accepted. Eighty years before Hitler became chancellor, the English son-in-law of Richard Wagner, Houston Stewart Chamberlain, influenced millions of readers with his treatise entitled *Foundations of the Nineteenth Century.* He wrote as an oracle, not as an historian or a scientist; his analyses were not the consequence of research, but of insight. He "knew" intuitively that he had discovered nothing less than the mechanism shaping the historical process. According to Chamberlain, the essential traits of a people were determined by the proper or improper racial components in their biological heritage. Creativity, moral fiber, character, and so on were fixed by the interplay of specific racial strains. The Jews, of course, were a hopelessly bastardized race, while the Germanic people were the inheritors of inevitable greatness. Once the theory had been stated, Chamberlain had no difficulty in corroborating it with many hundreds of pages of selected evidence.

The racist writers of the nineteenth century did not advocate mass murder, yet their theories played an important role in the coming disaster. Perhaps they exaggerated German greatness because, compared to France and Great Britain, the German people had underachieved. Perhaps they hoped to inspire nationalism strong enough to defeat the particularism which delayed unification until 1871. Whatever the motivation, they fostered the conceit that destiny had placed the German people on a separate course from the rest of the world.

Without Hitler, biological racism would have been worthy of a footnote in the history of modern Europe. The theory of an innate, unalterable Jewish malignancy would have remained the purview of quacks. But hatred for the Jews was at the core of Hitler's obsession. The claim that Jews were the bearers of an organic genetic flaw enabled the Nazis to rationalize their nearly successful genocide. If Jews were despicable merely because they did not accept Christ, then conversion or emigration were possible options for their survival. If Jews could not share the enigmatic ethos of the Teutonic past, the German *Volk,* they might be excluded from official positions or be subjected to social discrimination. But if the taint was congenital, if simply by their presence Jews contaminated society, then only their obliteration could make the world safe. And that delusion underlies the tragedy of the Holocaust.

Chapter 2

The World That Was Annihilated

The picture of families arriving at the Auschwitz death camp and lining up in front of the gas chambers to await their turn is one of the most familiar images of the Holocaust. The victims look into the camera with stunned expressions which make us wonder whether they knew that the rest of their lives was measured in minutes, hours at most. Some of the men and women are dressed in stylish clothing. They are carrying leather luggage and were it not for the fear in their eyes, they would be indistinguishable from any middle-class city dwellers. There are others in that line wearing workmen's shoes and peasant clothing; bundles are slung over their shoulders. Their women have knotted kerchiefs under their chins, their long skirts touch their shoes. Orthodox Jews cluster near each other. The men are bearded, in traditional black garb and wide-brimmed hats. Mothers and grandmothers share with the men the burden of looking after the children. They speak softly to the little ones, trying to soothe away fear, hunger, and thirst. If we were able to listen, we would hear them speak in many languages and dialects. Some voices reveal years of education, others are obviously unschooled. Murmured prayers rise from the lips of the devout but there are those who have enveloped themselves in stony silence. Perhaps they have abandoned all hope of help from God or man.

Who are these people? Or, more precisely, who were they? We know they were robbed of their future and that their present was compressed into moments, but what of their past? Unless we can give them human dimensions their deaths will remain mere statistics. To understand the meaning of the Holocaust, its victims must be more then entries in German ledgers. The dehumanization of the killing process must be reversed and the faces on the old photographs brought back to life, even if just for a moment.

THE VICTIMS

These men, women, and children were the Jews of Europe. With the exception of Finland, every country defeated by or politically linked to the Germans contributed to their numbers. They had been caught in a vast net which the Germans had spread over

Map 2–1 *Europe under Nazi occupation before June 22, 1941.*

most of the continent. In the east, it reached from the outskirts of St. Petersburg to the Ukraine, spread south along the northern rim of the Mediterranean Sea. With the exception of Switzerland, which the Germans preferred to leave neutral, the snare was laid eastward from the Pyrenees Mountains to include France, the Low Countries, across Germany to Poland and the Baltic states. The southern European nations of the Balkans, Italy, and Austria completed the encirclement (see Map 2–1).

The Jews who were massed behind the gates of the death and concentration camps were often strangers to each other. They had been brought here from any-where within the realm of German domination and were as diverse as any assemblage of Europeans. In appearance, in culture, in degree of assimilation, a Ukrainian, for example, was unlike his fellow Jew from Norway, and the world of a Polish Hasid was completely different from that of the assimilated dress designer from Paris.

Jews had lived in Europe since before the birth of Christ and had adopted, in vary-ing degrees, the customs and mores of their host countries. There had been intermar-riages as well, how else could one explain the great differences in physical appearance among them? There were blue-eyed blonds and dark-eyed brunettes, tall and short, stocky and slender men and women; some featured the high cheekbones common among the Slavic peoples, others were olive-skinned with narrow Semitic noses. The oval faces of the Norsemen were represented as well as the black eyes associated with Mediterranean natives. Culturally, too, they depicted a wide range of differ-ences. Most Polish, Russian, and a considerable proportion of the Balkan Jews spoke and wrote Yiddish, while many from the South used Greek or Ladino. Western Euro-pean Jews had experienced a greater degree of acculturation. It must be remembered that they constituted a small minority, less than 1 percent among their countrymen in France, Holland, Belgium, and Germany. In the process of assimilation they had adopted the vernacular and became integrated into the political and economic activi-ties of their nations.

In the arts, in science, and in literature the achievements of assimilated Jews were generally acclaimed. Social acceptance was growing, though still a questionable mat-ter for many Gentiles. The continuing process of industrialization was breaking down ancient class barriers and many Jews were clearly a part of the rising middle classes. Often they became fervently nationalistic and they fought in the uniforms of both the Allies and the Central powers during World War I. At the turn of the century, they confidently expected that their religious faith would not block full acceptance by their Christian neighbors; achievement of full equality was merely a matter of time.

Clearly, there was no monolithic Jewish culture. Any attempt here to re-create its diversity, country by country, within the context of a single chapter would serve to confuse rather than clarify. It is preferable to opt for a narrower aspect of the life that vanished, namely Polish Jewry. This choice is justifiable for two reasons: first, because three million Polish Jews were murdered, no other country sustained such losses; and second, because the once-thriving culture they had created no longer exists. Whereas pockets of Jewish life remain in western and southern Europe and a revival of Jewish culture is emerging in Germany, Poland is barren. How strange indeed, that Hitler, who despised the Poles, achieved his greatest success there; it is Poland, not Germany, that is nearly *Judenrein* ("cleansed of Jews").

HISTORY OF POLISH JEWRY

The term *Polish Jews* requires definition. The three partitions of Poland in the eighteenth century divided the land and its people among Prussia/Germany, Russia, and Austria. However, even without a political homeland, the Poles continued to foster their native culture and did not merge with the nationality of their conquerors. As a result, Poles, and that included Polish Jews, lived for almost 150 years under the flags of Russia, Germany, and Austria. Thus, it is possible to speak of Polish Jewry even when such a designation might refer to Galicia in the Austrian south, to Pinsk in western Russia, or Posen which sometimes was part of Germany.

According to German sources, of the nearly 6,000,000 Jews killed, 4,300,000 came from occupied Russia and Poland. In percentages, 85 percent of Polish and 71 percent of western Russian Jews were murdered. Their civilization has vanished. The few thousand Polish Jews who survived the Holocaust were met with hostility when they made their way back to their hometowns. The Polish people who occupied their former homes and places of business often greeted them with derision, even hatred. Clearly, the remnant could not reestablish itself on Polish soil. Emigration to Israel and even to Germany was preferable to continued anti-Semitism. Cities, towns, and hundreds of villages which had been depositories of a distinct way of Jewish life no longer have Jewish communities. Only traces of the past remain, a half-ruined cemetery, a former synagogue now used as a civic center, perhaps a defunct Talmud-Torah school where Polish poetry is recited.

Nor was the situation of Holocaust survivors from western Russia conducive to a revival of Jewish cultural life in their former homes. Since the Communists achieved power in 1917, their regimes had a long history of attempting to homogenize their people under the guise of equal aversion to all religious worship. The official attitude toward Jewish cultural distinctiveness vacillated between outright persecution and official discouragement. That policy did not change after the war. In fact, Soviet authorities refused to acknowledge that Jews specifically had been singled out for total destruction by the Nazis. Soviet commemorative monuments pay homage to Russian victims only. Thus, it is hardly reasonable to anticipate a reappearance of traditional eastern Jewish ethnicity in the Communist world.

Jewish history in Poland has deep roots. When the Crusaders attacked Jews with the same zeal they brought to the conquest of the Holy Land, many of the victims fled eastward. They brought with them the medieval German vernacular. From this base, Yiddish was developed and became the universal language of central and eastern European Jews. The kings of Poland, eager to foster a mercantile middle class, welcomed the refugees. The most enlightened of the Polish medieval kings, Casimir the Great(1333–1370), granted the Jews complete freedom to work, to worship, and to prosper despite objections from the church. Even when less enlightened monarchs restricted the economic and social life of the Jews, medieval Poland offered more promise than most other European states. Throughout the Middle Ages when west European rulers persecuted and expelled their Jewish populations, Polish Jews could work and worship in relative peace. Not restricted to peddling and money-lending, they could live decently in villages as well as towns. From the thirteenth century to the eve of the Nazi invasion, they satisfied many of the needs of a largely agricultural society. They represented a vital segment of the middle class. As craftsmen, from blacksmith to goldsmith, tanner to cobbler, miller to baker, weaver to tailor, merchant to banker, they supplied the rich and the poor with their handicrafts and their monetary services. The items they manufactured were usually crafted in the homes and small workshops. Some of the Jews plied their goods from village to village, others opened stalls in the market square and sold to the peasants on designated market days.

AUTONOMY OF JEWISH LIFE

The Jews of Poland were granted a charter by King Sigismund Augustus in 1551. In accordance with that document and others written with similar intent, they could govern themselves by means of an elected council of elders. These local assemblies organized themselves into regional conventions which, in turn, chose a supreme council. Thus, a sophisticated, well-ordered administrative machinery was set into motion. Jews were designated as a separate social group and given a great deal of autonomy. They chose their leaders annually, usually from among their prominent residents. Since the Jews lived in ghettos, sometimes by choice, more often by decree, local government was simplified. Their own bureaucracies regulated such social services as education, religious functions, relief for the poor, and hospitals; they supervised trade and manufacturing, organized civil and criminal courts, and collected taxes for their own and the royal governments.

Contemporary descriptions of life in the ghettos and small Jewish towns, the *shtetl,* strike us as grim. But it must be remembered that such problems as insufficient diet, polluted water, overcrowding, lack of sanitation, and the absence of privacy were the norm for all but the aristocratic few. Life was short and harsh, peace was rare, and class distinctions rigid. The Jews, as aliens, were always the most vulnerable amid the native population.

THE END TO PEACEFUL COEXISTENCE

It is estimated that a half-million Jews lived in Polish lands by the middle of the seventeenth century. Depending on the precarious balance of power between king and church and the influence of German merchants who disliked competition, Jewish survival fluctuated between prosperity and subsistence. Their numbers increased despite periodic outbreaks of anti-Semitic violence. The most devastating attacks occurred in the decade between 1648 and 1658 when the Cossacks revolted against their Polish oppressors and included the Jews in their fury. These massacres in the Ukraine were followed by a Swedish invasion from the north and Russian incursions from the east. In the Polish counterattacks, once more the Jews were accused of complicity with the enemy and their blood ran freely. It was always easier to destroy the defenseless suspect in their midst than the armed enemy without. From the seventeenth century on, the promise of peaceful coexistence between Poles and Jews was marred by officially sanctioned and privately enforced anti-Semitism. Fear of the Gentile world came to live permanently in the Jewish communities of Poland. Only from God could come relief. Only through strict observance of his laws could they hope to reach the ears of the Almighty. Only from each other could they expect help. Only in family life was there joy and comfort. The Jews turned their eyes inward. The authorities demanded that they live in distinct communities, therefore, the *shtetl* evolved. As the Jews were legally and physically separated, so they separated themselves from the Polish environment. The gulf between Jews and Christians widened. Immediately recognizable Jews came into being, they spoke a different language, wore odd clothing, and kept their eyes downcast in the presence of Christians.

SHTETL LIFE

A rhythm of life developed in the *shtetl* which interwove the spiritual and prosaic functions of survival in a pattern so intricate that it is impossible to separate the threads. This was not a theocracy, the rabbis were not the sole or complete authority. Yet, God and his commandments were part and parcel of every activity. The Torah and its commentaries were the basis for the laws, religious as well as temporal, which held the community together. Hundreds of prayers were uttered, not merely during synagogue services, but as part of such mundane activities as washing ones hands or eating the first apple of the season. The search to understand the word of God was a sacred obligation for those able to cope with the intricacies of commentaries piled upon commentaries. The Almighty of the *shtetl* was not an unknowable deity who dwelled on high, he was the heart of everyday life.

Family life was the source of happiness. Children were treasured long before Western civilization discovered the child-centered family. The celebration of the Sabbath was joyful, even in the poorest household. The mother was honored, she made it possible to observe the holy days with special foods, the white table cloth, and candles. Every home was extended by uncles and aunts, grandparents and cousins; supportive, quarrelsome, lively. Suppression by external forces seemed to compress life so that internal sources, the family and the community, supplied the consolation necessary for survival.

CULTURAL ACHIEVEMENTS

The fact that during the late Middle Ages many generations of Poles and Jews had lived more or less amicably side by side is not well-known. The modern history of Poland with its institutionalized and grass-roots hatred of the Jews overshadows the earlier centuries of coexistence. But it was Polish soil that nourished several vital and enduring elements of Jewish culture. As that soil became more and more barren, the Jews reacted effectively so that Jewish life in Poland continued. Among their responses were the following:

1. The mysticism of *kabbalah*
2. The preservation of rational orthodoxy and Talmudic studies
3. The Hassidic reaction to sterile observance
4. The advocacy and promotion of Zionism
5. The acceptance of *Haskala,* enlightenment of Jewish practices, and modernization

Although not all of these movements originated in Poland, it was here that abstractions were forged into powerful forces. When the SS troopers emptied Lodz or Warsaw or the hundreds of villages of their Jewish population, a rich and diverse cultural heritage ended. Jews who cherished every word of the Scriptures as emanating from God stood next to atheists during concentration camp rollcalls. Doctors who graduated from Polish universities rubbed shoulders with professional beggars, and judges suffered next to thieves. They had come from different circumstances and now they moved toward the same conclusion.

The clash between the traditionalists and the modernists is the wheel that turns history. In the case of Polish Jewry, it severed the progressive, reformist factions from the adherents of an ancient heritage which often had degenerated into the splitting of Talmudic hairs. The Orthodox feared that faith would be weakened if Jews went outside their own society, but they agreed on little else. Judaism was not exempted from the profusion and confusion of candidates who claimed to possess the only keys to heaven. The faith is littered with the false promises of so-called messiahs and religious visionaries who were certain they, and they alone, knew the path leading to a perfect understanding of the relationship between man and God.

KABBALAH

The quest for God's blessings is as ancient as man himself. For Jews, it has been bound up with living according to the religious precepts of the faith and with study of the Scriptures. The examination and contemplation of God's word has been and continues to be an honorable, even venerated, pursuit. But side by side with the philosophical, logical, and pragmatic search for God has been the allure of mysticism. The most firmly established form of Jewish mysticism is called *kabbalah.* Although the invocation of magic symbolism can be traced to the very roots of Judaism, its medieval and modern formulas are mainly based on the *Zohar,* a book attributed to a thirteenth-century rabbi, Moses de Leon. From the *Zohar* have emanated centuries of occult conjecture.

The kabbahlists sought to pierce the mystery of life and death and all the unanswerable questions by searching for the "true" meaning of the holy texts. Magical powers were assigned to the individual letters of the Scriptures and hidden meanings were assumed. The Hebrew symbols were manipulated, read upside down, superimposed upon one another, and read backward to reveal their magic. What was believed to be concealed became more important than what was revealed. A form of numerology developed wherein letters were given numerical value and kabbahlists charted these numbers and tried to extract their secrets.

The concept that the universe is understandable through mathematics strikes a sympathetic chord in the age of space exploration, but Jewish mysticism had no scientific basis. The numbers from one to ten were believed to have radiated directly from God and were assigned supernatural qualities. The longing to penetrate the mystery of God all too often turned into superstition. Mankind has always searched for a shortcut to understanding the inexplicable, and *kabbalah* promised an answer. In times of great suffering, the need to understand God's seeming indifference to human anguish grew especially strong. After the expulsion from Spain, the devotees of *kabbalah* increased rapidly. Like medieval alchemists, men spent their lives in search of the right formula and like astrologers they patterned their behavior to conform with heavenly signs.

The 16th and 17th centuries abounded with false messiahs who deceived hundred of thousands of followers. The most outrageous claims of imminent redemption found disciples only too eager to be deluded. Men and women gave up their livelihoods and their homes and embarked for the Holy Land in the expectation of messianic deliverance. Had not the Holy Scripture prophesied that great evil will precede the day of salvation? How else could one explain the miserable conditions of the Jews? By remaining faithful to God's commands, they had incurred misery and hatred; surely their suffering was the prologue to redemption. And each time that a pseudo-Messiah turned out to be either a fraud or a fanatic, the despair of his believers grew deeper.

RATIONAL ORTHODOXY AND THE GAON OF VILNA

Jewish scholarship of the eighteenth century consisted largely of pedantic, formalized repetition. The teacher, usually the *rebbe* (rabbi), accepted boys to his school who were as young as four or five years of age. They studied Hebrew, while Yiddish was their vernacular language. Learning was largely a matter of rote memorization. Although it was permissible to question the meaning of the text, one did not dispute the explanation of the *rebbe*. The boys sat all day in cheerless rooms, repeating words they often did not understand. They were expected to quell their natural desire for activity and remain obediently and submissively bent over their lessons. A boy's pale, earnest face was deemed to be handsome and the perpetual student was the joy of his parents.

Advanced scholarship was equally uninspiring. Endless recitation, argumentation over minutia, and the exaltation of ritual had taken the place of philosophical, even theological disputation. And yet, the spark for love of learning remained, uninspired and barren though it was. Young men who excelled in their knowledge of the holy books were encouraged to study all their lives. Since marriages were arranged by parents and since learning was valued above all other attributes, a bright student could hope to make a good match. It was entirely acceptable that he never earn a living for his family. A scholar was either supported by his father-in-law or his wife. Such a wife turned breadwinner would see herself in a natural and proud position, not at all demeaned by her husband's lack of economic contribution.

Education for girls was largely neglected. Their future role as wives and mothers was fixed. There could be no question of equality between the sexes. This was a patriarchal society. But since the home was truly the castle in which the family found solace from the hardships of poverty and prejudice, women were cherished for their life-giving and home-making duties. They could earn communal respect for goodness and wisdom but they performed few religious rites. In the synagogue, the sexes were separated and Orthodox men avoided looking at women in order to curb any inappropriate desire. Actually, Jewish women were probably less subjugated than their Christian contemporaries. Judaism does not acknowledge the concept of original sin. Eve is viewed as the mother of mankind rather then the temptress. The connection between sin and sex, which has rested so heavily on Christian women, does not exist in Judaism. God commanded man to multiply and his sexual urges were the God-given means to that end.

The sterility of intellectual life of the Polish Jews in the eighteenth century was alleviated by the reforms of Elijah, the Vilna Gaon (wise man). Elijah sparked the revival of Jewish learning by widening its inquiry to include all fields of knowledge. He created an approach to study which reformed the barrenness of repetition and endless arguments over minute points in the Scriptures. He urged the cultivation of scholarship rather than memorization. His influence left a permanent imprint on the evolution of

Jewish boys entering school in Vilna, 1929.   (Courtesy Yivo Institute for Jewish Research.)

Eastern Jewry. Fine minds, bound to become dissatisfied with the sterility of Jewish lore, were now able to find within Orthodoxy the challenges of a wider education.

Elijah established in Vilna, the capital of Lithuania, a model center of scholarship. His Talmudic academy opened the narrow windows of petty dissection of ancient texts to the world. Under his leadership and that of his followers, the study of philosophy, science, theology, and the Hebrew language swept away the years of sophistry and preoccupation with the obscure. From his academy a new breed of rabbis was graduated whose disciplined direction influenced generations. But the broadness of Gaon's intellect was not suitable for the masses. His erudition was fit for the intellectual elite, it was not accessible to the common man who also needed the solace that came from performing his religious duties. The Baal Shem Tov answered that longing in the creation of Hasidism.

THE HASIDIC CHALLENGE

Almost everyone has some knowledge of Hasidism. In recent years, Hollywood has produced two movies which depict Hasidic life in the United States. Certainly, many residents of large cities have seen the bearded men in black suits and their modestly attired women. Hasidic veneration of their leader, the *rebbe,* is celebrated and/or decried by Jewish and Christian observers. Sometimes hailed as committed fundamentalists or condemned as religious fanatics, Hasids have carved for themselves a conspicuous and worldwide niche. Their devotion to each other and to their form of Orthodoxy is impressive and so are their almost crime-free, drug-free neighborhoods, often located in the midst of old and crowded inner cities. In several ways, the modern adherents of Hasidism vary from the intent of the founder of the sect, the Baal Shem Tov ("Master of the Good Name"), but these differences are not part of this discussion. Be it understood, however, that rather then declining in numbers, Hasidism today is strong and still growing.

Hasidism exemplifies the inevitability of success when a great need is filled by a great man. The need was double-edged. First, Jewish life in Poland was growing more insecure thus intensifying the search for spiritual consolation. Second, the unlearned had no access into the tight circle of Talmudic scholarship. Hasidism began as a revolt of the unschooled against the aristocracy of the erudite. To serve God was the highest and almost universal goal of ghetto and *shtetl* Jewry. To fulfill one's obligations to God involved prayer, observance, and arduous, intensive study of the Scriptures and its numerous commentaries. But the mastery of such esoteric knowledge demanded years of single-minded commitment as well as intellectual aptitude. The ordinary head of a household could not meet such requirements. He could but wishfully press his nose against the window of the room in which wise men pored over holy books. The fact that these men were the social elite of the community could only add to his yearning.

The charismatic founder of Hasidism freed such a man from the frustration caused by the elitism of scholarship. Israel of Moldavia, the Baal Shem Tov, believed that devotion to God is rooted in the emotions, not knowledge. Prayer was joy and joy was prayer. Worship could be expressed through music and dancing. The beauty of nature, seen as a distraction by the Talmudists, was deemed a manifestation of the love bestowed by the King of the Universe. The father of Hasidism elevated faith over law and fervor over ritual. Actually, the sect did not rewrite the Scriptures; the changes its members brought to their form of worship were a matter of reinterpretation rather than innovation.

To the Hasids, the presence of God is everywhere in the universe and they may communicate with God anywhere and any time. This approach to religion was essentially democratic, since wealth and distinction avails one nothing in the eyes of the Almighty. The emotions of optimism and exultation replenish the whole man, body and soul. Yes, man needs rituals, but the essence of religion is faith which can be expressed from the depth of feeling. In enthusiasm, ardor, and communal excitation, the Hasids resemble the religious zeal exhibited by revivalist churches.

The Baal Shem Tov wrote no instructions for his followers. His personality was the center of the community he created. After his death, the administration of Hasidic life continued to revolve around the central figure of a leader. As the movement spread throughout eastern Europe, it split into several groups. Each chose its own rabbi, a position which developed into a dynastic seat of power. Although such a rabbi reigned without a constitution, without an army, without any but moral force, he had a great deal of power. His word was law, his decisions final, the loyalty of his followers absolute, his sphere of jurisdiction wider than that of any monarch. His disciples awaited his judgment on all questions affecting their lives, be they of an economic or personal nature. The source of this authority was the conviction among his followers that their rabbi stood in a special communion with God which allowed him to intercede on their behalf. It is not surprising that some critics compare the rabbi's hereditary position to absolutism, while others censure Hasidism as a religious cult that deprives its members of spiritual independence.

The Holocaust wiped out the Hasidic communities of Poland and western Russia. Their remnants established new and flourishing centers in Israel and in the United States. Obviously, the teaching of the Master of the Good Name continues to meet a deep emotional need. This phenomenon is particularly astounding when contrasted with recent achievements of greater rights for women; Hasids make no pretense of endorsing equality between the sexes.

THE IMPACT OF ZIONISM

The two major events in Jewish history in this century are the Holocaust and the creation of the state of Israel. The 1948 vote by the United Nations which sanctioned the formation of a national homeland for the Jews was certainly linked to the Holocaust, but political Zionism had begun much earlier. The struggle to create a national homeland for the Jews had been carried out on an international scale in which Polish Jewry played a vital role.

The passionate nationalism of the nineteenth century touched the long-buried longings of many subjugated peoples. Several waves of revolutions engulfed Europe reaching from France to Poland and culminating in 1848. The Poles had dreamt of liberation from the heavy hand of Russia, but like Italy, Prussia, Hungary, and Austria, the moment to realize the ideal of self-determination had not yet come. Among those Poles whose dreams and hopes were shattered when the uprisings of 1830 and 1848 failed were a number of urban Polish Jews. They had chosen the path of *Haskala*, the enlightenment, and expected to enjoy full equality with Christian Poles. The largest component of Polish Jewry, however, was still confined in their almost autonomous enclaves. They did not believe that their conditions would be improved by the efforts of Gentiles. Their poverty, insecurity, and well-founded fear of pogroms were, after all, inflicted on them by the Gentile world. Nor could anyone deny that most Catholic Poles were very reluctant to accept Jews as equals. Assimilation of Polish Jews into Polish society was feared by the Orthodox rabbis on the one hand and opposed by the church on the other hand. The Jews needed to find their own answer to their dilemma. When the summons came to support the creation of a modern Jewish homeland through Zionist organizations, a responsive chord reverberated in many hearts.

The hope of going back to the land of Israel had been kept alive for nearly two thousand years, ever since the Romans exiled the Judeans. Hundreds of generations had uttered the words "next year in Jerusalem" at the end of the seder meal. But until the closing years of the nineteenth century, these words implied an abstract longing, not a blueprint for action. Political Zionism, that is, the organized effort to bring about a national Jewish state, resulted from the confluence of several historic streams. There was the unhappy realization by large numbers of Jews that the spirit of enlightenment had not halted anti-Semitism. Also, ancient religious antipathy had eased but had never disappeared. Even a secularized Europe had been unable, perhaps unwilling, to end prejudice. Instead, new forms of the old plague had arisen. The Dreyfus trial in 1894 in France demonstrated in the very birthplace of liberty, equality, and fraternity that bigotry still flourished. A new form of bias claimed that Jews were racially and ethnically different. The modern nation-state could not integrate the alien Jew. Despite the success of the American experience, the notion that diversity could be a source of strength had not taken hold.

The search for an answer to the persistence of anti-Semitism was accelerated by the policies of Tsar Alexander III. His father, the Great Emancipator, had freed the Russian serfs and eased the most repressive measures against the Jews. His tragic assassination in 1881 was blamed on the Jews and was followed by years of officially condoned, perhaps instigated, pogroms. The death toll of these riots in the Pale of Settlement, the southwestern region set aside for Jews, was appalling. Once more, the physical survival of Russian and Polish Jews was in question.

In the final decade of the last century the idea to create a Jewish homeland in Palestine had the support of growing numbers of young Jews. When the English government expressed interest in such a scheme, its feasibility was strengthened. Considering the fact that at this time the region was under Ottoman rule and not part of the British Empire, this was merely a gesture. Nonetheless, a number of young Russian Jews actually translated the dream of creating a homeland by taking up plowshares.

They settled as farmers on the barren Palestinian land; the first small trickle of pioneers. A nation, however, was not built by the earnest efforts of a vanguard, it required massive support, political negotiation, and excellent leadership. It required, in other words, the ability of Theodor Herzl.

Theodor Herzl (1860–1904) was a Jewish journalist from Vienna who had been assigned to cover the Dreyfus trial in Paris. Captain Dreyfus, an assimilated French Jew, had been falsely accused of treason. His prosecution unleashed an upsurge of anti-Semitism that astounded and dismayed the young journalist along with many of the supporters of assimilation. Herzl concluded that only a Jewish state could solve the Jewish problem. The nations of Europe, he argued, should support his agenda because the persistence of anti-Semitism would undermine their internal peace. Persecution of the Jews would deliver them into the ranks of revolutionary socialists and even the most liberal governments would be thrown into turmoil. Herzl devoted the remainder of his life to effect legitimization of the concept of nationhood for the Jews.

Herzl's book, *Der Judenstaat* ("The Jewish State"), outlined the practical steps by which his vision could be realized. The work created a sensation although much of the response was critical. The Orthodox Jews protested that the in-gathering in the Holy Land could occur only when the promised Messiah appeared. Herzl was not an observant Jew, how dare he suggest conventional statehood for the chosen people? Other critics contended that Judaism was a religion, not a nationality. Leaders of the assimilated communities held that integration into the society of the various countries would take place eventually, patience was called for, not demands for separateness. And then there was the segment of the Jewish population which wanted only to remain invisible, who feared any publicity lest it give rise to more persecution. Among many eastern Jews, however, particularly the young, the idea of a homeland met enthusiastic support. Here the ideal of returning to the land of the Scriptures had already taken tentative root. Now a man of action had emerged from the west to provide the essential political leadership.

The First Zionist Congress met in Basel in 1897. For the first time in eighteen hundred years, Jews from throughout the Diaspora gathered to plan their future, rich and poor, capitalist and socialist, Orthodox and Reform. They spoke many languages, but their voices were unified in their aim to establish a national home for their people. They marveled at the white flag with the blue star of David, wept upon hearing a Jewish national anthem, and came away believing the impossible dream. They elected Herzl as the first president of their World Zionist Organization. Thus they laid the foundation for the future state of Israel.

Meanwhile, difficulties mounted. Palestine was Turkish and land sales for proposed settlements required the sultan's consent. That consent was never given. Herzl believed in diplomatic solutions to the deadlock and tried to enlist the rich and the powerful to promote his plans. He played on the kaiser's egotism to win his good offices to intercede with the sultan. In vain, he faced the palpable hatred of the Russian foreign minister. He even applied to the Pope for help. All was fruitless. Only Great Britain showed a sympathetic interest by offering Herzl a haven in Uganda, in East Africa. Should Uganda be accepted? Perhaps as a temporary refuge for the suffering eastern Jews? Or was Zionism unshakably committed to Zion, that is, Palestine? The organization was split by this controversy when, suddenly, just forty-four years old, Herzl died.

Theodor Herzl did not live to establish a Jewish state. In terms of concrete accomplishments, nearly all his diplomatic missions failed. Nevertheless, he is a founder of the state of Israel. His spirit ushered in a dramatic change in the self-perception, and in much of the world's perception, of what it means to be a Jew. The organization he founded spread from village to town, from west to east. The greater the oppression, the greater the impact of the message: We shall be as other peoples with a national state of our own. Young Jews, mostly Russian and Polish, prepared themselves for a future in Palestine. They studied Hebrew thus making vital contributions to the transformation of a dead language so that it would fit the modern world. They learned to farm, to irrigate, and to apply practical knowledge to practical problems. Instead of the Talmud, or law or medicine, they read treatises on soil erosion, reforestation, and horticulture. They split rocks, built roads, they sang and danced and rejoiced in the cooperative kibbutz life. The older generation often disapproved, particularly as their children's devotion to religion wore thin; but these young people were done with the meekness of their parents. These new Jews had no faith that assimilation would win them equality within the Gentile world. They would not accept the misery of persecution and poverty with docile hopelessness and look to God for deliverance.

It was difficult for their elders to condone this new activist youth. Religious education had been idealized for hundreds of years, while physical labor was seen as the lot of the intellectually barren. But now their children turned these ancient values upside down. In addition, the focus of the family was the hope for grandchildren, but these young Zionists planned to go to far-off Palestine. They chose their own mates and resented interference in their private lives. Often, the political views of the future pioneers made the older generation uneasy. The creation of a Jewish homeland required a cooperative spirit which was expressed through democratic socialism.

The religious attitudes of these young men and women ranged from liberal to Orthodox, each group creating its own cooperatives. They trained in collective agricultural camps in Poland and Russia and upon completing their preparatory course expected to make their way to Palestine, to make *aliyah.* Some emigrated legally, others illegally, to become the forerunners of the massive immigration that would follow the First and the Second World Wars.

THE THEORY AND PRACTICE OF *HASKALA*

A philosophical element, briefly referred to earlier, was the enlightenment, the *Haskala.* Imported from Germany, the concept of Jewish regeneration had crossed into Poland where it had particular attraction for city dwellers. *Haskala,* a Hebrew phrase meaning "let there be light," was largely based on the work of the philosopher Moses Mendelssohn (1729–1786). Mendelssohn was a friend of the great dramatist Gotthold Lessing who was the very personification of the spirit of tolerance and liberal thought. Both men devoted their considerable talents and fame to teach their contemporaries the meaning of humanity. Mendelssohn struggled against both Jewish and Gentile bigotry. His philosophy challenged the circumscribed beliefs of his day. His devotion to the cause of mutual understanding and his forbearance opened the door through which German and Jewish intellectuals could enter each other's realm. Jews began the process of participating in the mental world of Germany. German Christians acknowledged that Jewishness and Germanness might be compatible. Mendelssohn remained a devout Jew and saw no conflict between Jewish values and Western humanism. With his heart, mind, and powerful pen, he attacked the strictures of empty rituals and the binding confines of rabbinical power. As he sought to widen the world of his people, so did he fight for their economic and political emancipation, a goal he did not live to see fulfilled. Predictably, his work earned him the opposition of the Orthodox who feared that exposure to a Gentile environment would dilute the traditional visions of Judaism. Mendelssohn's insistence that his daughters' education equaled that of men certainly marked him as a man ahead of his time.

But Mendelssohn's impact could not be contained. Gradually, his concepts made their way eastward where a largely urban strata of Polish Jews fell under the influence of *Haskala*. To whatever degree the reluctant Polish authorities permitted it, these were the Jews who learned to speak Polish, attended Polish schools, and took part in every aspect of Polish national life. Many entered the middle class and were active in the professions and as owners of medium-sized businesses, while others became part of the urban proletariat. They operated the sowing machines in small factories, delivered goods by horse and wagon, and finished textiles in their homes. Most were patriotic Poles who chose to live outside the walls of actual or spiritual ghettos even though they rarely cut their Jewish cultural ties. In hundreds of organizations they transplanted the closeness of *shtetl* life to the city. They united into associations to serve every human activity, from birth to burial, so that no one needed to be alone. Some went to synagogues where they prayed from the time-worn books of the Orthodox, others were drawn to the new books issued by the Reform congregations, and still others did not pray at all. Nevertheless, all were Jews.

THE REBIRTH OF POLAND

The twentieth century opened with unprecedented optimism. Western Europeans fully expected to expand their domination over the political and economic life of much of the globe. They predicted an end to such anachronisms as war and poverty, even disease would be conquered in the foreseeable future. Science and logic would triumph over all the ills that had escaped from Pandora's box. But then the fantasy was shattered by the catastrophe of World War I. The insanity of a devastating war was followed by a hypocritical peace. After American idealism had raised hopes too high, disillusionment and disappointment were inevitable. Few of the promises for a better world were kept when the victors met to write a peace treaty at Versailles in 1919. Among those few was point thirteen of Woodrow Wilson's Fourteen Points, the restoration of Poland.

The new Poland had a bloody beginning. From north to south, its plains had been turned into battlefields of the German-Russian conflict. Already exhausted by the

Business courtyard on Nalewki Street in the Jewish quarter of Warsaw, Poland. (Courtesy United States Holocaust Memorial Museum.)

Great War, Poland's newly constituted sovereignty was challenged by its neighbors. Fierce border disputes with the Soviet Union, with Lithuania, Estonia, and Czechoslovakia disrupted the attempt to establish an economically viable and politically stable government. The entire interwar period, the twenty years between the rebirth of Poland and its defeat by Nazi Germany in 1939, was a period of constant tension and limited progress. The anticipation that political liberty would be accompanied by economic well-being could not be fulfilled. The euphoria sparked by independence turned to bitter frustration in the face of a difficult reality.

The Polish nation incorporated 27 million inhabitants, of which 70 percent were ethnic Poles; the rest of the population consisted of minorities with the Ukrainians and Jews comprising the largest percentages. The ordinary Pole could not understand the complexity of the problems his nation encountered. City workers struggled with unemployment; capitalists lacked money to widen the industrial base. An unstable parliamentary system composed of too many political parties and too little administrative experience tested the patience and the endurance of the population. Millions emigrated, relieving the pressure somewhat. The democratic constitutional government adopted in 1921 was overthrown by a coup in 1926. For the next few years Poland experienced some economic growth, but just as the recovery was giving encouragement to investors, the hope for further economic gains was dashed. The international Great Depression of 1929 caused severe hardships to the newly established industries of Poland. The origin of the collapse was beyond the comprehension of the masses and a scapegoat needed to be sacrificed. The Jews, of course, were the obvious selection.

The Polish government between the two World Wars had been a moral failure even before the economic disaster. The treaty which had reestablished Polish sovereignty had specifically stipulated that the rights of ethnic minorities must be protected. But the promise was not kept. The minorities were oppressed by policies of attempted Polinization instituted by a government bent on forcing them to abandon their distinctive ways of life. For 150 years, the tsars had attempted to turn Poles into Russians without success. How quickly that prolonged and painful lesson was forgotten.

THE INTERWAR DECADES

Politicians of the right and left became more radical and although these extremists agreed on little else, they were as one in their embrace of anti-Semitism. The Jews were held responsible for every calamity that beset the nation. The government sanctioned and encouraged such prejudice and used its legal powers to institutionalize the most irrational scapegoating. Laws were passed to restrict the Jews' economic freedom until fewer and fewer means to earn a livelihood remained. With the exceptions of the textile and some food-refining factories, Jews were denied industrial employment. All wage earners' job security was precarious as mechanization was introduced into growing numbers of industrial establishments, but Jewish workers were the last hired and first fired. Higher educational opportunities were severely limited by a quota system. Jewish students who managed to be accepted into universities were forced to sit on special "ghetto benches" placed in back of lecture rooms. The social services of the impoverished Jewish communities tried desperately to prevent outright starvation, but only the charity of foreign Jews kept a large percentage of the three million Polish Jews from pauperism.

The impact of this renewed persecution resulted not only in the growth of Zionism, it was also expressed in the organization of the *Bund.* This was a socialist political party, founded in 1897 to promote the welfare of the Jewish proletariat. It mirrored other socialist parties in its goals: better wages, improved working conditions, and promoting the election of a socialist government. Obviously, the Jewish workers established their own organization because the conventional socialist parties could not or would not meet their needs. Among the special demands of the Jewish workers were their wish to keep their holy days, including the Sabbath, equal educational opportunities for their children, and cessation of the government's official anti-Jewish posture. Unlike most of the proletariat, Jewish laborers were well informed, avid readers, and active in a variety of social and cultural activities. In most societies, only the upper and middle classes patronized the arts, but these working people loved literature, art, theater, and music. In western Poland many Jews spoke, read, and wrote Yiddish, Polish, Hebrew, and German, while in the eastern provinces the Russian language replaced German.

Rarely have an oppressed people been as creative as was Polish Jewry during the interval between the two great wars. Odessa and Warsaw became centers of Hebrew literature and Isaac Leib Peretz its master in poetry, drama, and the short story. He also wrote in Yiddish and authors such as Sholem Asch, Isaac Bashevis and his brother Israel Joshua Singer continued the genre. Theater developed from amateur status to professional productions and popular performers achieved fame as the darlings of their audiences. Libraries, trade schools, religious education, and magazines and newspapers to satisfy every political leaning flourished in spite of the tenuous economic and repressive anti-Semitic atmosphere. Concerts were performed in simple rooms with wooden benches or in gilded halls with plush seats to give pleasure to rich and poor. Jewish composers and musicians were in the forefront of Poland's musical resurgence. Even photography and filmmaking were fostered by Jewish artists. Endless philosophic and political disputations were, of course, accompanied and enhanced by uncounted cups of tea and mountains of cake.

While Polish urban Jewry discovered its great diversity, the *shtetl,* where God ruled without challenge, still existed in great numbers. Clearly, any attempt to speak of Polish Jewry as homogenious springs from a flawed premise. The world that vanished had many different faces. A Polish Jew might be Orthodox or atheist, socialist or capitalist, Zionist or patriot. In their dying, however, all differences disappeared. Young or old, healthy or ill, wise or foolish, honest or corrupt, it did not matter. The eyes looking back at us from the photograph of Polish Jews lined up outside the lethal showers of the death camps were the eyes of Everyman.

Chapter 3

The Nazi Rise to Power

There are almost daily news reports concerning the resurgence of neo-Nazi groups, both in Europe and in this country. The swastikas smeared on walls and grave stones send a shiver of fear and revulsion along the spines of the older generation, the generation that fought or experienced Naziism. Invariably, these hate crimes raise some difficult questions: Can a Holocaust happen again? Can it happen here? Should the skinheads and their ilk be ignored or punished? Where is the obscure line that separates overreaction from neglect of danger?

Some of the answers may be found in the history of the Third Reich. The Nazis were able to reverse the path of Western civilization when they met two conditions necessary to carry out the killing of millions. First, the unthinkable had to appear to be not only doable, but desirable. Persecution, even murder, had to be cloaked as a worthy ideal. "For the good of the many, some few must suffer." (This topic will be explored in the next chapter.) Second, the government must be totalitarian and exercise unquestioned and total power over every aspect of the life of the people. When the slogan *Die Juden sind unser Unglueck* ("the Jews are our misfortune") was accepted by most Germans, either as truth or as possible truth, the removal of this misfortune became merely a question of *when, where,* and *how.* The all-important *why* was no longer in doubt. Since authority radiated outward from the will of the *Fuehrer,* his word constituted the law of the land.

The Holocaust required an unqualified commitment by a totalitarian government and a passive population. Also essential were the men and the means to carry out murders on such a massive scale. The logistical problems of transporting and killing millions of people while fighting a war were formidable and required the cooperation of numerous officials and industrialists. Legal, psychological, and technical expertise were required to define who were Jews; the process of removing them from the economy called for financial specialists; the SS and military were needed to hunt them down and imprison them in ghettos; professional murderers had to be trained to machine-gun them in open fields; and finally, the construction and operation of concentration and death camps demanded willing hands and minds. The process of dehumanizing the killers and the attempt to reduce the victims to the level of subhumans was possible only in the absence of even the most basic civil liberties.

THE TOTALITARIAN PREREQUISITE

The wide-ranging apparatus of authorizing and implementing the destruction of the Jews was possible because the German people had relinquished to their government the right to make all political, economic, and many personal decisions. They had handed their individual and public liberties to Hitler like an unwanted gift they wanted to return. No doubt, many Germans believed that their personal noninvolvement absolved them of all responsibilities; those nebulous "others," those in charge, had the power, the glory, and the blame. If reprehensible action was required, their hands were clean, since they had neither ordered nor caused enactment of mass killings. The Reichstag had abdicated its power; it no longer represented the German people and merely tried to disguise the Nazi dictatorship with a rubber stamp. The concept that it was evil to permit evil to flourish without an effort to resist was not acknowledged. Not until the end of the war did men like Elie Wiesel arouse the world's conscience to the realization that the bystander cannot escape guilt or shame.

An understanding of the Holocaust necessitates a comprehension of the theory and practice of the Nazi movement. However, before discussing what it meant to be a German during the Third Reich, we must consider the circumstances which allowed Hitler to take control. The *Fuehrer* did not forcibly overthrow a legitimate government; he was the rightful successor to the Weimar Republic. There was no coup d'état, no revolution. The Nazi party won a plurality which resulted in the choice of Hitler as the chancellor. Those who voted the NSDAP ticket could not claim ignorance of Hitler's true aims. The press and radio had reported on his promises and tirades for years. His book, *Mein Kampf,* was in fact a blueprint of his intentions. Both his enormously well-received speeches and his writing were punctuated by a loathing for democracy, communism, peace, and Jews. Although it is debatable when he planned the destruction of the Jews, just when their extinction became imperative in his mind, it was always clear that their persecution was a cardinal theme in his program.

The question why a literate, well-informed electorate chose to throw away its freedom puzzles those of us who value liberty. Why did so many Germans decide to renounce democratic government and vote for a man whose qualifications were at best questionable? Were the circumstances which led to the demise of the Weimar Republic so exceptional, so singular, that their recurrence is nearly impossible? Or, might history repeat itself? Is it likely that the conditions prevailing in Germany in 1933 could be duplicated somewhere else at some other time? If the answer is yes, than it is our obligation to study the German situation with self-interested concern.

And the answer is yes. The German scenario was neither so exceptional nor so extraordinary that it could not recur. The circumstances experienced by Germans in the early 1930s were not unique; other nationalities faced similar difficulties. True, a number of events conspired to bedevil the German electorate at the very time that the charismatic *Fuehrer* emerged from obscurity. The combination of troubled times coupled with the lure of Hitler's magnetism allowed the Nazi tragedy to take place. It is not impossible that such a blending of economic, political, and psychological circumstances might be repeated in the future. The cost of such a disaster would be even higher because technological advances could easily enable another Hitler to exceed the eleven million civilians murdered, and the economic and social consequences would be impossible to estimate.

THE TREATY OF VERSAILLES

The government which preceded that of the Nazi Party was called the Weimar Republic. The Republic had been born in blood, hunger, and defeat at the end of the First World War. After four years of exhausting warfare, the Allied armies defeated the Germans in 1918 and the monarchy of Kaiser Wilhelm II ended. The emperor abdicated amid political agitation and fled to Holland. The armistice and peace negotiations were the unhappy responsibility of members of the new government. The German people wanted an end to hostilities and expected terms to be based on Woodrow Wilson's promises of peace without victory. The actual treaty which the German representatives were forced to sign was, in fact, punitive and hardly designed to give the fledgling Republic a much-needed vote of confidence. The war-guilt clause, placing the blame for the war solely upon Germany, infuriated every level of German society.

The Treaty of Versailles saddled the infant Republic with a burden it could not shake. Many Germans never absolved the signatories for their "betrayal." In fact, the German representatives were not permitted to participate in the negotiations; the first Republican government resigned rather than sign the treaty. But the German people were near starvation. Shipments of food were withheld until the signatures were affixed. None of this made any difference. The mark of Cain was on the men who signed the Versailles *Diktat*. How clever of Field Marshall von Hindenburg to refuse to represent the nation at the signing ceremony in the Hall of Mirrors. The civilian head of the Center Party, Matthias Erzberger, led the unhappy delegation. Within three years, that valiant man was assassinated in payment for his courage. The German army was not held accountable by the public for losing the war, for standing aloof at Versailles, or for its failure to support the new government.

The treaty was harsh, that is, unless one considers the terms of the agreement the Germans forced on the defeated Russians in 1918 at Brest-Litovsk. That was indeed a severe imposition of terms. One may well wonder whether Germany would have been impelled to adhere to President Wilson's Fourteen Points if it had been the victor. The Versailles settlement cost Germany one-eighth of its land along the eastern and western borders, her colonies, and her overseas investments. The German army was limited to one hundred thousand men; her navy was drastically curtailed, and the German people were obligated to pay an enormous, as yet unspecified, reparations bill. In light of today's understanding of international economic connections, the treaty could not help but obstruct and delay the process of German, even worldwide, recovery.

ORGANIZATION OF THE WEIMAR REPUBLIC

The government of the Weimar Republic consisted of a legislature, the Reichstag, elected by universal suffrage whose members represented the German people as a whole. A president, also chosen by the voters, served a seven-year term. The president, unlike his American counterpart, was not involved in the day-to-day running of the government but stood above political parties. Following national elections, he usually appointed the leader of the majority party in the Reichstag as chancellor. The chancellor then chose his cabinet and thus created the executive branch of government. Because it was difficult for any one party to have a clear majority in the Reichstag, all the Weimar governments were coalitions. The constitution also provided for representation from the eighteen states to sit as the Reichsrat, but that body played a secondary role in the interwar period. Article 48, a constitutional provision sometimes referred to as the suicide clause, permitted the president to suspend the constitution during emergencies. As will be seen later, this stipulation would play a critical part in the final destruction of the Republic.

As a document, the Weimar constitution was an admirable achievement. It provided for the civil liberties of the people, equality before the law, free elections of a representative government, education guaranteed for all, and safeguards for religious freedom. Despite such a commendable instrument of government, the problems faced by the Weimar administration were grave. With the caveat that classifying such difficulties may oversimplify some very complicated situations, the following summaries provide an overview.

THE POLITICAL SPECTRUM

Since the political designations *right, left,* and *center* vary in time and place, an understanding of their meaning during the first half of the present century is in order. These definitions clarify the aims, though not necessarily the practice, of political parties. Members of the extreme or radical left, mostly communists, Marxists, and the radical wing of the socialists, believed that their party must dictate policy in order to benefit the proletariat, that private property must be abolished and wealth redistributed to achieve greater economic and social equality, and that revolution was an acceptable means to that end. Supporters of the moderate, or liberal left, called themselves socialists. They advocated government control and ownership of all major public services, raw materials, and the means of production and distribution. They believed it was the state's duty to provide support from the cradle to the grave for all citizens. Despite their radical declarations, they valued stability and domestic peace. The major socialist parties of Germany expected that ballots, not bullets, would bring them to power.

On noneconomic issues, their views often coincided with policies of the center. The Catholic Center Party consisted mainly of middle-class Catholics. Its members favored gradual, constitutional changes that assured national stability and prosperity. Obviously, they also wished to protect the large Catholic minority within the Reich. The radical right, that is, ultra-nationalists, Nazis, and fascists, believed in a totalitarian, monolithic dictatorship. According to their credo, it was necessary for a single political party to use every possible means, including terror, to attain conformity and obedience from the citizens. National glory, war and conquest would be achieved under the leadership of the *Fuehrer* (leader). Democracy was judged a hated failure, the solace of the weak. Aside from these major political divisions, splinter parties moved in and out of the spectrum, forming and discarding coalitions according to the demands of practical politics.

DANGER FROM THE LEFT

The communists were disappointed that German socialism was not modeled after Soviet communism. Their support came from the urban workers who favored revolutionary methods to bring down the middle class Weimar regime. In order to prevent a Leninist revolution, the Social Democrats, under Friedrich Ebert, made a fateful deal with the German army. Generals Groener and Hindenburg agreed to support the Republic against any danger of a communist insurrection. When, in fact, the threat materialized, the army crushed the communists. From this moment on, German democracy was unable to make itself the master of the armed forces. Weimar's civilian government was under constant pressure from its conservative, ever-critical military. Swelling the ranks of the disillusioned regular soldiers were returning veterans. Unable to find work, they joined the *Freikorps*, a disruptive, often vicious volunteer corps dedicated to street fighting for rightist causes. They were part of the force the government used to crush the communists, a phyrric victory for Ebert because it alienated many of the workers from the Social Democrats. The murders of two of the communist leaders, Karl Liebknecht and Rosa Luxemburg, by former cavalry officers, merely intensified the mistrust. To the upper- and middle-class German, however, communism was the dreaded specter haunting Europe. This resulted in a rather sympathetic, almost forgiving attitude toward political assassinations.

DANGER FROM THE RIGHT

The political right was composed of ultra-nationalists. They glorified all things German to appease the wounded pride of a defeated, and from their point of view, cruelly betrayed people. In 1920, members of the old military-aristocratic alliance were secretly joined by industrialists in an attempt to overthrow the government by a coup d'état. Known as the Kapp putsch, it was a total failure. The ill-conceived plan misfired because the workers staged a general strike. While the military refused to respond to the call to defend the Republic, the labor unions united to crush the rebellion when they refused to provide the city of Berlin with basic services: no power, no mail, no transportation. Within five days, Wolfgang Kapp found that he could not establish a government in a paralyzed city. This fiasco, however, did not spell an end to rightist politics. Other, ever more extreme parties emerged. Among these was the Nazi Party whose actual name was *NAtionalsoZIalistische Deutsche Arbeiterpartei* ("National-Socialist German Workers' Party").

THE STRUGGLING CENTER

The Center's major objective was the protection of religious and civil rights of Catholics in a nation dominated by Protestants. The number of centrists usually were second only to the Socialists in national elections. Seen as moderate, they actually furnished more chancellors than any other party during the Weimar years. Without their cooperation and/or leadership, no government could effectively function. Trying to meet the needs of all Catholics meant that the party tried to serve some opposing interests beneath one umbrella. While the working classes were courted to join Catholic trade unions, their Catholic employers and members of the old aristocracy feared and opposed major industrial reforms. Agricultural, military, and commercial concerns also were frequently at odds. Only on the issue of communism was there unanimity; here party opposition was absolute. Obviously, it was difficult to find a single virtuoso to direct so many diverse voices. The brilliant Mattias Erzberger had been an outstanding leader of the Center. Unfortunately, he had believed it was his duty to sign the Treaty of Versailles, thus sparing the army and Marshall von Hindenburg the pain and humiliation of doing so. In the eyes of violent nationalists, that act tainted his name. He was murdered by young rightists in 1921.

The Social Democrats suffered from the brutal politics of the 1920s as well. One of their most gifted statesmen, Walter Rathenau, head of the Foreign Office, was assassinated in 1922. The fact that Rathenau was a Jew and that his religion became a point of anti-Semitic inflammatory rhetoric was an ill omen. He incurred the hatred of the extreme right because he believed that the signature of German delegates on the Treaty of Versailles obligated the nation to honor its provisions. His murder was hailed by the nationalists as a victory despite the fact that Rathenau had made international history by concluding the Treaty of Rapollo with the Soviet Union. This 1922 rapprochement of two pariahs in the family of nations benefited both participants; it broke their international isolation and provided Germany with an outlet for her industrial output so badly needed by the agrarian Soviet states.

The death of the first president of the Republic, Friedrich Ebert, might be called murder by defamation. This man deserved the gratitude of the German people, but in the poisoned atmosphere of the period, he was vilified instead. The right and the left opposed him for doing his duty, namely trying to make democracy function in Germany. While working people accused him of catering to the middle class, conservatives despised him for his humble beginnings as a saddler. He was publicly denounced as a traitor and went to court to defend his name. Ebert sued the libeler and won the verdict. But the court also found that since Ebert had taken part in an illegal strike in 1918, he was technically guilty. The actions and counteraction cost Ebert his life; he delayed a necessary operation for too long and died in 1925 at the age of fifty-four. His successor was the elderly Marshall von Hindenburg, the man fated to hand the government to Adolf Hitler.

ECONOMIC PROBLEMS OF THE WEIMAR REPUBLIC

While the questions concerning payment or nonpayment of the huge reparations bill aroused intense debate in the Reichstag, the French declared Germany in default over a rather minor delivery deficit. No doubt, memories of their defeat during the Franco-Prussian war and the German attack in World War I still festered in France. Supposedly to assure future payments, the French sent troops to occupy the industrial German Ruhr. This action escalated the long-standing enmity between Germany and France. The German public was incensed at this insult to German sovereignty. Although the former Allies opposed the French move, they did nothing. The inability of the Weimar administration to exercise control within its borders emphasized its weakness. But more serious still was the terrible inflation triggered by the occupation of the Ruhr.

THE WILD INFLATION

The German government urged the workers of the French-occupied Ruhr to strike and they complied. Such cooperation, however, was costly. Thousands of miners and industrial workers had to be supported through payments from the national treasury. This burden accelerated the further decline of German fiscal health. In order to deal with the costs of the war itself, with the expenditures incurred during demobilization and the penalties demanded by the Treaty of Versailles, the government resorted to printing more and more paper money which was not backed by gold. The limited amount of goods on the shelves were bid up by buyers who had the money to spend on too few products. The effects of a lost war, the economic dislocation, and losses of territories all contributed to the problem of inflation. Debtors obviously like to get rid of their obligations with inflated currency, but as the problem intensified, the whole monetary system was undermined. Each rise in prices activated higher wages and the resulting spiral drove the economy to ridiculous extremes. People rushed with their wages to stores lest prices double within the next hour. At the end of the war the mark had been valued at 8.4 to the dollar; in 1922 the ratio was 70,000 marks to the dollar; by December 1923 the rate of exchange was astronomical, trillions of worthless marks for a single dollar.

This wild inflation ruined the German economy. Savings of the middle class intended to provide for old age suddenly bought a single loaf of bread. Investments quite literally were not worth the paper on which the certificates were printed. Labor unions were nearly destroyed, since they could not provide their members with job security and a living wage. Some of the industrial giants, on the other hand, profited mightily. Their debts melted away, paid off with cheap money, their workers were powerless, and real estate speculators increased their holdings. The political reverberation of the economic chaos resulted in the further polarization of right and left. As will be clarified below, the newly organized Nazi Party attempted and failed in its premature putsch to use this crisis as a steppingstone to usurp the Bavarian government.

Finally, beginning in 1923, the administration was able to control the runaway inflation by placing the mark on a par with its prewar currency. The medicine was strong and many of the already weakened businesses collapsed; the standard of living declined further as unemployment and low wages demoralized the breadwinners. But the bitter pill was swallowed and digested and resulted in a partial economic recovery.

MOMENTARY RECOVERY

The international community, somewhat belatedly, made an effort to support Germany's struggle to recover. The Dawes Plan and later the Young Plan, both formulated by Americans, provided for orderly and gradually reduced or altogether forgiven reparation payments. The French troops were withdrawn from the Ruhr and a major international crisis was averted. The ensuing recovery expanded as foreign investors acknowledged the fine performance of German business and labor. Industries extended their organization into giant vertical trusts, called cartels. These were conglomerates which brought together every process of manufacturing, from extracting raw materials to the distribution of finished goods. Among such successful, monopolistic international business combinations, I.G. Farben Industrie was probably the best-known. By concentrating great business and technical power in the hands of its managing directors, cartels were able to compete successfully in domestic and foreign markets. Prices and profits were controlled, competition eliminated, yet the quality of their output was high. The Weimar constitution provided for greater freedom for the labor unions and under its legal protection, collective bargaining secured higher wages and improved working conditions. Unemployment fell and optimism rose. It is fair to say that in the mid-1920s, despite political uncertainties, the German people were rebuilding their economic life. If this trend had continued, political stability might well have followed. But, disastrously, the period of revival was short-lived. Conditions outside the control of the German people plunged the nation into new danger. This time, there would be no last-minute reprieve.

THE GREAT DEPRESSION

The always shaky foundations of the German Republic were subjected to an unexpected shock by the worldwide Depression which began in the late 1920s. The Wall Street crash of 1929 destabilized the American economy and following a domino effect, the European economies were pulled down one after another. The Great Depression slashed production, employment, and individual as well as corporate purchasing power. Many banks struggled in vain to remain viable when debtors were unable to meet their obligations and the number of foreclosures and bankruptcies multiplied. Farmers, the first to suffer economic decline, saw the ghost of forced sales of their land materialize at their doorsteps. Hunger once more undermined the physical and mental health of millions of people. Despair and rage competed for the hearts of men and women who had worked hard all their lives and now faced a daily struggle for survival.

The German recovery had relied heavily on foreign loans and exports. Financial institutions from the United States had been the most generous creditors but now called in their outstanding loans. Many importers who had bought German products now shut down these markets, thus deepening the downturn of the economic cycle. Doubts were voiced about the ability of the capitalistic free-market system to provide industrial societies with economic security. The wide swings of the boom and bust cycles obviously harmed too many people. Centrally planned economies which could function without foreign interference or dependence found new supporters. The industrialists, of course, wanted no part of communist state planning. The mere thought of the possible nationalization of their companies sent these conservative barons into a search for alternatives. Even the rhetoric of the Nazis seemed to promise a possible solution. The NSDAP and other ultra-rightist parties promised to place no restrictions on private property but claimed that they would manage the nation's business life without foreign meddling.

CONTINUING POLITICAL CRISIS

The Weimar Republic could not cope with the destitution of millions of its people. The unemployed who were affiliated with labor unions received a small income through the social security system, but the self-employed and unorganized workers were reduced to poverty. Once more, the middle class, barely emerging from the chaos of inflation, was victimized by economic disaster. No wonder the quick-fix solutions offered by the Nazis appealed to these groups. The Social Democrats, in power since 1928, were unable to alleviate the problems. They were replaced by the Center Party under Heinrich Bruening. When the new chancellor was unable to get several of his projects through the Reichstag, he persuaded President Hindenburg to invoke Article 48 of the constitution which declared the nation to be in a state of emergency and suspended the parliamentary system. The measure was to be temporary, but in effect, marked the beginning of the end of the Republic. Officially, the takeover by the Nazi Party did not take place until 1933, three years later, but the democratic process ground to a standstill as the nation tottered from crisis to crisis.

THE ART OF DEFEAT

The rise of Hitler to national prominence is best understood within the context of the prevailing mood of hopelessness in Germany. World War I had begun with expectations of a quick and easy victory and ended with disillusionment. The urge to escape the stark reality of a world gone awry gripped the nation. Some Germans found comfort in blaming a scapegoat for their ills; the communists, the Jews, and the Weimar Republic ranked high on that list. Others sought to bury their despair at the bottom of the liquor bottle and excesses of every kind. The nightlife in Berlin clubs was notorious for its dissoluteness. The craving for entertainment was inexhaustible. Long-held sexual mores broke down in an atmosphere of "anything goes except boredom." The pleasure seekers, of course, were censured by conservatives who shook their heads and recalled the gilded versions of the good old days when people knew how to behave decently.

The arts, particularly literature and painting, mirrored the turmoil of the generation. Several great literary figures, among them Erich Maria Remarque (*All Quiet on the Western Front*), Thomas Mann (*The Magic Mountain*), and the poet Rainer Maria Rilke distilled the pessimism of the age. Had the suffering of the war changed nothing? Were militarism and materialism the new gods of German culture? Like so many other writers in the Western world, German authors reflected the age of the lost generation.

German artists were among the leaders in using new forms of expression. Dadaism exhibited the concept that life and art have no meaning when millions are senselessly slaughtered on battlefields. Jean Arp, Max Ernst, and George Grosz used paint to introduce shapes and contours, angles and distortions which pointed expressionism toward new directions. Dreams and nightmares, disjointed human forms and nonrepresentative abstracts depicted a world where nothing was beautiful in the traditional sense. These paintings may have disturbed the viewer but they are glimpses into the artists' anguished conception of this world.

THE NAZIS ENTER HISTORY

The soil in which the Nazi Party took root and grew powerful was well tilled. Since their defeat at the end of World War I, the German people had experienced international humiliation, political convulsions, economic disasters, and cultural escapism. Every calamity left a trail of discontent which fueled the hope that something new, something extreme would set the world right. Conservatives remembered the past in ever more glowing memories, extremists on the left looked with yearning and rose-colored glasses toward the Soviet Union, and rightists lent their ears, their conscience, and their money to the several ultra-nationalist parties. The success achieved by Hitler and the Nazi Party was the result of a historic convergence of a man and his time.

THE NAZI VICTORY

By any measurement, Adolf Hitler's career was phenomenal. He became the most hated man in the world, the irrational dictator of a cultured nation, a malevolent figure who left the world much poorer than he found it. His qualifications for any work were minimal. If ever he had filled out a job application, it is unlikely he would have been granted an interview. Technically, as an Austrian citizen, he was an alien in Germany. His education was incomplete, he had not graduated from high school, nor did he ever hold a paying job. Hitler's appearance, except for the power of his eyes, was ordinary at best.

In a nation that values family background, his *Kinderstube* was barely commonplace. He was a Catholic who came to rule a nation with a Protestant majority. Those who knew him agreed that his work habits were deplorable. He did not meet any criteria for the vaunted Nordic superhero, and most of the men who occupied high places in the Third Reich were ambitious misfits.

Adolf Hitler was born in 1889 in Lower Austria the son of a minor official and his third wife. The boy showed no special promise and he failed the entrance examination which would have admitted him to the Vienna Academy of Fine Arts. This rejection turned the young Hitler into a homeless vagabond. For four years he tried to earn pennies peddling the picture postcards he painted. The Vienna interval was also associated with the development of his violent anti-Semitism. The capital of the Austro-Hungarian Empire had been a magnet for many poor Jews from the provinces and from Poland. As is usually the case, the newcomers, often with odd customs, unfamiliar religious practices, and a strange mode of dress, were resented. Between 1895 and 1910 the political life of the city was dominated by its Christian Socialist mayor, Karl Lueger. To stay afloat in the caldron of Austrian politics, Lueger tied himself to the hopes and frustrations of the lower classes. Among his formulae for retaining the support of the masses was anti-Semitism. The young destitute Hitler was deeply impressed by Lueger's simplistic solution of ascribing all calamities to the evil influence of the Jews. Lueger was popular and powerful, he was also an eloquent speaker; all in all a notable model for the future dictator.

World War I gave Hitler's life the direction it had lacked. He had moved to Munich in 1913 and had volunteered for the German army when the war broke out. From all accounts, he was a good soldier. The fact that he only achieved the rank of corporal would indicate that although he was awarded an Iron Cross first class for bravery, he did not impress his superiors as outstanding. When the armistice was reached, Hitler, by his own admission, was devastated. He returned to Munich and he joined a small political party, the German Workers' Party. Its membership was comprised of almost penniless veterans who advocated some rather vague notions of extreme nationalism. Although Hitler was their seventh member, he very quickly reshaped this company of malcontents into an effective organization. Here he discovered his exceptional powers as an orator. His words, his gestures, his blazing eyes had an almost hypnotic effect. Time and time again his own inner conviction transfixed his audience. He spoke with certainty when others equivocated; he offered simple, bold solutions with an air of absolute assurance. His world was black and white, full of love and hate. Germany was the object of his love which he was destined to rescue from the clutches of communist and Jewish depravity. His appeal was emotional, not logical, but his words moved his listeners to the heights and depths of his will.

THE PARTY PLATFORM

In 1920, the party, soon to be renamed the National Socialist German Workers' Party, or Nazi Party, drafted the program designed to attract money and members. There was something in this agenda to appeal to nearly every discontented or frightened German.

Among the twenty-five enumerated principles, the following are of particular interest in light of future events:

1. We demand on the basis of the right of national self- determination, the union of all Germans in a Greater Germany.
2. We demand equality for the German nation among other nations and the revocation of the peace treaties of Versailles and Saint Germain. (the latter concluded between the Allies and Austria). . . .
4. Only a racial comrade can be a citizen. Only a person of German blood, irrespective of religious denomination, can be a racial comrade. No Jew, therefore, can be a racial comrade.
5. Noncitizens shall be able to live in Germany as guests only, and must be placed under alien legislation.
6. We therefore demand that every public office, no matter what kind, and no matter whether it is national, state or local must be held only by citizens. . . .
8. Any further immigration of non-Germans is to be prevented. We demand that all non-Germans who entered Germany after August 2, 1914, be forced to leave the Reich without delay. . . .
10. It must be the first duty of every citizen to perform mental or physical work. Individual activity must not violate the general interest, but must be exercised within the framework of the community, and must be for the general good. . . .
25. To implement all these points (these included confiscation of war profits, mandatory profit sharing of large business enterprises, old age insurance, land reform, death penalty for many criminals, educational and health service, newspaper censorship, and circumscription of religious freedom), we demand the creation of a strong central power in Germany. A central political parliament should possess unconditional authority over the entire Reich. . . .

Considering the fact that most party platforms contain empty verbiage rather than a plan for governing, this document came close to a blueprint for the conduct of the Nazis in office. The need for union with Austria was cited, also the scrapping of the treaties ending the First World War. Discrimination against the Jews was clearly delineated although the magnitude of persecution remained vague. Hitler's preoccupation with so-called German blood, so vital in his Aryan superiority ideology, was deemed worthy of several references. Article 10 asserts that the citizens exist for the nation, not vice versa, a concept of central importance in the Third Reich. The last proposition alludes to dictatorship by the party and is just short of endorsing totalitarianism.

THE SA

In 1921, Hitler created the SA, a semi-military band of men to protect Nazi Party meetings and to harass rival organizations. These troopers wore brown shirts, pants, and boots and were often referred to as the Brownshirts. Most were unemployed toughs, some had seen military service, others could be labeled as perennial losers. Their antisocial behavior was glamorized as heroic acts in the defense of the fatherland. In fact, they brawled in the streets with the militant members of opposition parties, threatened voters near the balloting places, and beat up Jews and other targeted civilians. Under the leadership of Ernst Roehm, their numbers had swelled to four hundred thousand in 1932. When Hitler became chancellor, he enhanced the SA's powers by converting it to a national, political police force. While policemen were expected to enforce the law, the SA was beyond and above the law. But Roehm's ambitions were greater than Hitler's view of the role of the SA. Roehm aspired to create a truly military force, one to rival and equal the regular armed forces. As will be noted later, the feud between the *Wehrmacht* and the SA was decided in 1934 during the *Night of the Long Knives,* in favor of the regular army. The function of terrorizing the public was taken over by the SS, the better-trained, better-schooled elite of Hitler's private army.

THE FAILED BEER HALL PUTSCH

Hitler's first attempt to attain political power was a local affair. He planned to unseat the Bavarian administration by staging an attempted coup d'état in 1923 in Munich. Named after the beer hall where the event began, its scenario resembled a comic opera performance rather then a serious political exercise. Act I opened in the cellar where some three thousand Bavarians, including several political, military, and social leaders, had gathered to hear a speech by Gustav von Kahr, the state commissioner. Outside, six hundred members of the semi-military units of the Nazi Brownshirts, the SA, surrounded the building. They set up a machine gun with its muzzle pointed toward the door of the building. In the beer hall, in the meantime, there was shock and high drama. Von Kahr was droning on when suddenly an excited man with a mustache jumped on a chair, fired a shot toward the ceiling, and shouted that the national revolution had begun. Hitler, with a few followers in tow, then claimed that the SA had already taken over the police and army barracks and that soldiers and police had joined the revolution. This statement was a lie. Several dignitaries among the assembled chiefs hustled Hitler into a back room. There a very tense Hitler informed them that the new head of the German nation was the renowned General Ludendorff. The stunned circle of officials recovered enough to tell Hitler to stop his nonsense. The enraged leader of the Nazi Party screamed that tomorrow would find Germany with a new government or he and his comrades would be dead. Neither prediction was accurate. One by one the heads of the Bavarian government managed to escape the beer hall and prepare for the coming showdown with these would-be revolutionaries.

Ludendorff, the war hero turned right-wing eccentric, arrived in time to lend his considerable prestige to the coup. Meanwhile, news of the Bavarian uprising had reached the head of the national army. The military promised to stand by the Republic and declared its willingness to commit troops to quell the insurrection in the event that Bavarian authorities needed help. As it turned out, such assistance was not required.

The next scene was enacted on the streets of Munich. The SA, led by Ludendorff and Hitler, marched toward a confrontation with Bavarian police. Three thousand Nazis were stopped by a barricade of one hundred policemen. Hitler's demand that they surrender was answered with bullets. The line of Brownshirt marchers melted away. Neither Hitler nor Ludendorff were injured, but the putsch was over. The sixteen Nazis killed that November morning became the glorified martyrs of the movement; their praises were sung many thousands of times in the "Horst Wessel Song," the Nazi anthem.

The last act of the putsch was played out at Hitler's trial. Indicted for treason, he did not stand as a penitent at the bar of justice. Quite the opposite, he used the public prosecution as a propaganda platform and turned failure into a publicity success. The whole nation suddenly knew who he was. He was found guilty and sentenced to five years imprisonment. Actually, he served less than two years but he used that interval to further advance his cause. While rather comfortably confined, he dictated the holy writ of Naziism, *Mein Kampf* ("My Struggle"), to his friend and secretary, Rudolf Hess. The lesson of the failed takeover was not lost on Hitler; he was now certain that it was his undeniable fate to resurrect Germany but only by legitimate means. The acquittal of Ludendorff, so obviously a conspirator against the Republic, was a clear indication that the judicial system remained unduly awed by the military. Hitler's brief sentence was another example of the indulgence with which the established government viewed the extreme right.

MEIN KAMPF

It is difficult to judge the actual impact of Hitler's book. During the Nazi era it was found in most German households; it replaced the Bible as an almost mandatory wedding present. Every student could quote passages from its pages. Hitler became a millionaire from the number of copies sold. How much of the volume was actually read and understood by the general public one cannot guess. The first edition was almost unreadable. It was a jumble of Hitler's racial and administrative notions, of his admonitions for the German people, of his economic and political aspirations, and of his love for his mother. It was so poorly organized and contained so many grammatical errors that subsequent editions had to be cleaned up by the editors. In retrospect, the German people, in fact, the entire world, would have done well to pay greater heed to Hitler's stated objectives. Those who actually bothered to plow through the volume received few surprises when Hitler ultimately achieved power.

Among the major propositions postulated in *Mein Kampf* are the following:

1. Unconditional authority belongs to the leader. This concept, often called the *Fuehrer Prinzip*, regards democracy as a despicable form of government and the Weimar Republic one of its most depraved examples.
2. The Germans are a superior race. As Aryans, they are the bearers of the highest expression of racial fulfillment. Aryan racial purity must be maintained at all cost. No diseased or weak people must be allowed to have children.

3. The Jews are the essential enemy in Hitler's pseudo-Darwinistic concept of survival of the fittest. Jews aim to ruin Germany and all civilization; they have no culture, and Jewish men desperately seek to seduce Aryan women.
4. All life is a struggle for survival; war is the natural and honorable expression of that struggle.
5. Marxism is the other great enemy of Germany. Often the Marxist and Jewish menace are depicted as one and the same.
6. Germany's economy must become self-sufficient. Dependence on foreign loans and trade was designed to keep the nation enslaved to interest payments.
7. Nationality and race are a matter of blood and soil. Only birth and heritage can bestow the German birthright, not language or religion or cultural imitation.
8. Large economic complexes must be broken up and all businesses must share profits with their workers.

With the exception of the last item, most of the ideas expressed in the book became Nazi policy after 1933.

THE ARYAN SUPERIORITY MYTH

At the center of Hitler's dogma was the racial doctrine. Since it was the theoretical basis and the rationale for the destruction of so many millions deemed unfit to live in the Nazi universe, it requires further understanding.

There is no *Aryan* race. The term was adopted by the Nazis from the designation of an Indo-European language group. By virtue of skillful manipulation, a falsehood was elevated into a so-called science. From kindergartens to universities, racial studies were presented to students as objective truth. Aryan superiority was "proven" with concocted data of biological measurements and historical "evidence" of past greatness. The ideal men and women were depicted as blond, blue-eyed, tall, straight-backed, with high foreheads and straight noses. Side by side with the physical attributes of the Aryans were their spiritual qualities: courage, honesty, intellect, inventiveness, and artistic excellence. These traits were genetically embedded in the bloodline. The superiority of the Nordic race permitted, no, demanded, the right to subjugate less advantaged people such as the eastern European Slavs. Thus, counterfeit biological factors were given momentous significance in this perverted form of Darwinism: The race most fit to dominate had the natural right to mastery over lesser races.

AUTHORS OF THE ARYAN THEORY

The spurious scientists of the Third Reich elevated the theories of the fertile minds of Houston Stewart Chamberlain and Alfred Rosenberg to the level of doctrine. Chamberlain (1855–1927) was born an Englishman who turned his back on his native country. He married the daughter of the composer Richard Wagner and became fanatical in his admiration of all things German. His mental acrobatics were astounding. He admired Galileo, Dante, Michelangelo, and Leonardo da Vinci, and insisted that these historic figures were racial Teutons. In fact, all benefactors of mankind, all gifts enjoyed by humanity stemmed from the Nordic race. Even Jesus was given an Aryan heritage. The Teutonic/Germanic people stood in direct opposition to the destructive power of the only other pure race, the Jews. In his lofty, metaphysical style, Chamberlain rewrote history. Racial impurity was assigned the blame for the fall of ancient Rome, and the Jews had inherited the ethnic disorder that felled mighty Rome. It is difficult to believe that such nonsense found so many advocates; nevertheless, his books were best-sellers and won critical praise.

Alfred Rosenberg (1893–1946), a Lithuanian by birth, was the chief ideologist of the Nazi party. After a stint as editor of the Nazi newspaper the *Voelkischer Beobachter,* Hitler awarded him several political positions. His final post was as *Reichsminister* for the Eastern Occupied Territories where he promoted the brutal Germanization of conquered Poland, supervised slave laborers and aided in the mass murder of Jews. His dreadful career ended on the gallows, a convicted criminal of the International Court of Justice. Chamberlain's influence on his thinking was obvious. Rosenberg's best-seller, *The Myth of the Twentieth Century,* reiterated the claim of Nordic racial superiority but added a new concept: namely a virulent anti-Christian element. The Catholic church was held responsible for accepting and spreading the destructive spirit of a Semitic/Latin faith. In pseudo-scientific terms, Rosenberg reshaped Christ into an Aryan warrior who, with sword in hand, fought rather than preached of non-Germanic love, pity, and meekness. From this convoluted reasoning, Rosenberg leaped to the conclusion that not only were the Jews answerable for their own crimes, but also for all evil, past and present, committed by the Christian world. His attempts to return to the ancient pagan faith, called rather paradoxically, *positive Christianity,* was cut short by the war. One must seriously doubt that the god Wotan of Norse legend could have replaced Jesus even among ardent Nazis. Rosenberg's theories sounded confused and even deranged. Nonetheless, Hitler allowed him a great deal of power. Just how many Germans actually shared his vaporous imagination is impossible to tell.

LEGITIMIZING HITLER

The Depression gave the Nazi movement the opportunity to increase its strength dramatically. The electorate turned to radical parties in increasing numbers. City workers found their way into both the Nazi and the Communist Parties. The radical left and its *Rotfrontkaempferbund* ("Red Front Fighter Group") and the SA of the Nazis fought pitched battles on the streets of Berlin. Speakers representing every political point of view harangued the public with their rhetoric. Every sort of uniform was resurrected from attics and cellars. Prominent among these was the gray worn by the *Stahlhelmers* ("the Steel Helmets"), a paramilitary umbrella organization of nationalist ex-service men. Their smart marching ranks accommodated many monarchists as well as other assorted antagonists of the Weimar Republic. Rarely did the Steel Helmets clash with the Nazi militia; Hitler had ordered that such collisions must be avoided. The connection between the *Stahlhelm* and the military was too close for comfort and Hitler had no wish to alienate the army.

Political warfare was costly, even in the 1930s. The Nazis campaigned hard in every local and national election. The SA, the propaganda campaigns, the sea of swastikas on flags and posters, the uniforms, all these trappings necessitated fund-raising. Hitler needed money, or preferably, he needed support from people with money. But would members of the financial and industrial establishment take him seriously? Could their snobbish attitude toward an Austrian upstart be overcome?

Fear of communism gave Hitler the passport into the world of power and money. He became a possible champion, a counterweight against the dreaded Red Menace. When the number of Nazi Reichstag representatives rose from 12 to 107 in the 1930 election, making it the second largest party in the parliament, the mighty took heed. The communists too had made dangerous gains, from 54 to 77 seats. *Herr* Hitler, the magnates believed, would have to do. Indeed, he was a little uncouth, not from the background they preferred, but he would be useful as their tool, their means to fight communism. No doubt, this Austrian corporal would be malleable in their experienced hands, a man to be molded to their will.

Two events contributed to the improved standing of the Nazis among the upper classes. The first occurred in 1931 when a conclave of political rightist party leaders allowed Hitler into the vaunted company of well-established nationalists. In attendance were the *Stahlhelm's* chief, Franz Seldte; the director of the United Steelworks, Fritz Thyssen; the renowned banker and economic wizard, Hjalmar Schacht; and the head of the Nationalist Party, Alfred Hugenberg. The meeting took place in the small town of Harzburg, thus was dubbed the Harzburg Front. Hitler, always an impressive speaker, made a good impression on the assemblage. Acceptance, endorsement, and financial support by the mainstream of rightist organizations allowed the Nazis to take a giant step on the ladder to power.

During the following year, Hitler was invited to address the members of the elite Industry Club. Here, in Duesseldorf at the center of German manufacturing, Hitler again worked his oratorical charm. He spoke for two and a half hours, shouting much of the time.He persuaded his audience that his party would safeguard capitalism, protect private property, end once and for all the communist danger, and keep the trade unions in check. Surely, this was music to the ears of the coal and steel barons of the Ruhr. Hitler was given a standing ovation, and more importantly, his future political campaigns were well financed.

THE END OF THE REPUBLIC

The moderate parties of the Weimar Republic had been unable to convince the German voters of their ability to solve Germany's economic distress and the political morass. At this juncture, in 1932, Hindenburg's first presidential term ended. Hitler decided his time had come and ran against him. It was an election campaign characterized by frequent violence, particularly between Communists and Nazis. The voters at the polls were threatened by the Brownshirts, who swarmed around the polling places. Hitler won 30 percent of the vote and this necessitated a run-off election with Hindenburg. The aging war hero was returned to office but his was a hollow victory. Later that year, in the Reichstag elections, the Nazis won 230 seats. They had become the largest single party.

By tradition, Hitler should now have been appointed chancellor but the venerable president of the Republic could not bring himself to hand the government to this ex-corporal from Austria. Hindenburg was eighty-four and his mind and body had lost much strength, yet, he had an almost instinctive mistrust of this gesticulating man with the black mustache. So, he tried to give Germany a government without Hitler.

Chancellor Bruening had been dismissed. Who could fill the post? The Machiavellian role played by General Kurt von Schleicher underlined the continuing deterioration of German politics. Schleicher (his name in German means "the sneaky one") had been at the periphery of power for years. He now suggested that Hindenburg proffer the chancellorship to a mediocre member of the aristocracy, Franz von Papen. The debonair von Papen sought to curb the power of the Nazis by bringing Hitler into his fold. The maneuver failed; Hitler did not want the vice-chancellor's job because he was certain his time would come—and soon. Von Papen took note of the latest political straws floating in the wind and decided that a new election would reduce the Nazi vote. He was only partially correct. The number of NSDAP members in the Reichstag was cut by only thirty-four seats. A small victory, but it changed nothing. Von Papen resigned and Schleicher moved up into the chancellor's office. His was the last administration of the Weimar Republic.

Schleicher tried to check the Nazi menace by creating an anti-Nazi coalition between the army and the trade unions, but even fear of Hitler could not hold together such an awkward pairing. Finally, the chancellor tried to convince Hindenburg that only a military dictatorship could save the fatherland but the old field marshall had sworn to uphold the constitution and would not sign such an order. Schleicher had no choice but to offer his resignation. Hitler did not forget this attempt to obstruct the Nazi rise to power. In 1934, during the Blood Purge, six Nazi murderers entered Schleicher's home and killed him in front of his family.

The curtain fell on the Republic when Hindenburg was finally persuaded to ask Hitler to form a government. Von Papen, still under the illusion that his titles, his background, his experience would impress Hitler, had a hand in the machinations. He took the vice-chancellor's office, certain that he could keep *Herr* Hitler in check. The field marshall's son, Oskar, also pressured his father to submit to the inevitable, namely turning the government over to the Nazis. It must have been a bitter pill for the old soldier to swallow. On several occasions, Hindenburg had stated that never, absolutely never, would he ask Hitler to be chancellor. Hitler's response was tragically prophetic when he replied: "Hindenburg is eighty-five years old, I am forty-five. I can wait." Actually, he did not wait very long. Within a year he would occupy the president's office as well.

Chapter 4

Careers Built on Hate: Hitler and His Instruments

The Holocaust was implemented by men, not mechanical robots or spineless puppets. Men planned, executed, and exulted in the commission of history's most despicable crime. The more we learn about the savagery necessary to translate Hitler's mental picture of a world without Jews, the more insistently does the question recur: Who could have done this? The answer is as haunting as the question. An American visitor to Berlin, sitting in a cafe some forty years after the liberation of the concentration camps, found himself staring into the faces of men and women whom he judged to be in their seventies, wondering, wondering, wondering. . . .

HITLER AND THE JEWS

The Holocaust was Hitler's most persistent passion. The man and the event cannot be separated. The suggestion that the *Fuehrer* did not order, in fact did not know of the mass killings flies in the face of all we know about the administrative apparatus of the regime. No one would have dared to execute such a momentous scheme without Hitler's actual or tacit order. Even though a written directive for the mass murders of the Jews has, as of this writing, not been uncovered, veritable mountains of research indicate that Hitler's elite vied with one another to do their master's will. Often, the heads of agencies dealing with Jewish issues anticipated Hitler's thoughts and converted accepted ideology into actuality, always remaining within the context of well-established policies.

In *Mein Kampf*, Hitler gave little indication of how his early personality was shaped. He generated the impression that upon passing a group of religious Jews on the street during his stay in Vienna, he realized with mystical insight that these bearded, black-garbed men were a cancer upon Germanic life. Actually, during the period from 1907 to 1913, the young Hitler in Vienna adopted his racial and political concepts from ideas promulgated by others. For example, an ex-monk who called himself Lanz von Liebenfels wrote extensively on Aryan superiority and flew a flag with a swastika over his castle. Liebenfels insisted that Jews headed the list of inferior races who must make way for the Aryans. Making way included the very same methods of deportations, slave labor, sterilization, and killing which were later decreed by the Third Reich. Another precursor of Nazi theory was Georg Ritter von Schoenerer. He was the leader of the Austrian pan-German movement who urged the union of all Germans into a single nation. He too exhorted his followers to recognize Jews as a national menace. The previously mentioned mayor of Vienna, Karl Lueger of the Austrian Christian Social Party, became Hitler's mentor in two areas; first, his allegation that the Jews engaged in shameless financial exploitation was adopted by the adult Hitler; and second, Lueger's manipulation of the masses was a prototype for the masterful use of dramatic, emotional propaganda techniques of the Third Reich. Karl Lueger's effectiveness in haranguing crowds amid the display of symbols and finely tuned pageantry was not lost on young Adolf.

The historic origins of Hitler's war against the Jews can be traced easily enough; anti-Jewish hostilities in the ancient, medieval, and modern world had foreshadowed everything except the death camps. But regardless of where Hitler's vision of Europe without Jews originated, the problem remains, why was it a matter of the first priority for Hitler to physically destroy the Jews? He was the *Fuehrer*, the unquestioned head of a powerful nation that was admired for its cultural heritage, feared for its military establishment, advanced in its industrial institutions, and peopled by a literate, hardworking citizenry. Why was that not enough for this upstart, this nonentity who burst upon the political scene from nowhere? During the dozen years of Hitler's control, German society faced staggering domestic, foreign, and military problems. Nonetheless, the destruction of Jews remained a central preoccupation for Hitler. Why?

WHO BENEFITED FROM THE HOLOCAUST?

As a rule, governments enact policies which, at best, are presumed to profit the nation, or at worst, promote the wealth, the power, or other self-serving motives of its leaders. Some sort of rational agenda, even when ill-conceived and badly mismanaged, underlies the national policies. This was true of the Nazi regime in all areas but one: the Aryan superiority myth. No logical measure of what was good or bad for Germany was applied here. The force driving Germans to commit genocide was Hitler's will, but we do not know what drove Hitler with such relentless fury.

What advantage was to be gained by making Germany and its conquered lands *Judenrein?* What economic, political, or social purposes would be served by the annihilation of a defenseless, highly productive minority? The search for an answer has evoked some invalid conclusions which must be exposed and laid to rest.

ECONOMIC MOTIVATION

Among the explanations erroneously put forward was the view that Hitler's motives were economic. The Nazis coveted the wealth of the Jews to fuel their military plans. That reasoning is flawed. Hitler seized the Jewish properties and bank accounts, in fact any item of value from jewelry to wool coats, but why resort to mass murders? To place Aryans in jobs and businesses held by Jews was simple enough and done efficiently wherever German armies established dominion, but how did the nation profit by the death of six million? As a matter of fact, the killings exacerbated the critical labor shortages on farms and in factories. Large numbers of skilled and semi-skilled workers became casualties when Germany was at war and the demand for ever-increasing production required an inexhaustible pool of manpower. Keeping the Jews alive and utilizing them as an unpaid labor force would have made economic sense. Instead, the effort required for the process of annihilation cost the Germans many millions of working hours.

POLITICAL MOTIVATION

Were the Jews killed for political reasons? Hitler once stated that if there were no Jews he would have needed to invent them. In other words, the political use of the Jews as scapegoats for every setback suffered by Germans was of great value. But what good are dead scapegoats? Once gone, they can no longer absolve the living of their failures. A new scapegoat would then be required, but Jews were historically peerless as objects of hate.

Did the Jews at any time present an actual political danger to the Third Reich? There is no evidence to support such a view. Goebbels, master of the big lie, denounced them as Marxists, Communists and saboteurs, and as traitors in league with the enemy. At the same time, they were accused of being exploiters of the working poor. Actually, Jews were in no position to pose a danger, not for Germany nor anywhere else. During the Weimar years, they did not support any single political ideology; they did not vote as a bloc. Their diversity prevented them from exerting real political clout. As a group, they did not conspire to overthrow either the economic or the political order. The Nazis refused to see the conflict in their portrayal of the Jews as both Communist agitators and capitalist plotters. The rather well-worn accusation that Jews had actual plans to overthrow the Christian civilizations of the world was an echo from that old tsarist forgery known as *The Protocols of the Elders of Zion*. Hitler often coupled *Jew* and *Communist* to form a single word, a device which played upon the fears of the German middle class. In truth, there was no Jewish political threat. The very success of the Holocaust speaks convincingly of the weakness of the Jewish people in exerting any influence within the German nation or internationally.

CULTURAL MOTIVATION

We have already dealt with the cultural phenomena of religious, nationalistic, and racial anti-Semitism. The hostility created by this ancient and modern antagonism provided the groundwork upon which Hitler built the organization of annihilation. Some scholars assert that German philosophers during the past two centuries prepared a uniquely Teutonic predisposition to the Holocaust, but their arguments are not convincing. It is questionable how much influence was exerted by the learned professors from Kant to Fichte, Hegel and Treitschke over the minds of ordinary Germans. Until the rise of Hitler, the ebb and flow of anti-Semitism had washed the shores of Spain, France, Germany, Poland, and Russia without partiality. More authoritative research is needed before it is possible to accept the existence of a distinctly German and particularly vicious form of anti-Semitism. One could make an equally dubious case for the opposite *Weltanschauung* by quoting from the works of Germans who urged tolerance and acceptance of differences among people. Finally, we must not assume that Hitler's racial ideology was derived from reading the works of philosophers whose theories were often unintelligible to most Germans. Neither Hitler nor the men who sat at his feet were philosophical thinkers. They took pride in action, not debating, and they often sneered at the intellectuals whom they considered useless baggage.

THE CASE FOR A PSYCHOLOGICAL EXPLANATION

The economic, political, and cultural rationales do not answer the essential question: Why did Hitler hate the Jews with such an all-encompassing rage? Only the realm of psychology is left to us. Many historians view with suspicion the intrusion of that discipline into their bailiwick. The difficulties are many because, at best, a psychological analysis of Hitler would result in a theory, a probability, a presumption. As social scientists, historians prefer to place their emphasis on the term *scientist*, that is, one whose findings stand on provable grounds. Dissecting a dead man's motivation cannot yield a measurable definitive conclusion. But since a study of the Holocaust cannot evade the central question of Hitler's state of mind, and since psychiatry holds the best clues, we are compelled to step into these uncertain waters. Always, however, the student must be aware that psychological judgments are open to debate, to be accepted or rejected, wholly or in part.

The concept that early childhood experiences have a role in the development of personality is widely accepted. Although Freud's theory of psychosexual development has not survived unchallenged, it remains a thesis which contending psychologists may dispute but can never ignore.

Among the several psychological analyses offered, this writer finds the most compelling is argued by Robert G. L. Waite in his book *The Psychopathic God: Adolf Hitler.* Waite reconstructs Hitler's early years and presents some very persuasive conclusions. According to Freud, the evolution of a normal personality requires that the child pass successfully through the oral, anal, Oedipal/Electra, and latency stages. Nature itself has set the timer for each individual and damage can be done to character development when extraneous forces, most likely the parents, interfere with the process. Waite and others have maintained that the paradoxical, irrational, sexually aberrant Hitler was reared amid circumstances which were destructive to proper maturation.

Before outlining the possible psychological causes for Hitler's all-consuming hatred of Jews, it is important to sound a word of caution. There is an important difference between understanding and exonerating criminal behavior. Even if we accept the premise that certain childhood events twisted and deformed an individual, such past events do not absolve the adult from responsibility for his actions. It is very dangerous to excuse evil in the name of illness. We may comprehend the roots of anti-social, or even cruel, behavior, but civilized society must also protect itself from destructive elements within it. If the conditions of Hitler's childhood appear to make him a victim of circumstances, we must counter that assertion with the observation that human beings are not straws in the wind, blown this way and that without some degree of free will. Choices do exist; even in Auschwitz the victims made choices,

Hitler, the orator.
(Courtesy AP/Wide World Photos.)

often only concerning the manner in which to meet death. For the religious funda-mentalists who see God's handiwork in every event in the universe, nothing said here or anywhere will change their views, not even the obscenity of making Hitler an agent of the creator.

A MAN OF PARADOXES

Biographies of Hitler delineate his personality as paradoxical. He was brutal and also capable of kindness, particularly to children and animals. Sometimes his honesty could be disarming, but lies served him with equal ease. His grasp of reality was a matter of timing, sometimes it seemed firmly based, other times his fantasies seemed to overpower his mind. His life was marked by acts of courage as well as of cow-ardice. In public, he exhibited superb self-assurance, in private, he worried about the impression he made. He saw others in only two diametrically opposing shades, black or white, vassal or enemy. His moods could swing from rage to gentleness in a moment. His capacity for hatred, coupled with his conviction that destiny had singled him out for a messianic role, made him the most dangerous man in a perilous century.

Hitler glorified the concept of the perfect Aryan specimen but he hardly met his own criteria, and furthermore, he surrounded himself with misfits. When a truth con-tradicted a concept in his mental world, Hitler did not change his mind, he altered his truth. Thus, for example, it became Nazi lore that Jesus was not a Jew, that Jews were infectious vermin, that Franklin D. Roosevelt and most of the English nobility were Jewish, that Judaism was a race not a religion, that only Aryan blood was creative and non-Aryans were merely fit for enslavement. The determining essence of good and evil, right and wrong, was blood and blood alone. His preoccupation with blood, and Jew-ish blood in particular, runs like a refrain through his mind. One cannot but wonder why.

THE FATHER

Hitler's father Alois was the illegitimate child of Maria Anna Schicklgruber. The uncertainty of his own ancestry may have contributed to the son's fixation on his genetic inheritance, raising the question of the purity of his blood. Austrians have a long history of anti-Semitism. It is probable that Hitler was taught to despise Jews during his childhood. Such early indoctrination, when coupled with insecurity concerning his ancestry, may have caused Hitler's fascination with blood. If he feared that his own blood could be tainted, then his many references to poisoned blood, his refusal to father any children, and his strange eagerness to endure leeches as part of medical treat-ments become more understandable. Whether consciously or not, doubts regarding his own Aryan purity may have resulted in some strange personal habits. For example, he was obsessively clean (Jews are dirty); he covered his nose with a mustache (Jews have large noses); in 1935, just two years after he became chancellor, he banned Gentile

females under the age of forty-five from work in Jewish households (his grandmother had been a maid, although not in a Jewish household); sexual intercourse between Jews and Gentiles was declared a capital crime. The razing of the entire village where his father was born was certainly bizarre. Surely, there were other sites where an artillery testing ground could have been installed without moving the residents to new homes. Did Hitler hope that the disappearance of the village would cause his father's memory to go up in smoke as well?

Alois Hitler had risen from peasant stock to become a minor customs official. As best as we can ascertain, he was a mean and cruel man. Clara, Adolf's mother and Alois's third wife, was twenty-three years younger than her husband. Alois expected, and usually was given, total and silent obedience. He was often drunk, and regardless of whether he was drunk or sober, apparently beat the children and their mother. It is difficult to reconstruct which must have been more painful for the child Adolf, to see his beloved mother terrorized or feel the blows on his own back. The adult Hitler rarely mentioned his father. As a matter of fact, he did not commonly refer to Germany as the *fatherland*, it is the *motherland* he promised to save, the *motherland* he extolled endlessly.

Alois's notion of parental responsibility seemingly was to either ignore his son or browbeat and humiliate him. Eric Erikson used the term *negation* in such a context and the renowned psychologist stated that a child who is negated develops the desire to destroy.

THE MOTHER

Hitler's mother was a deeply troubled, pious Catholic. She had lived with her husband before they were married and the sin consumed her conscience. She probably interpreted the death of two of her children as God's punishment for her weakness. Adolf was not only the object of her maternal love, he also represented the possibility of God's forgiveness. So she clung to him, doted on him, adored and spoiled him. She hoped the boy would enter the priesthood, but Adolf was expelled from the religious school he briefly attended; he was caught smoking.

While there is no doubt that the boy loved his mother, he surely must have hated her as well. Why did she allow herself to be beaten? Why was she so powerless? And even more tormenting was her inability to protect her children. How could she love them and do nothing when the father abused them? Why did this wide-eyed, pale woman work so hard to please her despicable husband? What secrets did the mother and the father share when they closed their bedroom door?

Growing up with a brutal, all-powerful father and a loving, indulgently permissive but weak mother does not bode well for the future of any child. The resulting confusion is commonly identified by family counselors as receiving "double messages." Hitler's mother died when he was nineteen, by then the ingredients for future neurosis were likely to be in place.

A PSYCHOSEXUAL VIEW

According to Freudian analysts, the personality of the adult Hitler reveals behavior which points to unresolved problems in his psychosexual development. The *Fuehrer* was a compulsive talker; he was given to uncontrolled tantrums (German anti-Nazis called him *Teppichfresser*, "one who chews on carpets"); the line between imagination and reality often blurred in his mind; his sniffing of his own body and repeated washing were neurotic. His personality was rigid, and he was unable to change his mind. He spoke about the "granite foundation" of his philosophy and prided himself on his inflexibility. He never admitted to any mistakes; failures were never his, others had to bear the blame. Unable to be a friend, he had no friends.

Nor did Hitler resolve his Oedipal conflict; his relationships with women were never normal. There is general agreement that the most important woman in his life was a young niece, Angela Rabaul. Hitler kept her a virtual prisoner until she succeeded in her efforts to kill herself. His most lasting attachment was to Eva Braun. She was his mistress for twelve years during which time she too attempted to end her life. Eva was Hitler's wife for one day, April 30, 1945, the day the newly married pair committed suicide in their Berlin bunker. Eva matched Hitler's concept of the ideal woman: quiet, loyal, disinterested in politics, undemanding, and shallow. Hitler commented to Albert Speer, his personal architect and wartime production chief, that a highly intelligent man should take a primitive and stupid woman. The wording is revealing not only in connection with Eva, but that a man should *take* a woman. . . . This contemptuous statement was made in Eva's presence.

POSSIBLE DIAGNOSES?

Was Hitler mentally ill? Unfortunately, a simple yes or no is not possible. Within the legal context, he would have been pronounced sane. He knew right from wrong and chose wrong. Had he lived to face the judgment at Nuremberg, he would have been hanged because he understood the consequences of his actions. Could the psychiatric community have argued the legal findings? Possibly, because Hitler was a borderline personality, neurotic but not consistently psychotic. In other words, he was able to function effectively despite certain obsessive and sado-masochistic traits. In the early years of his regime his very pathology, his certainty that heaven itself had mandated his mission to save Germany, gave him the appearance of commanding authority. As *Fuehrer,* he brushed aside all opposing opinions in favor of the dictates of some inner voice only he could hear. After the German armies had failed at Stalingrad, reports on his behavior described it as aberrant. Like a demented man, he ordered armies about that no longer existed, had uncontrollable fits of rage, and saw treachery everywhere. Defeat pushed him from the realm of neurosis into madness.

While German soldiers were freezing to death from the rigors of a terrible

Russian winter, while supplies were urgently needed at the front, the German railroad system delivered trainloads of victims to German installations in Poland. Shipments of Jews to the death camps had priority over the requirements of the army. One day before Hitler died on April 29, 1945, while Berlin turned into blazing rubble, he wrote his so-called political testament. The final sentence reads as follows:

> Above all I charge the leaders of the nation and those under them to the scrupulous observance of the laws of race and to the merciless opposition to the universal poisoner of all peoples, International Jewry.

SELF-HATRED TURNED OUTWARD?

Hitler was host to various mental and emotional problems. Since he did not fit into any level of society, he felt isolated, inadequate, and at the same time, vastly superior to the common man. It is possible that the ferocity of Hitler's hatred of the Jews may have stemmed from an overpowering feeling of self-loathing. No one can map the unconscious mind, but the damage done by his parents, his early anti-Jewish environment, his failure to achieve any status, his ecstasy followed by desolation during his stint in the army all contributed to create a warped personality. The possible role of genetic factors must be left in abeyance; future researchers in this field may add additional pieces to the puzzle. What emerges at this point is a hypothesis that the troubled child and unhappy teenager grew into a man burning with self-hatred. The human ego, however, is very fragile; it protects itself from unpleasant truths and builds elaborate defenses. Among such defensive mechanisms is scape-goating, the transfer of guilt and shame upon the shoulders of others. But loading the sacrificial animal with all the unresolved problems solves nothing in the long run. Hitler's self-hatred, constantly fed by his dreadful crimes, turned outward upon the Jews whom he saw as representing everything loathsome within himself.

Individuals who despise themselves, whose spirits are awash with vague guilt and free-floating anxiety, seek an outlet for their destructive, often suicidal, conflicts. Since ancient times, the scapegoat has been the reality as well as the symbol for shedding evil and misery. The greater the offenses, the greater must be the suffering of the sin-offering. If we accept the premise that Hitler needed a scapegoat, not merely as a political convenience, but as a result of a deep-seated personal neurosis, then the Jews were well suited to play that role. The sacrificial goat must be docile, without powerful friends or allies. As the history of the Holocaust has demonstrated, the great majority, though by no means all of the Jews, were docile. Obviously, they had no powerful protectors, and the old and familiar precedents of punishing innocent Jews lent historic justification and examples to the process.

The theory of Hitler's self-hatred externalized into anti-Jewish hatred permits a glimpse into the irrationality of the Holocaust. In Hitler's mind, the death of every single Jew destroyed some atomic particle of the self he wished to obliterate. It thus may become possible to understand why a million victims could never be enough, nor ten million. All Jews everywhere had to die, but even then, he could not be satisfied. Other scapegoats would have to be driven to their death. A terrible image strikes the inner eye; a picture of Europe if Hitler had won the war. . . .

THE EXECUTIONERS

If we accept the explanation that Hitler tried to extinguish the fire of his self-hatred with the burnt offerings of European Jewry, the insatiability of his destructive impulses becomes comprehensible. This, however, leaves the historian with the still unanswered questions concerning the motivations of the men who so willingly carried out the orders to commit genocide. Excluding the officials who "merely" expedited the paper trail that ended in mounds of human ashes, many thousands of SS troopers, organized into the special killing squads of the infamous *Einsatzgruppen*, were involved in the physical execution of men, women, and children who were guilty of nothing at all. What do we know about members of these special task forces? Their work was not abstract, their own eyes met those of the victims, their hands held the guns which killed an estimated 1,500,000 Jews. What did such men say to their wives, their children, or their parents at the end of a day's work? It is inaccurate to dismiss them as brutes, savage animals outside the perimeter of civilized society. The commanders of the four individual detachments of mobile killing units, the *Einsatzkommandos,* were professionals with many academic degrees, men who were quite at home among Germany's cultural elite. Many members of the *Einsatzgruppen* were volunteers, others had been conscripted into this ghastly duty. A few objected to the assignment of supervising and participating in mass killings and were given other duties, as far as we can determine, without penalty. Once again, students of the Holocaust must face with incredulity the chasm that separates morality and education.

Within the scope of this book it is not possible to examine the motivation of all or even any of the *Kommandos*, some three thousand strong, or their many counterparts who worked in the death and slave-labor camps of the Nazi world. It will have to suffice to discuss, albeit briefly, three criminals at the top of the Nazi hierarchy. The choice of Goering, Goebbels, and Himmler was based on their prominence in carrying out the Final Solution, the Nazi's euphemism of annihilation of the Jews. Did they hate the Jews? Why? How did they achieve personal and political power which enabled them to climb to the heights of Hitler's world? Were there similarities in family background, in neurotic behavior, in education, in attitude toward religion, in ambition, in failures in earlier enterprises? Should a pattern emerge, could it help future generations to reject potential villains at the polls? Unfortunately, at this point we cannot identify a Nazi archetype. Perhaps further study will be more fruitful, for now, it seems clear that evil comes in as great a variety of packaging as does the rest of humanity.

HERMANN GOERING: RISE TO POWER

Life is struggle. Hitler, in the very title of his book, proclaimed this to be true. Leadership in the upper Nazi circles was achieved only by men who shared that *Weltanschauung*. Struggle required fighters. Goering, although he liked to call himself a Renaissance man, began his rise to power as a fighter. According to Aryan ideology, the true warrior did not shun, rather he welcomed violence because the new world order of conquest demanded that enemies must not only be defeated, they must be annihilated. Goering, who was never burdened with ideological scruples, was a mercenary who found his war, first during the campaigns of World War I and later in the Nazi movement and its continuous warfare. He craved power and the adulation of the masses who saw only a whitewashed version of his character, the smiling, overweight, avuncular officer who combined the attributes of a hail-fellow-well-met with that of a war hero. His ridiculous vanity, his appetite for luxury, and his megalomaniac cruelty were unknown to the public. In the end, Hitler called him his greatest disappointment and deprived him of all honors and authority.

Hermann Goering (1883–1946), was born into a "good" Bavarian family. Among the political and social nonentities of the Third Reich, he stood out as the welcome exception to the rule. His father, a distinguished colonial official, had been the first governor of the German protectorate of West Africa. Hermann's first wife, Karin von Katzow, had come from a well-connected background. Young Goering's career, before he discovered the Nazi Party in 1922, had been in the military. He was a much decorated fighter pilot in the newborn *Luftwaffe* and commanded the group which had won fame under Germany's World War I ace, the Baron von Richthofen, after the baron's death. At the end of the war, Goering, like so many of his contemporaries, found it difficult to adjust to civilian life although his air force experience enabled him to find employment. He joined the fledgling Nazi Party in 1922, and thus qualified as an "early fighter." Hitler was delighted with this supposedly wealthy, famous new recruit and made him commander of the SA. Goering was by his *Fuehrer's* side during the Beer hall putsch, the failed Nazi attempt to overthrow the Bavarian government. In the melee, Goering was severely wounded but managed to escape from the country. Apparently, these injuries caused his addiction to morphine. When a declaration of political amnesty cleared the way for his return, he was assured of high rank in the Nazi Party.

GERMANY'S NUMBER TWO MAN

Goering's rise was rapid indeed. Among the positions he held were president of the Reichstag, Reich's minister without portfolio, commander in chief of the *Luftwaffe*, minister president of Prussia, and Prussian minister of the interior. He created the Prussian Political Police, which was soon (1934) incorporated into the Gestapo. These were not empty titles. Goering enjoyed the exercise of personal power. If ever he had scruples, they did not prevent him from directing the execution of old comrades. He directed the assassinations of the SA leaders during the Night of the Long Knives in the Berlin region. It was Goering who established the first concentration camp at Oranienburg. To the delight of many Germans, "our Hermann" was made a full general in 1936 and shortly thereafter he became the tsar of the Four Year Plan for economic development. In that capacity he directed German industry and its effort to achieve self-sufficiency and military preparedness. As chief executive of the state-owned Reichswerke Hermann Goering, a huge mining and industrial complex, he amassed enormous personal wealth. He became an avid collector of great works of art, sometimes by purchase, sometimes by forced gifts, and finally by theft from the great collections of defeated nations. He built a small palace, Karinhall, named after his deceased first wife but presided over by Emmy, his second wife. Emmy had been an actress who continued to perform in style as Hitler's official hostess during state functions. The Goerings became notorious for the exorbitance of their entertainments, so lavish, so outrageous, they rivaled the circuses of the emperors of ancient Rome.

Goering did not advocate Hitler's policy of expansion through war although he played a central role in the annexation of Austria and Czechoslovakia. The day before the attack on Poland, Hitler, never at a loss to take advantage of a dramatic moment, declared that in case he, the *Fuehrer*, died in the fighting, Goering was his designated successor. A new title, chairman for the Reich council of national defense, was added to the many already held, and within the year he was named *Reichsmarschall*.

The mantle of success did not suit Goering very well. His love for the decorative aspects of power was not in tandem with his disinclination to work. Although he relished his titles, he did not enjoy the performance of the accompanying duties. The search for wealth to enhance his personal pleasures occupied his time and energies while rivals for Hitler's favors, such as Goebbels and Himmler, whittled away at his authority. Goering's tailors created fantastic costumes and uniforms in every color, but it was impossible to hide his ever-increasing girth. Not only did he change his wardrobe many times a day, but with each new outfit, a different set of jewels adorned his fingers and glittering waistband. By the 1940s, the ace of World War I had grown fat and fatuous.

Some early doubts notwithstanding, once Germany was committed to war, Goering gave it his full support. In fact, the *Reichsmarschall's* power and popularity reached their greatest heights during the Polish and French campaigns. The *blitzkrieg,* or "lightning war," (adopted from the theory of mobile warfare suggested by a French officer named Charles de Gaulle and rejected by the French General Staff) depended largely on the air force. After the fall of France and Poland, the German media used every word of praise in its vocabulary to laud the *Luftwaffe* and its chief. But unexpectedly, the promised quick defeat of England did not happen. First, Goering's fliers were unable to prevent the escape of British and French troops from Dunkirk, and then the English Royal Air Force refused to yield its domination of the skies over the English Channel. As a result, the invasion of the British Isles had to be delayed again and again and finally abandoned. Goering's inability to protect the fatherland from Allied bombing raids further diminished his popularity and Hitler turned cool toward his erstwhile comrade. Perhaps, if the *Reichsmarschall* had boasted less and paid more attention to his duties, his star might not have descended so rapidly. He even neglected to keep his darling *Luftwaffe* from staying abreast of new developments in the field of aviation. By 1943, it was clear that Goering was a shell, left standing with empty titles and a chest full of medals but no authority.

GOERING AND THE JEWS

Despite the fact that Goering was not a fanatical anti-Semite, he played an important role in the persecution of the Jews. His participation in almost every aspect of the destruction of European Jewry was not born from conviction but from subservience to the stronger will of the *Fuehrer* coupled with unqualified greed. In 1938, he had actually played the major role in international negotiations between the German government and an intergovernmental committee proposing to speed up the emigration of German Jews to foreign countries. Nothing came of the negotiations, but Goering's action refuted the notion that he had always been convinced that the annihilation of Jews

Hermann Goering. (Courtesy UPI/Bettmann.)

was necessary to secure Germany's future. His personality seemed to have no inner core. Self-gratification masqueraded as principle. If others had to pay a price, any price, to assure his obscenely grandiose lifestyle, that was his due. Thus, the *Reichsmarschall* joined and often led the crusade against the Jews which included the appropriation of their possessions.

Whenever Nazi policy presented possibilities of increasing his personal wealth, Goering was certain to be in the picture. As head of the economic Four Year Plan, he controlled the profitable Aryanization campaign. *Aryanization* was the euphemism for the legalized theft of Jewish assets. Jewish-owned property was taken over by ethnically correct buyers at a fraction of its actual value. The state then withheld even the reduced payment from the sellers who received a small percentage in monthly installments. Obviously, Aryanization was replete with opportunities for private bargain hunting.

In 1938, Goering commented that it might be necessary to place Jews into ghettos at some future time. Within two years he called for the physical separation of the Jews from the Aryan Germans. The idea of using Jewish work brigades also germinated in his mind, a concept he rephrased into an order in 1938. After the destruction of Jewish property during the *Kristallnacht* pogrom, it was Goering who proclaimed that the insurance companies must pay for the damages, but the payments would be made to the state instead of the policy holders. The wrecked stores had to be repaired at the owners' cost, while insurance compensation was collected by the national treasury. The legal rationalization was that the Jews were responsible for causing the pogrom in the first place.

Goering hoped to maintain permanent control over the Jews, but he was outmaneuvered by Himmler. It is doubtful, however, whether the Jews would have fared better if Goering had retained command. In 1939, he appointed Reinhard Heydrich, one of the fiercest Jew baiters, to head the Reich Central Office for Jewish Emigration. The selection of this man to positions of ever-expanding power was in itself a crushing blow against the Jews. Before Himmler and his SS usurped mastery over all the Jews within the Nazi grasp, Goering had directed Himmler's activities. Thus it was the *Reichsmarschall* who ordered the clearing of the ghettos and the deportations of its inhabitants to Polish concentration camps. And yet, Goering was not a fanatic. He never accepted Hitler's assessment that the Jews, by their very existence, threatened Germany. Jews had usefulness, first, by virtue of their possessions, second, as slave laborers. But whatever their value, their destruction was vital to Hitler and that was the final verdict concerning their fate. In July, 1941, Goering asked Heydrich to prepare for a "Final Solution" to the Jewish question. Although he did not attend the fateful Wannsee Conference of January 20, 1942, he shares responsibility for the death of six million Jews.

THE FALL FROM POWER

Goering brought on his own collapse. The war was going badly for the Germans, yet he paid less attention to his work than to his tailor. His behavior grew increasingly bizarre, even Hitler lost patience with him. At first, the Nazi leadership merely bypassed him in their decision-making processes, but that did not make an impact on Goering's lethargy. His drug addiction and regression into infantile theatrics intensified. Shortly before the end of the war, he was dismissed from all his posts. Hitler believed that his old comrade had conspired to replace him and ordered him to be shot, however, there was no opportunity to enforce that order.

For a few belated moments, toward the end of the war, some of the old vitality seemed to resurge in that bloated body. He claimed, upon hearing of Hitler's suicide, that he was the new leader, the only proper representative of the German government. He actually demanded a meeting with General Eisenhower. Instead, he was captured by American troops and placed before the International Military Tribunal at Nuremberg. During his incarceration, while awaiting judgment, he was cured of his addiction, his body regained some shape, and he defended himself with considerable vigor. Nevertheless, he was found guilty of crimes against humanity. In the end, his flair for theatrics prevailed. He managed to swallow a vial of poison two hours before his scheduled hanging and the mystery and drama of his final exit gave him a burst of the public attention he had craved all his life.

THE CAREER OF JOSEPH GOEBBELS

Among the intellectual lightweights at the top of the Nazi elite, Goebbels was an oddity. He was well educated, had attended several renowned German universities, and had earned a doctorate in literature. He was often called brilliant, even by people who despised him. Under his stewardship, propaganda, once merely the art of persuasion, became the medium for mass manipulation. He combined applied science and technology with total ruthlessness to create a mental vacuum in his audience. At the precisely timed moment, an emotional frenzy carried the public to the desired goal of Hitler worship and/or hatred of supposed enemies of the fatherland. Among all of Hitler's henchmen, Goebbels was the most able and the most cunning. He did not fit in among the dullards who surrounded the *Fuehrer*, not in mind nor body. His appearance was ill suited for leadership in the Reich which valued brawn over brain.

Goebbels could not live up to the image of the Aryan he so relentlessly acclaimed. He had neither the long, sturdy legs, the slim waist and wide chest, nor the fair skin, blue eyes, and blond hair of the ideal German. His importance to Hitler had to be great indeed to forgive his puny frame, the large head sitting atop a spindly body, the brown hair and eyes, and swarthy complexion. Worst of all, he walked with a distinct limp and had to wear a special shoe and braces. His left leg was several inches shorter than his right. This was the result of an operation he underwent as a boy when he was ill with osteomyelitis, an inflammation of the bone marrow. Even the most touched-up photos could not erase his physical shortcomings. Goebbels was well aware that behind his back he was called "mouse general," "malicious dwarf," and many Germans believed he was born with a clubfoot. Among his enemies, gossip was spread that he was partly Jewish and the clubfoot was cited as evidence.

Goebbels was a physical and mental misfit in Hitler's hierarchy; that he rose to great power nonetheless demonstrated the strength of his will. Ashamed of his body and reluctant to display his intellect, he lived a cynical lie. He often pretended that his lameness was due to a war wound; he appeared at public meetings in SA uniform at the head of a contingent of SA troopers. He expressed disgust for learning and stood proudly at the bonfire during the book burning hysteria where the intellectual heritage of Europe was incinerated. His diaries were filled with adulation for Hitler whose private conversations were notoriously long-winded and boring. Whether these entries revealed his true feelings remains questionable, after all, he was a professional liar.

YOUNG JOSEPH

Goebbels was born in 1897 into a devoutly Catholic Rhineland family. His father had been a manual laborer who rose to a lower-middle-class position. The young man, already painfully aware of his handicap, was desolate when other youths went to war in 1914 and he was rejected. He never came to terms with his inability to serve as a soldier. Success at university life gave him status, but it could not mend the anguish over his deformed leg. He was awarded a doctorate at Heidelberg and from then on insisted upon being addressed as *"Herr Doktor."* The attempt to win fame and fortune as a writer floundered when his book *Michael* and two plays were received with critical scorn. His career as a journalist was short-lived, merely the preliminary bout while awaiting the main event. His keen and restless mind was searching for a calling, for a way to show the world his brilliance. In 1922, quite accidentally, Goebbels heard Hitler speak in Munich. The die was cast; the Austrian with the black mustache and the hypnotic voice was the star in whose light his own would rise.

TRUTH AND PROPAGANDA ARE UNRELATED

Goebbels's first propaganda campaign was designed to penetrate Hitler's inner circle. The *Fuehrer* responded to his flattery despite such caustic references as "Wotan's Mickey Mouse" that were whispered behind Goebbels's back. The Nazi party could use a man who was not only an impassioned speaker, almost as intoxicating as Hitler himself, but whose mastery of the written word could manipulate passions. The fact that this new recruit combined a cunning mind with a complete absence of integrity increased his value. Goebbels edited a newspaper, *Der Angriff* ("Attack"), to promote National Socialism and did so with total disregard for the truth. Even his detractors were awed. Thus, even before the Nazis came to power, he had developed the concept of "the big lie," that is, a lie so blatant, so outrageous and repeated so often, the public could not conceive of anyone daring to tell a falsehood on such a scale.

When Hitler appointed him *Gauleiter* ("district party leader") of Berlin, Goebbels created the highly effective political theater which would later dazzle all of Germany and beyond. He is credited with the great gains in the Reichstag elections of 1932. *"Herr Doktor"* cheered when some twenty thousand books were burned in bonfires across the nation. Among the volumes thrown into the flames by university students and some of their professors were revered classics and the works of Jewish and Communist authors. Goebbels had an instinct for judging the mood of the masses and fed their appetite with instigated slander, false rumors, and personal attacks. Some of his SA Brownshirts walked the streets with bandaged heads, reddened with dye for more dramatic effect, to simulate injuries suffered during street fights with the Communists. He wrote articles under an assumed name in which he lauded Dr. Goebbels as a man of extraordinary valor; he used the death of an ignoble SA rioter named Horst Wessel and turned him into a martyr. For a dozen years, the German nation gave the "Horst Wessel Song" equal status with the national anthem. One of the lines in this hymn to a brawling low-life ran: "Yes, when the blood of Jews spurts from our knives, then things go twice as well."

In 1928, that is, five years before Hitler became chancellor, Goebbels became propaganda chief for the party. This assured his appointment as national minister of public enlightenment and propaganda in 1933. The title did not indicate the dimensions of power that Goebbels wrung from his position. He built an empire which encompassed jurisdiction over the cultural life of the nation in which propaganda was but one of many facets. His commitment to Hitler was total. He never abandoned his mission: to glorify the *Fuehrer* and his vision of the new Germany.

THE MINISTER OF CULTURE

As cultural tsar, Goebbels had the authority to dictate the literary, artistic, journalistic, and musical tastes of a nation. He decided which sports were proper for schoolchildren, which films the movie houses could show. His censorship extended to the written and the spoken word; he masterminded and managed the spectacular rallies which imitated the pomp of religious ceremonies. He was the arbiter of painting and sculpture, and decided what was acceptable Aryan artistic expression. Propaganda, he stated, had no relationship to truth, only to effectiveness.

The outbreak of the Second World War caused Goebbels's fortune to lapse for several years. He was jubilant over the early victories, but his public assurances of a quick end to the struggle were obviously wrong. The public could no longer rely on his pronouncements. He further blundered when he treated the Allied forces with contempt rather than with the respect due to a worthy adversary. Victories over an ignoble foe earn no glory. His pledge that German civilians would be safe in the fortress the *Fuehrer* had built around them flew in the face of reality as night after night Allied bombers delivered a message more potent that his words. Goebbels's enemies within the party believed the little man was finished.

But when the possibility of defeat, though unspoken, was no longer unthinkable, Goebbels's services were again in great demand. The nation must be readied to fight to its last breath. Now his approach was to instill fear and hatred for the enemies of the Reich: the Jews, of course, but also England, the Soviet Union and the United States. If defeated, he warned, the German people could expect no mercy. Rape and pillage, particularly at the hands of the "Asiatic hordes," would be their fate. In an effort to

Joseph Goebbels. (Courtesy UPI/Bettmann.)

reverse the spirit of weariness and hopelessness, he promised them a marvelous secret weapon that would turn the tide of the war. His glee at the death of Franklin D. Roosevelt was obscene; Hitler was still blessed by destiny, with the cursed "Rosenfeld" gone, the American war effort would wither away. But German defeat was inevitable. Goebbels's appointment in 1944 as general plenipotentiary for the war effort was, in effect, a gesture. Germany had no reserves left to prevent the invasions from east and west.

GOEBBELS AND THE JEWS

In his early life, young Joseph seemed indifferent to the so-called Jewish question. As soon as he realized that such an attitude would prevent his rise in the ranks of the party, he conformed to the required anti-Semitic stance. Whether he believed what he said and wrote is questionable but it hardly matters. His portrait of the Jew as a dehumanized caricature was certainly effective in persuading millions of Germans that there "must be something to it." The assassination of a German official in Paris by a Jew—the events will be more fully explained in Chapter 6—gave Goebbels the opportunity to demonstrate the sincerity of his anti-Semitism. He turned the shooting by a Jewish youth into provocation for a nationwide pogrom from which German Jewry never recovered. With his talent for brutal, often satanic, exaggeration, he answered those who claimed he did not hate the Jews enough. All the media under his control assailed the all-powerful, international, conspiratorial, Bolshevik *Untermenschen* ("subhumans"), the Jews who controlled the economic world from New York to Moscow. The pogrom he had initiated was presented as just punishment meted out spontaneously by an enraged German public.

MURDER AND SUICIDE

Certain aspects of Goebbels's life and death bore a resemblance to Hitler's. Both men appear to have been driven by self-hatred. In Hitler's case, Jews became his personal sacrificial scapegoats. For Goebbels, all of humanity was the enemy. Only Hitler was exempt from the sharp edge of his pen. He was a homely man, small and lame; the antithesis of the Aryan superman he so masterfully glorified and so consummately envied. Although the details differ, both men had difficulty in their relationships with women. Goebbels had many affairs, before and after he was married. As a politically powerful man, he had no difficulty in proving his virility with ambitious starlets eager to further their careers. His wife, Magda, was ready to ask for a divorce when his philandering became a public scandal. Only Hitler's personal intervention prevented the breakup of the marriage.

In their suicides, similarities between Goebbels's and Hitler's personalities were striking. Goebbels actually orchestrated Hitler's death. He urged his *Fuehrer* to die like a hero portrayed in German mythology, a godlike superman who leaves this world in a blaze of destruction. Only suicide and flames could feed the future legend of his greatness. The drama must end like a climactic scene from Wagner's *Goetterdaemmerung*. Afraid of capture by the Russians, Hitler agreed. He paid the faithful Goebbels a final tribute. In his final testament, Hitler appointed him to a leading role in a future German government, a nomination that can only be characterized as bizarre.

But Goebbels had decided to play out his own drama. In his last words he apologized for refusing, for the first and only time, an order from the *Fuehrer*. He had decided to die because life no longer had any value. His wife, he wrote, had chosen to die with him. Joseph and Magda had brought their six children to Hitler's underground bunker and refused to have them flown out to safety. Goebbels's final crime violated the most basic norms of humanity. He claimed that if his children had been old enough to speak for themselves, they too would rather die then live. The picture of the mother and father, going from bed to bed, handing their children a lethal drink, was the penultimate scene of Goebbels's life. The curtain came down on May 1, 1945. With Russian tanks entering the chancellery garden, his wife took poison and Goebbels shot himself.

HEINRICH HIMMLER

Himmler is often called the architect of the Holocaust. If that epithet denotes more than theoretical planning but also includes the organization and the day-to-day supervision of the killing process, then the title fits. Himmler was not the originator of the Holocaust, Hitler was; but the efficiency required to murder such great numbers in less then five years was Himmler's work. Some writers have called him the perfect bureaucrat, the man who carried out orders with the mechanical efficiency of a robot. But that characterization does not take into account the man's fanaticism nor his political acumen. The smooth implementation of the Holocaust required the resources of a master of deceit. Everything about Himmler, including his appearance, was deceptive. It must also be remembered that the threshold leading to Hitler's office was always crowded with ambitious men jostling to get nearer to the seat of power. Himmler's success in that perilous arena indicates that the man cannot be reduced to a single, simple caption.

Himmler was the most feared, hated man of the Third Reich. He inspired terror not only among Jews, but in the general population. The arm of his Gestapo, his SS, and all the police forces he commanded, seemed to reach into every home and workplace. Germany and the conquered lands were politically silenced by fear. Himmler cultivated the perception that no one was safe and even the slightest criticism of the regime would reach his spies. Only whispers repeated that this neighbor or that had disappeared because the ears of secret police were everywhere. There were hushed reports of terrible tortures during Gestapo interrogation and of unspeakable conditions in concentration camps. In the center of this atmosphere of dread was Heinrich Himmler.

SOME BACKGROUND DATA

Hannah Arendt, the author of *The Origins of Totalitarianism* and *Eichmann in Jerusalem*, saw the banality of evil confirmed in the person of Himmler. The man was so ordinary, so conventional that it is very difficult to see him as a fanatical mass murderer. His upbringing was comfortably middle class; a devout Catholic home, the father an educator with connections to Bavarian nobility, the mother attentive to home and her three sons. Psychiatry cannot point to cruelty or abnormality in the workings of this family. Heinrich was the middle child, born in 1900. The young man was unattractive, but not distressingly so; his small eyes, thin lips, and weak chin gave him a ratlike expression. He attended a technical college and was awarded a diploma in agricultural studies. He married a nurse who shared with him her interest in such para-scientific subjects as herbalism, mesmerism, and homeopathy. We know little of the marriage. Heinrich was not a faithful husband and fathered several children out of wedlock while neglecting his own family. When he had achieved great power, he exhibited an affinity for mysticism and superstition which often bordered on the ridiculous. His youthful contemporaries foresaw none of these peculiarities; they described him as methodical, hard-working, attentive to detail, utterly without charisma. He was a plodder, adequate but not outstanding.

At the outbreak of the First World War, Heinrich was in school. At age seventeen he served for a year in a Bavarian infantry regiment without duties at the front. Peace and the political unrest of the Weimar Republic disappointed the young man who, like so many others, joined a rightist paramilitary organization. He came to Hitler's attention and joined the National Socialist Party. At the beer hall putsch of 1923, Himmler stood next to SA Commander Ernst Roehm, thus he could claim the "early fighter" designation. For the six years following the failed coup d'état in Munich, Himmler functioned in various capacities in the Nazi party while earning a living as a chicken

Heinrich Himmler. (Courtesy AP/Wide World Photos.)

farmer and fertilizer salesman. Up to this point his career was in no way distinguished. His subservience and slavish loyalty had made an impression on Hitler and the "faithful Heinrich" was assigned to head the SS, or *Schutzstaffel* ("Defense Echelon") in 1929. With this appointment, a new chapter opened for Himmler, for Germany, and tragically, for the Jews.

THE SS

Himmler's advance cannot be separated from the evolution of the SS. The Black-shirts consisted of a mere three hundred men when Himmler became their chief. The troop's original duty was to protect Hitler during public appearances. Taking a page from the praetorian guards of ancient Rome, impressive, handsome men were selected to enhance the *Fuehrer's* presence. Their emblems, the double lightning, the death's-head insignia on collar and ring, the dagger in the belt, the black tunic and high boots were calculated to instill awe among civilians. But the paraphernalia was not a mere facade, it represented careful training, a code of conduct, total dedication to Hitler personally—as opposed to service for Germany—and a readiness to perform any assignment no matter how repulsive. Since the SS became the instrument of carrying out the

Holocaust, its development will be detailed elsewhere; at this point, suffice it to say that the SS as a cult and as an instrument of terror was Himmler's work. He created a state within the state where ordinary rules of morality and law did not apply. He brought a businesslike approach to fanaticism that made mass murder a product to be manufactured with all the efficiency of modern technology.

Himmler had a perfect opportunity to show Hitler his loyalty during the massacre of the SA leadership, the Night of the Long Knives. In this butchery (also called the blood purge), the SS proved equal to the task of murdering some of the veterans of the Nazi movement. The fealty of the SS could never be questioned again. The enlarged job description of the Blackshirts now included the pinpointing and destruction of all enemies of the regime. Himmler's personal interpretation of the Aryan obsession was the SS's role in ensuring German racial purity. His notions on race seem to have sprung from the brain of a lunatic. It is chilling to realize that the SS *Reichsfuehrer* used these bizarre ideas to plan his own version of a brave new world.

BREEDING THE MASTER RACE

Himmler, the student of agriculture, wanted to expand Germany by means of selective breeding. He was convinced that genetics, or as the Nazis called it, *the blood*, determined all the characteristics of a people. Valuable, that is, Aryan blood must be cultivated; inferior blood, that is, Jewish, Gypsy, or Slavic blood must be prevented from further polluting the Nordic race. Himmler not only believed this, but devised plans to realize this fanatical dream.

The centerpiece of his plan was the SS. Candidates for membership had to trace their racial purity for three generations; they took an oath to marry only "qualified" and approved Aryan women, and promised to father many children. Out-of-wedlock offspring were welcomed and became the financial obligation of the SS organization. Land taken from Poland and perhaps western Russia was envisioned as the homestead for this new caste of super-Germans. They would farm the land and their labor would be augmented by the dispossessed Slavic underclass. "Surplus" Poles had to be eliminated, moved eastward, or killed; it was immaterial which method was employed. These Aryan settlements were to Germanize in perpetuity the *Lebensraum* taken from Poland. In order to prevent the native peoples from rebelling against this new order, potential leaders among them—the educated, army officers, priests, and communists—would be exterminated.

Poland had a large Jewish population, of over three million. Since Himmler believed Jews to be the most dangerous enemy of the Reich, their end was necessitated. The vital role of the SS in the Final Solution dovetailed with Himmler's and Hitler's obsessions. The Blackshirts were vital to the destruction of the Jews. Accompanying the elimination of millions of racially inferior people was the plan to harvest the Germanic residue who lived in the eastern lands. A monumental process involving the transfer of hundreds of thousands of so-called ethnic Germans was well on the way between 1940 and 1944. These *Volksdeutsche* were settled in the former homes of Poles and Jews

who, for the most part, had been murdered in accordance with Himmler's blueprint. The same fanatical cruelty impelled Himmler to kill Germans whose imperfections made them unworthy of life. His so-called euthanasia program sanctioned the murder of children and adults whose genes could pollute the racial integrity of the nation. Himmler supervised the secret killings of mentally and physically handicapped people in a terrible distortion of Darwin's theory of the survival of the fittest.

EMPEROR HIMMLER

At the height of his power, Himmler commanded an empire. In 1939, he became the Reich's commissar for the consolidation of the German nation. The title was grandiose but so was the power it yielded: commander of an enormously expanded SS, including control over the "racial degenerates," concentration and death camps; chief of the *Einsatzgruppen*; political administrator of the eastern occupied territories; head of the Gestapo and all police organizations; minister of the interior; supreme commander of the People's Army, the *Volksturm,* or Home Guard, and of the *Werwolf* troops of teenagers who had sworn to defend the fatherland when all else was lost.

Himmler's power emanated from the single source of Hitler's will. But everything depended on winning the war and the *Fuehrer* could not order that miracle. When, finally, even Himmler realized that all was lost, he tried to approach the Allies with peace feelers. Apparently, he had no idea that he was the very last man with whom the victorious commanders would deal. Hitler was furious with the last-minute desertion of his paladin and ordered his arrest; a futile gesture reminiscent of Goering's fate.

CLOSING THE CHAPTER

The personal files of the *Reichsfuehrer* were destroyed at his orders. Nevertheless, enough evidence remains from other sources to give succeeding generations a portrait of a man who was slavishly devoted to Hitler, who was totally indifferent to the fate of millions, and whose unrealistic racial theories bordered on the demented. His rise to power from obscurity confirmed his stamina as an in-fighter and his skillfulness as an administrator. His character was devoid of any ethical code save that of loyalty to his *Fuehrer*.

Himmler tried to escape in disguise after the German surrender. He was captured by the British and while undergoing a physical examination, he bit down on the vial of cyanide hidden in his mouth. He had made the mistake of assuming the identity of a low-ranking Gestapo agent, unaware that the entire organization had been declared criminal. He died almost instantly, thus he, like Hitler, Goering, and Goebbels, slipped out of the hangman's noose.

Chapter 5

Germany under the Nazis

The once-popular assessment that the Nazis ran Germany with clockwork precision has been rejected by historians of the era. The uniformity of marching feet, of arms outstretched at a precise angle for the Hitler salute, the vaunted punctuality of the trains, and the conformity of the faces of Hitler Youth beneath the swastika banners all created the myth that these appearances mirrored German life. The facts, however, paint a different picture. Nazi German politics was muddied by conflicts, uncertainties, and unclear lines of authority. Hitler worked sporadically, often his orders were vague hints rather than commands, and he encouraged interservice rivalries among his deputies. As long as the men around him vied with each other for a scrap of his power, his own position was more secure. The fact that no serious contender ever challenged Hitler's authority indicated that this approach produced the desired results.

THIRD REICH POLITICS: DESTROYING THE REPUBLIC

On January 30, 1933, Field Marshall Hindenburg, president of the Weimar Republic, reluctantly agreed to the appointment of Adolf Hitler as chancellor of Germany. The government which now was headed by the former corporal achieved power through constitutionally proper channels. The choice of von Papen as vice chancellor had finally convinced the old president that Hitler could be reined in if necessary. After all, the Nazis held only three other cabinet posts out of eleven and the important ministries were in the hands of conservatives. Such reasoning was understandable in light of the fact that at the point of their greatest popularity in 1932, the Nazis polled only 32 percent of the votes. Their election rhetoric had emphasized nationalism, a vague socialism, vicious anticommunism, and the promise of relief from economic woes. The party's agitated Jew baiting had proved to be a poor vote-getter and was toned down.

How then was it possible that within a few years not only the political, but also the economic and intellectual life of Germany was set back by generations? In Hitler's Germany, civil rights disappeared, established institutions became unrecognizable, and long-held social and cultural mores faded away. The myth of Jewish degradation and its counterpart, Aryan supremacy, came to play central roles. The most absolute government in history was established and only defeat on the battlefield would dislodge it. We can only estimate how much this catastrophe cost the world, and it behooves us not to underestimate the ability, perhaps the genius, of the man who blighted Europe and much of the rest of the world.

The Nazification of the nation was a process, not an event. As processes go, the transformation was implemented at breakneck speed. Although the assignment of blame for the origin of Hitler's rise is an imprecise study, three possibilities are worthy of consideration. First, the opposition parties in the Reichstag were unwilling or unable to put aside their differences and present a united opposition to the Nazis; second, the leaders of the Weimar Republic could not convince the German public to preserve their democratic freedoms; and third, in their narcissism the conservative upper class overestimated its own power and underestimated the Nazi Party and Adolf Hitler.

THE LAST ELECTION

In order to win a larger constituency in the legislature, Hitler asked for and was granted new Reichstag elections. The date was set for March, 1933. With the resources of the government behind him, the new chancellor could run a very effective, forceful campaign. But, of course, there was always the need for more money. Hitler addressed a conclave of Germany's industrial magnates and pledged to the heads of such giants as Krupp, I.G. Farben, and United Steel Works that the coming election would be the last one. He vowed to preserve private property and hinted broadly that regardless of the outcome of the election, he would stay in power, if necessary by extra-legal means. It seems inconceivable in retrospect that such a speech was applauded. When Goering passed the hat, he collected three million marks.

The last election of the decade merely buried the Republic. Communists and Socialists were unable to present their candidates to the public effectively; their meetings were disrupted or shut down by the SA; many of their leaders were arrested or went into hiding, and their printing presses were smashed. In Prussia, that state's Minister of the Interior, Hermann Goering, urged the police to shoot anti-Nazi suspects. Although the words "Socialist Workers" were part of the proper name of Hitler's party, trade unionists were beaten regardless of their political affiliation. Street fights escalated into murders and still the German people or any of their institutions did not rise in protest. The churches, professional and labor organizations, university faculty and students, civil servants, and most importantly, the armed forces remained passive, and by their moderation, (or was it cowardice?) encouraged the illegal tactics of the Nazis. Actually, Hitler had hoped to provoke the Communists into some action

Hitler addressing a giant Nazi demonstration, 1933. (Courtesy AP/Wide World Photos.)

which would allow him to destroy their organization once and for all. They held one hundred seats in the Reichstag out of a total of six hundred, and if these delegates could be dislodged, then the Nazis would have a clear majority. The problem of eliminating them, the most committed foes of Hitler, was solved by a dramatic event which literally and figuratively destroyed German communism and the Weimar Republic.

THE REICHSTAG FIRE

The word *Reichstag*, similar to our House of Representatives, denotes both the legislative body and the building. On February 27, 1933, just a week before the elections, the building was torched. Without question the blaze was the result of arson. The large amount of incendiary material found on the premises left no doubt on that issue. But who set the fire remains unclear to this day. The Berlin police arrested a mentally impaired young Dutchman, van der Lubbe, on the scene. Whether or not he was guilty remained uncertain. Hitler and company seized the moment they may well have created for themselves. The Communists were immediately accused and their Reichstag delegates were arrested. The Nazi press shouted Communist conspiracy and construed the illegal seizure of the duly elected representatives as a triumph of law and order.

There was a trial. Five men, the incoherent Dutchman, a former Reichstag deputy, and three Bulgarian Communists residing in the Reich were charged with arson and intent to instigate a rebellion. The world was watching which possibly saved all but the pathetic Van der Lubbe. No one who knew this confused and obviously disturbed young man believed him capable of high treason. Nevertheless, that was the verdict and his life was cut short by the guillotine. The other defendants were acquitted.

Did the Nazis set the fire and use the unfortunate Van der Lubbe as their dupe? Was it coincidental that the Dutchman, with an inclination toward pyromania, was in the building at the same time as members of the SA? The truth will never be known. It is, however, obvious who benefited from the crime. The day after the fire, Hitler succeeded in persuading Hindenburg to sign a decree "for the protection of the people and the state" which suspended the civil rights of the Weimar constitution. Thus, on February 28, 1933, the individual freedoms to speak, to write, to assemble, to have privacy in one's home, and to enjoy due process of the law were all swept away. The great majority of Germans cried no tears over the incarceration of the Communist leadership; many believed that even an abuse of power was laudable if it rid Germany of Communists.

ELECTION NAZI STYLE

Despite the unbridled election propaganda spewed upon the public by the National Socialists, their blatant scare tactics, the disruption of opposition party meetings, the disappearance of rival politicians, and the intimidation of the SA standing at the polling places, this last election did not give Hitler the victory he expected. The Center Party and the Socialists held their own; even the Communists' losses were smaller than anticipated. Instead of a landslide, just 44 percent of the votes went to the Nazis. Only in conjunction with another ultra-rightist party, the Nationalists, did they achieve a simple majority. It was Hitler's intention to nullify the Weimar Republic, that is, dismantle its constitution. Changes in the organic law of the land, however, required passage in the Reichstag by a two-thirds majority. Since the failure of the beer hall putsch ten years earlier, the regime consistently covered its actions with a cloak of legality. Nazi leaders and followers sought to protect themselves with the leitmotif "I was only following orders" and these orders had to originate from a legitimately constituted source.

THE ENABLING ACT

Hitler had planned to become the dictator of Germany without appearing to seize power illegally. Somehow the Reichstag must abrogate its own law-making functions in favor of the cabinet, which, of course, was headed by Hitler. In the hysteria created by the Reichstag fire, the Communist delegates had been prevented from taking

Adolf Hitler and Paul von Hindenburg, Potsdam, 1933. (Courtesy UPI/Bettmann.)

their seats in the legislature. Other anti-Nazi members were "detained" by the SA. The passage of the so-called Law to Remove the Distress of the People and the State, better known as the Enabling Act, required a large bloc of votes from parties which were not of the extreme right. Two days before approval of this important legislation was to be cast, Goebbels created a most disarming, seductive scenario. The ceremonial opening session of the Reichstag was held in the Garrison Church at Potsdam. This church was connected with everything dear to Hindenburg and the Prussian military establishment. Hitler, all sincerity and humility, paid homage to the spirit lingering in these hallowed walls, and the old field Marshall wiped a tear from his eye. When, on March 23, 1933, Hitler asked for a four-year suspension of the constitution, the Center Party voted yes. The Catholic delegates justified their support of the bill with the argument that their endorsement would allow them to exert some influence over the Nazis. Only the Social Democrats resisted but they could not prevent the passage of the Enabling Act.

Thus the legislature gave Hitler dictatorial powers. The four-year expiration date written into the Enabling Act was meaningless from the start. The provision that the president, not the chancellor, could exercise legislative veto power was equally useless. When Hindenburg died in 1934, Hitler assumed the presidential title and authority. Now he was well along on the road to making himself an absolute power.

DICTATORSHIP

The consolidation of political power, the *Gleichschaltung*, took place within the next few months. One by one, the separate strands of authority were pulled into Hitler's chancellery. All political parties except the NSDAP were outlawed in July, 1933. The fact that this was accomplished without serious opposition might be attributed to fear of Nazi terror as well as to widespread bitterness over the failures of the Weimar Republic. Many Germans were willing to give Hitler a chance; perhaps dictatorship would succeed where democracy had failed. State governments were reorganized. A unified, highly centralized administration replaced the previously federated system of government. Local legislatures were deprived of their autonomy. A single individual, the political *Gauleiter*, usually a reliable Nazi who took his orders from Berlin, headed each of the governmental units within the Reich. Bureaucracies were Nazified by means of a purge that was disguised as The Law for the Restoration of the Professional Civil Service. All Jews and many anti-Nazi employees were ousted from their positions. It was not possible to remove all "unreliable" officials and keep the government functioning, but whenever and wherever possible they were supplanted by party members. It must be remembered that teachers, including university professors, were also civil service appointees.

On May 1, Hitler celebrated the working man and his contribution to the future greatness of the Reich. With laudatory speeches and parades, the working class was lulled into wishful thinking about its future role. That was the calm before the storm. On the following day, all trade union headquarters were raided, their assets confiscated, and their leaders sent to concentration camps. Within the week, labor unions were dissolved and strikes were declared illegal. Without a choice in the matter, workers were enrolled in the German Labor Front headed by Robert Ley. The hidden purpose of the Labor Front was the suppression of workmen's time-honored and hard-won rights in the workplace. In due time, the Nazis forbid workers to leave their jobs, to demand better wages, or to complain about working conditions. Some historians have referred to this relationship as the "enserfment" of labor.

THE LEADERSHIP PRINCIPLE

Clearly, the actualization of the *Fuehrerprinzip*, a theory which held that total power must be confined to a single leader, was well under way within a year of Hitler's appointment as chancellor. In the next decade, the grip of the Nazi Party would grow tighter until party and government functions were indistinguishable. Not all Nazis approved of Hitler's ultra-rightist interpretation of the National Socialist German Workers' Party (NSDAP). Clearly, the industrialists were gaining ground at the expense of their workers. The promise of national socialism had been discarded and not all the "old fighters" were satisfied with Hitler's interpretation of Nazi goals. The challenge to Hitler did not come from outside his party, but from within.

THE BLOOD PURGE

Hitler's flirtation with the conservative, even reactionary, elite, namely the generals and the barons of industry, created problems. In the center of discontent was the SA and its chief, Ernst Roehm. No doubt, the swashbuckling adventurer and his Brownshirts had contributed greatly to his friend Adolf's victory. Roehm had been remarkably successful in attracting young men to the ranks of his troopers, two million strong in 1933. Despite past contributions, Roehm was becoming a liability. He had taken seriously the socialist pronouncements of the *Fuehrer* and had urged a second revolution to bring about the promised leftist shift of the nation. Obviously, the regime had no intention of curbing the profits of the few in order to further the interests of the workers. In addition, Hitler and Roehm differed in their view of the SA. Hitler wanted the corps to function as a political army, the paramilitary strong-arm of the party. Roehm was ambitious and demanded a greater arena for himself and his men. He wanted his units incorporated into the regular army, a suggestion the generals found totally unacceptable. The officers of the high command were appalled at the notion of a "people's army" under the personal command of Roehm, whose homosexual lifestyle raised eyebrows. It was no secret that he and other leaders of the SA engaged in all sorts of debauchery. This alone made them quite unacceptable to the great majority of Germans.

Faced with the choice of appeasing either the regular army, which had the power to unseat Hitler if it had the will, or Ernst Roehm, Hitler made his decision. Goering and Goebbels agreed that the old comrade and his cronies had to be sacrificed. The fact that Himmler's SS was willing, perhaps even eager, to carry out the assassinations removed the practical difficulties. Without leadership, the power of the SA would be broken and the generals would be satisfied.

The arrests and most of the executions took place on June 30, 1934. The event is known as the Night of the Long Knives. Hitler himself participated in the arrest of Ernst Roehm. Some SA leaders were murdered immediately, others within a few days. The liquidation of the chiefs of the SA also served as a screen to settle some old scores. The SS had been issued a list of men condemned for the crime of disagreeing with Hitler at some time during his life. The exact number of victims has never been firmly established, perhaps as few as one hundred or as many as one thousand were killed. No indictments were filed; no due process of the law was granted. After the assassinations were carried out, the public was told that Roehm and the SA had planned to usurp the government in a counterrevolution. For the sake of public peace and order the authorities had been obliged to strike quickly. Since almost all of the alleged plotters were surprised in their beds, no credence can be given this official explanation for the blood purge. The SS, of course, earned the *Fuehrer's* gratitude and its growing importance stemmed from this moment.

As always, the Nazis attempted to mask their crimes as legally sanctioned acts. An obedient Reichstag passed a law which retroactively legitimized the murders.

Members of the Nazi party would not again challenge its monolithic leadership, no matter how despicable its depravity.

THE PARTY AND THE CIVIL SERVICE

Who was in charge of the day-to-day functions of the government, the party commanders or the bureaucratic administrators? It suited Hitler's concept of rivalry among the services to leave that question unclear as long as it was understood that his authority was supreme. The cabinet ministers continued to meet, but Hitler was not interested in supervising their affairs and did not participate in their sessions. A state secretary for the chancellery ferried papers between the ministers and the *Fuehrer*. The difficulty in carrying on the business of governing was further complicated by Hitler's appointments of particular favorites, riding roughshod over established bureaucracy. Fritz Todt, who built the famous German road system the *Autobahn*, for example, was responsible to no one but Hitler and received his funds directly from the chancellery. Thus, Todt could ignore the established ministry of transport. This sort of dual authority existed in many departments and created personal and interdepartmental controversies.

In order to prevent a collapse of the governmental functions it was necessary to permit many nonparty members to remain at civil service jobs. Officials serving in such institutions as the foreign ministry, the national banks, economic department, post offices, railroads, police, education, courts, and public health were all needed to conduct the nation's business. The more responsible the position, the more eager were the *Gauleiters* to install their comrades. Many of the older bureaucrats found that their duties were hampered by the constant interference from party officials. The framework of the Nazi Party resembled a pyramid; Hitler stood at the apex of the national organization. Beneath were the *Gaue,* which roughly matched the old German states. These, in turn, were partitioned into provinces and further divided into the smallest units, usually county-wide party wards. Lines of authority were often blurred, and the judge, the school principal, the museum director, the post master, et al., worked in a morass of conflicting directives. Many civil servants solved their dilemma by becoming active members of the Nazi Party and following orders issued by the party.

Von Hindenburg was eighty-seven when he died on August 2, 1934. Hitler used this opportunity to declare that the office and functions of the presidency were henceforth merged with those of the *Fuehrer.* Members of the armed forces were required to swear a new oath of obedience, not to the fatherland but to the *Fuehrer.* The generals, with that act of subservience, lost whatever independence they had long claimed. This was one of those historic moments when the fate of many millions was decided. The personal allegiance of the generals and their troops to the former corporal allowed the events of the next decade to unfold. Hitler must have concluded that the Night of the Long Knives was a gamble that had paid splendid dividends. When the voters were asked to legalize the dictatorship by means of a plebiscite, 90 percent gave their approval. A totalitarian Germany had officially and legitimately replaced the last trace of the Weimar Republic.

THIRD REICH ECONOMICS: FINANCIAL MANIPULATIONS

Hitler had no patience with and no understanding of the intricacies of economics. He simply wanted to realize certain highly visible objectives, regardless of the long-range economic implications. Foremost was the goal of an immediate reduction of the unemployment rate. When he came to power some six million Germans were out of work. Within the next four years that number was reduced to one million. Production rose more than 100 percent in this period and a sense of hope and expectations for the future kept the rather poorly paid working people acquiescent. Public works from grandiose construction schemes to the innovative *Autobahn* road system were partially responsible for these gains. Certainly, the revival of the armament industry played a major role. Hitler's ambitions for Germany were in the arena of foreign affairs; the aggrandizement and glorification of the Reich could be realized only through war. Both industry and labor were the means to that end; the details of financing his aims were other people's problems. Indeed, he was fortunate to have the wizardry of Hjalmar Schacht at his disposal.

Dr. Schacht was the mastermind behind the achievement of the early economic successes of the Reich. His career in finance was indeed impressive. At age thirty-nine he had become a director of the National Bank of Germany and within seven years was appointed director of the Reichsbank, the foremost monetary institution in the nation. He had been largely responsible for curbing the runaway inflation of 1923. Since he had opposed the financial policies of the Weimar Republic, he resigned his post. Then Hitler appeared on the horizon. Although Schacht objected to some of the programs initiated by the Nazis, including their violent anti-Semitism, he was willing to give them his support. Hitler, of course, was delighted to have such a renowned banker in his service. Schacht initiated the subordination of the total German economy to a war-readiness status. In one capacity or another, he provided Hitler with the economic means to pursue his aggressive schemes. He printed money and manipulated the foreign currency. When creditors feared that they might lose their German investments, Schacht convinced them to invest more money to recoup a shaky debt.

Schacht became disillusioned with Nazi methods and after the attempt on Hitler's life in July, 1944, he was arrested and spent the remaining war year in concentration camps. Much of his authority had already been usurped by Goering who was in control of the Four Year Plan. This plan attempted to make Germany self-sufficient and independent of foreign imports. Despite the creation of various synthetics and *ersatz* fabrications, Germany was never able to free itself of the need for certain imports. Only conquest could provide the nation with the petroleum and food products it lacked. But the foundation upon which the German war machine was created sprang from the mind of Dr. Schacht.

FARMERS

In his campaign speeches, Hitler promised small farmers land reforms. Included among these were the breakup of the huge estates held by the Prussian Junkers, the abolition of interest on farm loans, and the termination of land speculation. Such assurances of aid were welcomed by a deeply indebted peasantry. Fear of foreclosure was constantly confirmed as friends and neighbors were driven from their ancient holdings. Additionally, the loss of social status caused great distress when landowners, no matter how small their plot, dropped down into the ranks of farm laborers or joined the unemployed. The Nazis' promise to ease their condition had won the party much support from the farming community. Hitler had charged Walter Darré to head the Reich's agricultural and food ministries. Darré believed that the Aryan race sprang from some mythical interaction of German blood and German soil and thus the preservation of the small farmer was a racial as well as an economic necessity.

Darré instituted price controls and production quotas. The former enabled the farmers' income to rise, the latter deprived them of their freedom of operation. The Reich's Hereditary Farm Law was, at best, a mixed blessing. To ensure that farms of less than 308 acres remained intact, the owner could not sell his property but was forced to pass it on to a single heir, the oldest or youngest son according to local custom. The heir was then obligated to provide for the basic needs of his siblings. Such inherited farms could not be divided, mortgaged, or foreclosed upon. While this legislation provided security, it also tied the farmer to the soil. A certain similarity to medieval serfdom is an inescapable observation.

WORKERS

As was noted earlier, the working class lost its right to organize, to bargain collectively, and to strike. In place of independent unions, the German Labor Front was proclaimed the successor to the established "Marxist dominated" organizations. Hitler appointed Dr. Robert Ley to head the Workmen's League which was designed to assure the subservience of labor to the nationalistic goals of the regime. The Nazification of trade unions was enacted with a carrot-and-stick approach. The more than twenty million workers were promised better wages, an end to industrial strife, emergency financial assistance, greater educational opportunities, and stable wages. Factory managers were urged to make working conditions more pleasant and government pressure resulted in a variety of improvements. Wage earners whose records were deemed perfect by the party could participate in a recreational program called Strength through Joy. Highly publicized and well-financed by the state, it allowed selected workers to go on luxurious vacations, visit theaters, and participate in various sports. Perhaps the greatest incentive to support the Nazis while increasing productivity among the workers was the Volkswagen scheme. Participating workers signed up to allow deductions from their wages to be collected. When enough money was saved, the worker would receive a Volkswagen. Ownership of a car was an important status symbol, rare among working people. Goebbels's propaganda press waxed ecstatically about the respected status of workingmen and issued posters depicting the well-muscled worker as the indispensable counterpart of the soldier.

But Germany was not the new Eden for the working class. No Volkswagens rolled off the assembly lines for the workers; the money withheld went into the production of tanks instead. Wages remained low as the civilian sector was subordinated to the rearmament demands of Hitler's foreign policy. After 1939, war requirements determined employment policies. German men who were not inducted into the military were pushed to work to the limit of their endurance. There were no pay raises, only the declarations of gratitude from the government. No longer could a worker choose his occupation freely, a state agency had the right to approve or disapprove changes of employment and residence. As a good soldier must do his duty without complaint, so must the German laborer. The effectiveness of that appeal may be judged by the fact that workers remained at their tasks until the Allies destroyed their factories.

BUSINESS INTERESTS

The gulf between election rhetoric and the substance of governing was clearly exemplified by the Nazi attitude toward small businesses. The craftsmen and small store owners had been promised the breakup of their giant competitors such as chain and department stores. Large numbers of the lower middle class had voted for the NSDAP expecting protection for their vulnerable businesses. Such help was never given. The associations of shop owners were dominated by Nazi Party members who discouraged political action among their membership. Even when the Jews had been driven from the economic life of the nation, the position of small enterprises did not improve. The economic welfare of individuals was never a concern of the Nazi hierarchy; the emphasis was always on doing what must be done to assure Germany's victory in the coming war.

The subordination of domestic needs to foreign policy goals, however, enabled the great manufacturers and industrialists to thrive. In the first six years of the Third Reich they increased their profits from 175,000,000 marks to 5,000,000,000 marks. Although the government issued innumerable rules and regulations dealing with production, import and export, prices and wages, allotments of raw materials, and the size of the work force, the great cartels flourished. No attempt was made to break up the giant combinations or curb their profits. Hitler knew that their productivity was a vital component of his policy of foreign conquest. If, in the pursuit of his larger goals, the hopes of the workers for a better life were sacrificed, so be it. Without unions, without the right to strike, the workers were powerless against the combined strength of employers and the government.

The rearming of Germany was to be carried out with a maximum of self-sufficiency and a minimum reliance on imports. The manufacture of substitute products, the *ersatz* materials, resulted in various synthetics yet could not meet the fuel and food requirements of Germany. The people could drink coffee made from grain, but tanks and planes could not operate without gasoline. What Germany needed it would take by force as soon as that force was irresistibly strong. Meanwhile, no matter how eloquent Dr. Goebbels's homage to the virtue of labor, the gap between rich and poor grew wider.

THIRD REICH CULTURE: EDUCATION

It is an almost plaintive cry heard time and again: "How could the Holocaust have happened in the land of Goethe and Beethoven?" The question seeks to define the relationship between culture and ethics. A people's culture, that is, its art, music, literature, institutions, values, and prevailing attitudes, are passed from one generation to the next to be accepted, questioned, or altered. Education plays a dominant role in this process of acculturation. The Nazi leadership was well-aware of the importance of training the young to ensure the continuity of their vaunted Thousand Year Reich.

It is not an exaggeration to claim that education underwent a revolution at the hands of the Nazis. Before 1933, in conformity with other European schools, Germans learned that intelligence was laudable, that degrees from universities opened the way to success in life. The good students earned their parents' pride and hope. As was noted earlier, the Nazi ethos adapted an antiintellectual posture which flew in the face of long-held traditions. In the Nazi scheme of education, the strong body was valued above the brilliant mind, obedience above critical thinking, patriotism above family loyalty, and conformity above individualism. German youth was to be recast in a new image.

CHANGES IN THE PUBLIC SCHOOLS

The man appointed to Nazify the educational system was an old friend and supporter of Hitler, Bernhard Rust. He had not been a successful pedagogue; his teaching career had ended when he was fired for molesting a schoolgirl. Nonetheless, Rust supervised the centralization of the educational system and the dissolution of local school boards. All professional decisions, all appointments, were under his jurisdiction. He promised to do no less then effect a transformation of German education. To a rather frightening degree he succeeded.

Rust was able to rely on the enthusiastic support from faculty members who were already committed Nazis. In fact, the percentage of educators in the party before it was mandatory to join was considerably larger than the 20 percent membership of the general population. Remarkably, the proportion of university professors was highest of all. The partnership between school and parents, so familiar to Americans, rarely existed in Germany. The teacher knew best—period. Most educators fell in line with Rust's new directives, the rest conformed to keep their jobs or left the profession. Parents did what they had always done: allowed the system a free hand.

Eventually, all teaching staff were required to enroll in the party and obliged to swear an oath of obedience to the *Fuehrer*. Faculty, from kindergarten to graduate school, attended special courses of intensive training in the new educational goals. The will of the state, not the welfare of the child, was the basis of Nazi pedagogy. To guarantee classroom application of this philosophy, only the politically reliable were permitted to teach. Jews were excluded immediately. Teachers with records of democratic or socialist sympathies were dismissed as soon as replacements became available. All academic associations were automatically incorporated into the National Socialist Teachers Organization. In effect, they became valuable and dangerous extensions of Goebbels's propaganda network.

Rust initiated some fundamental changes in order to transform German youth into chauvinistic, anti-Semitic, obedient Nazis. Physical education was given top priority, usually it was scheduled for five hours per week. Students who did not complete their PE requirements, regardless of physical handicaps, could not receive their graduation diplomas. Girls too were compelled to participate in the rigorous body-building programs. As the fatherland needed healthy soldiers, so it needed strong, fertile mothers. Curricula were rewritten to conform with the national ideology. Particular emphasis was placed on changes in history, biology, and German literature. Aryan racial theories acquired the aura of science and students were required to trace their personal racial inheritance as far back as possible. Readings were purged of the works of Jewish and liberal authors. Every field of instruction was twisted to follow Nazi ideology. For example, a geography lesson emphasized Germany's need for *Lebensraum*; an ancient history class instructed students that the culture of the Germanic tribes was superior to that of the Romans; the physical sciences became a vehicle to demonstrate the biological inferiority of the Jews, and mathematical problems related to the number of bullets needed to kill Germany's enemies. If Jewish children were present, they were called to the front of the class to have their subhuman features analyzed. The racial superiority of Germans found expression in almost every topic and a pupil could not spend a single day without learning something about the perfidy of all Jews. Questioning the teacher was discouraged. Boys and girls who wore their Hitler Youth uniform to class were made especially welcome. Physical punishment, usually caning, was not discouraged. Boys and girls who wore glasses, were physically weak, had parents who were not members of the Nazi Party or were serious about scholarship found the atmosphere in school to be hostile.

CREATING THE PERFECT NAZI

The most intense ideological indoctrination of German youth took place within the Nazi Youth movement. The young Baldur von Schirach, a poet by avocation and professional Nazi by vocation, had been Hitler's choice to head the Hitler Youth organization. In

1936, all other youth organizations were outlawed and membership in the Hitler Youth became compulsory. Many young people enjoyed themselves within its ranks. The programs included camping, hiking, day and nighttime marching, and many sport competitions. Some groups offered instructions in flying model planes, and participation in marching bands and singing contests. The camaraderie and the variety of activities drew most German youngsters like moths to a flame. Parental complaints that their children had so little time at home merely assured the troop leaders that they were doing well. The party expended large amounts of money to mold the next generation in the Nazi image. From the ages of six to nineteen and often beyond, the greatest influence on the development of German youngsters was not the parents, not the schools, but the youth group. It had first call upon their time and energies; nothing was permitted to interfere with the activities it sponsored.

Between six and ten years of age, little boys learned to aspire to become members of the Hitler Youth. Games, marches, camping and singing, and of course, indoctrination which took place under the Nazi banner filled the hours, often pleasantly. At ten, the *Pimpf* advanced to the status of *Jungfolk* after demonstrating his knowledge of bits of Nazi dogma, and his physical fitness. Within three years he was eligible to become a member of the *Hitler Jugend*. Once again, highly competitive examinations determined his acceptance. Strength, courage, and the ability to follow orders without question were tested. In a more practical vein, some youngsters demonstrated their competence in completing such tasks as laying telephone wires and reading semaphore. Graduation at eighteen promoted the young man into the NSDAP and/or the SA.

Even at this point his political education was not complete. All young men and women between the ages of nineteen and twenty-five, were obligated to give six months of national service by working on farms or in factories. No one was exempt from the *Landjahr*. The aim of this program was to promote a social leavening of all Germans, to encourage the objective of a single, unified *Volk*, regardless of intellectual, economic, or religious heritage. Young people from the cities learned about life on the farms, country youths were expected to relate to their counterparts in the cities. After the *Landjahr*, most men were conscripted into the armed forces and only upon completing their army training were they ready to pursue individual careers.

Girls were subject to similar regimentation including separate Hitler Youth organizations and the *Landjahr*. They were not accepted into the military service. The ideal woman was depicted with her children, the helpmate to her husband, the homemaker, the mother who willingly sacrificed her sons for the glory of the fatherland. She was expected to marry and produce healthy offspring. If there was no marriage, out-of-wedlock children were fully accepted by the party. Girls could deliver their babies in special, cost-free maternity homes. If they wished, they could rear their children and receive help from the government, or could offer them for adoption. Nazi ideology held that the natural spheres of women's activities were in the nursery and the kitchen. All university enrollment declined during the Nazi era, but that of women dropped most sharply.

SCHOOLING THE LEADERS OF THE FUTURE

To ensure the proper leadership for the next generation, a series of elite Adolf Hitler Schools was established. Selection of students was rigorous, only the most dedicated were chosen. The boys (only three institutions enrolled girls) were placed under the complete control of their instructors. For four years, between the ages of fourteen and eighteen, they were housed and trained in special castles. The philosophy underlying the system is best summed up by their motto: "Believe, Obey, Fight." The SS ran a number of these institutions and expected to have its graduates join their officer corps.

Anyone visiting Germany in the prewar Nazi years would be charmed by its polite, good-looking youth. Healthy and active, they compared favorably with children of other nations. That is one side of the coin. The other side involved the rapid decline of the intellectual standards in German schools and universities. Everyone was overtaxed with rounds of endless activities which had no connection to studies. One might assume that juvenile delinquency had disappeared, young people seemed to be in a perpetual, albeit highly regulated, summer camp. The facts refute such assumptions. Gangs were still active and juvenile lawlessness continued to exist—an interesting puzzle for the sociologists.

THE CHRISTIAN CHURCHES

Much has been written about Hitler's campaign upon the churches, but this war was waged against the Christian spirit, not the institutions. Even though the official philosopher of the NSDAP, Alfred Rosenberg, denounced Christianity and tried to promote a cult of pagan worship, the German masses rejected his *Mythus*. Rosenberg's claim that Jesus was an aggressive, revolutionary Nordic whose essence was perverted into a faith of Christian meekness, fell on deaf ears. Rosenberg convinced few Germans to accept his Aryan creed of the gospel of blood and racial purity. Not even the Protestants accepted his denigration of Popes as mere merchants of false medicine.

Hitler wanted no confrontation with the churches. It was enough to bring them into line by restricting many of their functions. The Nazis closed most religious schools and outlawed religious fraternal organizations. Freedom to teach the tenets of the faith was severely curtailed. But persecution is a relative concept. The doors of the churches remained open. Some individual members of the clergy, both Catholic and Protestant, suffered greatly for preaching anti-Nazi sermons. The vast majority however, went about their business as best they could and kept clear of dangerous topics. In effect, the churches continued to observe Christian rituals while ignoring the spirit of Christianity. Individual members of the clergy who spent years in concentration camps for resisting the Nazis deserve the accolades of their congregations, but their heroism was personal. German religious institutions did not battle the Nazi anti-Christ, instead, by their silence they permitted the perpetration of terrible wrong. While hymns were sung, masses said, and baptisms celebrated, the doctrines of mercy, love, peace, and equality before God were all but extinguished.

HITLER AND THE PAPACY

The Catholic Center Party had opposed the Nazis and even after the *Gleichschaltung* of all political parties, Hitler appreciated the potential opposition of the centrists. Although he did not practice the faith of his parents, he did not underestimate the power of religion. Not only was it his wish to avoid an all-out conflict with German Catholics, he courted their support. Shortly after coming to power, in 1933, he concluded a concordat with Pope Pius XI. This agreement guaranteed the free exercise of the Catholic religion in Germany, the right for Catholic instruction in public schools, and the protection of church institutions. The Vatican, in return, recognized the regime and promised to dismantle its church-sponsored social and political organizations.

The immediate benefits were Hitler's; his reputation for diplomacy was considerably enhanced. Before long, however, the Nazis violated many provisions of the agreement. The Pope's hope of safeguarding the faith in Germany ended in humiliating failure. The Catholic Youth League was dissolved, classroom religious instruction was banned, and publications were prohibited. Often the Nazis harassed worshippers and the text of sermons was censored by the presence of uniformed SA and SS men in the churches. The concept of a perfect race ran counter to the Christian obligation to love all the Lord's creations, no matter how impaired. When the Nazis activated a plan to sterilize those Germans judged too defective to have children, the churches objected strongly. But the medical procedures continued; by 1937 some two hundred thousand people had been sterilized for reasons such as schizophrenia, alcoholism, and a range of physical deformities. The objective of racial superiority took an even more heartbreaking turn when it was decided to stop the feeding of "useless eaters." So-called misfits were quietly, secretly murdered. The Catholic church became aware of these "euthanasia" killings and warned the Nazis to cease and desist. Fear of public reaction did bring an end to lethal injections and gassings of children and adults, but this victory came too late for an estimated one hundred thousand victims.

The persecution of Catholics grew more pronounced over the years. Arrests of individual members of the clergy were carried out in public view and the press carried stories of the alleged immorality of the accused. Priests and nuns suspected of trying to save Jews were sent to concentration camps, sometimes after a trial by a Nazi court, the so-called *Volksgericht*, sometimes without any trial. Pius XI issued an encyclical in 1937 entitled "With Deep Anxiety" in which he deplored Hitler's breach of the concordat as well as the illegal persecution of Catholics and the promotion of a cult of race and blood. Upon his death in 1939, Pius XI was succeeded by Pius XII. Several of his messages expressed concern over the fate of the non-Aryans but he declared that he could offer no other succor than prayers. The Vatican was later criticized for its silence on the fate of the Jews, while defenders of the Pope responded that his protests could only have harmed Catholics without benefiting the persecuted Jews. Obviously, the entire question of the official reaction of the papacy to the Holocaust remains a painful issue to this day.

PROTESTANT RESPONSES

The relationship between the Nazi state and the non-Catholic Christian communities failed to develop into a consistent policy. Neither the government nor the religious groups found a satisfactory method of dealing with the other. The official stance was to reduce the influence of traditional religion without causing serious opposition. Several different approaches were tried, sometimes at the same time. The attempt to crush the independence of the churches by placing them under the control of a synod of pro-Nazi ministers was not successful. The Nazis could not unify nor completely control the church federation they established. A second course of action by the authorities was the promotion of "positive Christianity." Known as the German Christians' Faith Movement, the *Deutscheglaubensbewegung* was based on the rather nebulous concept that an amalgamation between Christianity and Nordic paganism was possible. Alfred Rosenberg's muddled mind was at work here. Despite pressure from the party and their "German Christian" supporters, the great majority of the Protestants resisted the paganized version of the faith. Hitler himself kept aloof, he knew very well that moving too far and too fast from long-established tradition would cost him popular support. Finally, the Nazis had to settle for weakening the churches by the tactics they had found most successful: intimidation, harassment, and even terror. Reports of ministers arrested during services in front of their worshipers were whispered behind cupped hands. Both the fear and the reality of incarceration in concentration camps for recalcitrant clergymen stilled all but a few voices of protest.

German Protestants, numbering about 45 million of a total population of some 60 million were not a homogeneous group. The majority were Lutherans, followed by Calvinists, with smaller representations of Methodists and Baptists. The several thousand Jehovah's Witnesses deserve mention because the Nazis persecuted them relentlessly for their steadfast adherence to the doctrine of the superiority of God to man and for their dedication to peace. Further divisions occurred within the denominations over the issue of cooperation with the Nazis. It is well to remember that Martin Luther, the towering figure of the Reformation, was fiercely anti-Semitic. His unrestrained verbal attacks on the Jews were not equaled until Goebbels's rhetoric. The Nazis, of course, invoked these denunciations to fortify the concept that it was possible to remain a devout Protestant while becoming an equally devout Nazi. The great reformer had been an ardent German nationalist, who exhorted his followers to give unquestioning and complete obedience to civil authority. Thus again, Nazi aims dovetailed with Lutheran doctrine.

PROTESTANT PROTESTERS

The great majority of the Reformed churches tried to avoid running afoul of the authorities by preaching "safe" sermons which the uniformed Nazis in the back rows would tolerate. Thus, essential doctrine was watered down to rites and rituals in an atmosphere of disquiet. Some Christians, however, raised their voices in opposition.

The best-known among these was the Reverend Martin Niemoeller. A highly decorated U-boat captain of World War I, he had described his experiences in a best-seller, thus his name was familiar to most Germans. A fervent nationalist, he had supported the rising Hitler. But the actuality of Nazis in power, and their racial and anti-Christian policies offended and disillusioned him. An activist by nature, he became the leader of a religious resistance movement. His Confessional Church was a counterweight, albeit an ineffectual one, to Hitler's German Faith organization.

Niemoeller was the guiding spirit of the Pastors' Emergency League and the Confessional Church. In 1934, its members drafted a statement declaring their opposition to Nazi interference in church affairs, and to the doctrine that might makes right. They also declared that Christianity was irreconcilable with the Nazis' German Faith Movement. At its height, Niemoeller's organization included some 7,000 of approximately 17,000 Lutheran ministers. The Gestapo responded swiftly. More than 700 ministers were arrested, usually sent home after a brief but highly educational imprisonment. Pastors who were deemed unlikely to fall into line, numbering about 50, were sent to concentration camps. Hitler was concerned that the protests raised in favor of the arrested clergy could harm national unity. He preferred a gradual rather than an abrupt diminution of the power of the church. Direct pressure was eased. Niemoeller, however, was seen as the spark of the movement. He was apprehended in 1937 after preaching a sermon on obedience to God, not man. He was tried in a special court on charges of "abuse of the pulpit." Since his sentence was shorter than the time already served while awaiting trial, the court ordered his release. As he left the courtroom, however, he was arrested by the Gestapo and placed under "protective custody." He survived seven years in various concentration camps until, in 1945, he was finally liberated by the Allies.

It would be misleading to see Pastor Niemoeller as spearheading an army of Righteous Christians. During the seven years he endured in the Sachsenhausen and Dachau camps, he was almost forgotten by the German people. The brief candle of protest, the Confessional Church, was quickly snuffed out by the Gestapo. Only after the German defeat did Pastor Niemoeller become a hero once again. He had been a "good German," a symbol of German decency and courage. In the face of the general submission of the Protestants to the repression of religious freedom, martyrs were urgently needed.

NAZI JUSTICE

Every sphere of life in the Third Reich was subordinated to the ideal of the *Volksgemeinschaft*, that is, the ideological and organizational unity of the German people. Individual rights had to give way to communal rights; persons and institutions were measured only by the new criteria established by the Nazis: Did this person or institution promote the Nazi *Weltanschauung* of blood, race, *Volk,* and conquest? Those who failed to advance Nazi ideals were useless, those who stood in the way had to be rooted out. Ruthlessness, even cruelty, became a virtue in the battle to destroy the real and imagined enemies of the new order. Concepts of justice were no exception. The regime was based on the decisions of men, not the rule of immutable laws designed to secure lives and property in a civilized society.

The Third Reich did not issue a new legal code. The existing system was reinterpreted to suit the present realities. Most of the sitting judges were already nationalistic and conservative and some were committed Nazis. With the exception of Jewish jurists, there was no wholesale dismissal of judges. The courts continued to function. New harsh laws poured forth from Berlin in a constant stream, mainly in connection with safeguarding racial purity and protecting the regime from opposition. By 1945, there were forty-three crimes punishable by execution including *Rassenschande*, defilement of race by sexual intercourse between Aryan and non-Aryan. Crimes committed by juveniles were tried in adult courts. The criminal justice code sanctioned beating of prisoners during questioning—but not more than twenty-five blows delivered to the buttocks. This practice was officially approved and was not part of the tortures of the Gestapo and SS.

It was still possible to get justice in a German court in some civil and criminal cases, but that was by no means a certainty. If a party member sued a nonmember, the verdict was likely to be tainted; if an individual hoped to win against the community, his case was doomed. Those sworn to uphold the law became accomplices in crimes against humanity when judges approved the sterilization and euthanasia of Germans deemed unfit to live in the world of Aryan excellence.

The Nazis were unceasingly preoccupied with the possibility of political counteraction. The Gestapo alone employed thousands of informers whose identity was unknown. Remarks implying the slightest criticism, even a joke, could be interpreted as a political crime under the Law Against Malicious Attacks on State and Party. To deal with the spate of accusations, special courts were established whose judges were fiercely loyal to the regime. Cases involving so-called treason were heard by the Nazis' *Volksgericht*, the "Peoples' Court" which consisted of a combination of committed party jurists and ranking Nazi officials. The proceedings had little resemblance to our understanding of justice. Defendants were threatened, denounced, and shouted down by the judges. There was no appeal of the verdicts. When an attempt on Hitler's life misfired on July 20, 1944, the highest *Volksgericht* ordered the execution of between 180 and 200 accused conspirators. Cases involving party members were tried by yet another innovation, *Parteigerichte* (the "Party Courts"). These tribunals were generally used to discipline members of the NSDAP and punish administrative irregularities.

The most tragic perversion of justice was the Holocaust. The criminals, here were the SS, who acted as judges, juries and executioners. The question was never one of wrongdoing by the victims. Himmler had become the master of the Jews and other "enemies of the state." The SS had the right to take their possessions, their liberty, and their lives without the formality of accusation, trial, and verdict. Their victims are reckoned to number six million Jews and five million non-Jewish civilians.

THE COMPENSATION GAME

None other than Ronald Reagan, then president of the United States, stated that the German people were themselves victims of the Nazi regime. If his statement had read *some* German people, it might have had some legitimacy. The facts are that the vast majority of the Germans did not feel outraged or betrayed or driven to take action by the abuses of the Nazi regime. They pursued their daily lives within the limitations the government had established and talked about making the best of things. But the greatest calamity—Hitler's abuse of unbridled power—was never challenged by the German masses. No doubt, the Weimar years had been viewed by many Germans as a disaster. It was difficult to face the fact that in Hitler they had invited an even greater catastrophe. Rather than confront dire reality, it was comforting to concentrate on the successes of the regime and emphasize rationalizations, even apologies for the Nazis.

Our unions are gone, but at least we are working.

My child has time for nothing but the Hitler Youth, but at least his future is assured.

It's too bad I can't speak freely, but Hitler must know what he is doing, look at his successes in foreign policy.

I don't approve of all this anti-Semitism, but isn't it nice, I bought the Cohen's shop so reasonably.

Our neighbor has disappeared, his wife said she doesn't know why. That's nonsense, he must have done something to deserve it.

When the truth is painful, only the few and the brave will confront it.

Chapter 6

German Jewish Life to 1939

The term *anti-Semitism* originated in Germany. It was first introduced into the vocabulary in the 1870s by Wilhelm Marr in his book *The Victory of Judaism over Germanism* and popularized by the diverse factions that opposed the integration of the Jews into the life of the German Empire. The fact that hatred of Jews was given a new designation in the recently unified nation is of some significance. It acknowledged that an additional dimension had been added to an ancient prejudice. No longer was the ancient aversion based solely on its religious antecedents, but the taint of racial inferiority was now superimposed on long-accepted theological phobias. Anti-Semitism became the catchword which sanctioned the concept that an ethnic, that is, an inherent genetic incompatibility existed between Jews and Gentiles. Thus, the argument evolved that the proverbial negative "Jewish characteristics," from avarice to zealousness, were inborn and inbred. This implied that Jews could never be part of the Germanic people even if they converted to Christianity. Nor would their residence on German soil, be it of hundreds of years in duration, alter their inability to be part of the *Volk*. The acceptance by some Germans of such sophistry in the nineteenth century marked a reversal of the generally more liberal attitude of the era.

EMANCIPATION

The medieval persecutions of the Jewish people in Europe had been deeply rooted in the deicide myth. The refusal of the Jews to accept Christ was viewed as a sign of unforgivable perversion. The miserable state of Jewish life, though caused by severe economic restrictions, was explained in religious terms: It was God's punishment for the rejection of Christ the Messiah. All past sins, however, could be absolved through conversion. Beginning with the Age of Reason in the eighteenth century, Christian influences weakened and long-held assumptions concerning the Jews were challenged. The French Revolution and the Napoleonic conquests spread the ideals of equality before the law eastward and by the end of the eighteenth century, Jews in central Europe and England had been granted most civil rights. As the ghetto walls fell, its former occupants were grateful, and hopeful that the forces of rationalism would allow them to live peacefully as citizens in the Gentile world of their birth.

For more than a century, German Jews lived on a roller coaster of hope and despair. The achievements of Moses Mendelssohn (1729–1786) had raised their expectations of entering into the full rhythm of German life. Mendelssohn, the "German Plato," exhorted the Jews to emulate educated Germans; speak their language, read their literature, and study the natural sciences, history, and philosophy. In the intellectual salons where men and women of learning came together, Jews and Gentiles met as equals. The eagerness of German Jewry to be accepted animated them to embrace German culture enthusiastically. The voices of admonition raised by the Orthodox rabbinate could not hold back the desire of most German Jews to join the mainstream of national life. They hoped that cultural conversion could accomplish what religious conversion had done in the past.

CAN JEWS BE GERMANS?

Germany was not unified into a single nation until 1871. Bismark's political achievements were followed by rapid economic growth as German industry competed to manufacture goods for international markets. German Jews eagerly participated in these expanding economic opportunities. But as they entered and succeeded in various business and professional pursuits, the voices of opposition grew stronger. This renewed anti-Jewish agitation rested upon overt and latent religious antipathies but now claimed to be based on a national and ethnic incompatibility. Jews were different, "aliens in our midst," and could never be true Germans. Modern German anti-Semitism found a new theory to support an old resentment.

The second half of the nineteenth century was a period of great economic, social, and political upheaval. Power was shifting from the landowners to the middle class; factories replaced farms as the nation's preeminent workplaces; scientists and philosophers confronted and questioned many long-accepted articles of faith; the unpropertied classes were no longer quietly grateful for the opportunity to work, instead they organized to gain some political influence. The entire established social framework was under attack. Such far-reaching displacements were accompanied by stress and confusion, and as in bygone eras, there were people who held the Jews responsible for their losses.

ECONOMIC ANTI-SEMITISM

Throughout the Middle Ages and beyond, Jews had been subjected to severe economic limitations. The heads of the more than three hundred German principalities regulated the activities of "their" Jews. Generally, that meant confinement to petty trading, horse and cattle dealing, and money-lending. Some Jewish artisans provided for the needs of fellow Jews, but their numbers were limited. In south Germany, the law provided that only one son could enter into the business or occupation of his father. Permission for craftsmen, such as tailors, carpenters, shoemakers, furriers, goldsmiths, et al., to sell to the world outside the ghetto was rarely authorized. Generation after generation of Jews eked out a living as they competed with one another in the narrow economic perimeters allotted to them.

During the first half of the nineteenth century, the door to economic opportunity opened a crack wider. The Napoleonic wars were followed by the gradual emancipation of western and central European Jews. Most German states (their number was reduced to thirty by Napoleon) permitted Jews to do business with the Gentile world on a more equitable footing. The unification of Germany and the ensuing industrial expansion gave Jews entry into growing trade and manufacturing activities. The revolution in production required modernization of business methods, particularly in finance and banking. Now the middlemen, the traders, the storekeepers, the men who understood investments and the raising of capital were in demand. Workers were needed to man the machines and factory owners were not interested in the religious affiliation of their labor force.

For the Jews, economic changes were not obstacles, rather they were opportunities. Many took full advantage of these new possibilities and often they succeeded. Within a generation or two, many poor Jews had entered the middle class and a few had become rich and powerful. As they embraced bourgeoisie economic values, they usually adopted the prevailing German moral and cultural standards as well. With an enthusiasm often typical of newcomers seeking acceptance, they plunged into German art and literature as admirers and as contributors. German replaced Yiddish, modern dress was substituted for somber traditional garb. In the process much of the old religious orthodoxy waned. The ideal of a life dedicated to Torah was supplanted by admiration for the bounty of European culture and the achievement of economic ease.

German Jews, by and large, espoused emancipation and acculturation. Their successes, however, reawakened a barely dormant anti-Semitism. The economic upheaval which accompanied the development of German industry frustrated those who did not or could not benefit from it. Social and political power was no longer the intrinsic endowment of land-holding nobility as money challenged long-venerated family status. The cycles of boom and bust, the hardships caused by recurring periods of unemployment, the emergence of new wealth and new poverty, all were factors in creating insecurity and anxiety. Who could be blamed for ushering in this new and, for some, frightening state of affairs?

Since there is no connection between prejudice and reality, it was not difficult to target the Jews. Capitalists, unhappy with the growing socialist movement among their workers, noted that some of the labor leaders were Jews. Factory workers, protesting the avarice of the owners, pointed to the few Jews among manufacturers. When wild speculation resulted in the crash of 1873, the press singled out Jews for condemnation. Both monetary inflation or contraction can cause economic hardships; Jews were held responsible for both. Although the name of Rothschild was held in high esteem in financial circles, that banking house had become entirely too rich and powerful for the anti-Jewish conservative and reactionary forces in the nation.

POLITICAL ANTI-SEMITISM

Extension of the right to vote in national and state elections in the German Empire stimulated the development of political parties ranging from the reactionary to the radical. The majority of German Jews supported liberal politicians. This fact aroused the antagonism of factions within conservative and reactionary circles. Even Otto von Bismark, the architect of German unification and venerated leader of the Reich until 1890, was not averse to using the Jewish scapegoat. Bismark the politician had lost two major battles in his long and usually successful career; he was unable to reduce the influence of Catholicism *(Kulturkampf)* in Germany and he could not stem the tide of socialism among the working class. Since Jewish leaders had supported him in both these battles he found it convenient to transfer the reasons for his failure to the Jews.

The blue-collar middle class, shopkeepers, craftsmen, and petty officials were courted by conservative politicians who quickly realized the vote-getting power of anti-Semitic propaganda. Although many of the recently enfranchised workers followed the Socialists' banner, other parties vied to enroll them into their ranks. Among these was the Christian Social Workingmen's Party.

Founded in 1878 by Adolf Stoecker, the chaplain at the court of Emperor William I, this organization made vilification of Jews its centerpiece. Stoecker, like Hitler, was an eloquent speaker, a rabid anti-Semite, and good organizer. Several international anti-Semitic congresses convened in Germany with his endorsement. For the first but certainly not the last time, a delegate from an overtly anti-Semitic party appeared in the Reichstag. Stoecker demanded the revocation of citizenship for Jews and their removal from certain professions. But his diatribes were too regressive even for Bismark who declared that the nation would not permit religious affiliation to intrude on the rights of citizenship.

Anti-Semitism had considerable political appeal. The Catholic centrists joined with the Conservative Party to include a pledge in their platform to combat the so-called "oppressive and disintegrating Jewish influence on our national life." Ambitious politicians also gave assurances that their Christian constituency would deal solely with Christian magistrates and only Christian teachers would be permitted to instruct Christian pupils. The phrase, so often repeated by the Nazis, "the Jews are our misfortune," was given legitimacy when used by the renowned historian Heinrich von Treitschke. So forceful were the accusations coming from the extreme nationalists, from certain members of the clergy, and from the ever-present clique of opportunists, that anti-Semitic violence broke out. During the last quarter of the nineteenth century, these disturbances resulted in the destruction of property and physical injury to Jews. With the exception of the Socialists, no civil authority took these riots seriously. Many German Jews, however, recognized that they needed to exert themselves on their own behalf. What forms their self-defense should take remained a divisive question until Hitler supplied the answer.

JEWISH REACTION: THE REFORM MOVEMENT

The Jews of Imperial Germany, citizens under the law but attacked by powerful forces, were facing a dilemma. The great majority continued to await complete acceptance by their Christian fellow nationals. They believed that it was possible to serve two masters, to be patriotic Germans and retain their religious attachment to the ancient faith. There were Catholic Germans, Lutheran Germans, why not Jewish Germans? *Deutschtum* was not incompatible with *Judentum*. In order to facilitate the process of acculturation, German Jews initiated the modernization of religious practices. Rites and beliefs which were obsolete or considered to be contrary to the judgments of modern science were discarded or changed. Dietary prohibitions, the use of phylacteries in prayer, the separation of men and women in synagogues were held to be outdated. Choirs and organ music were introduced to enhance the service. Sermons were preached in German. Prayer books were revised and German translations of Hebrew texts were provided. Predictably, the Orthodox were appalled and accused the reformers of abandoning Judaism for Germanism. The fact that members of Reform congregations were more likely to marry outside their faith and often were lost to the Jewish people gave substance to their fears.

But there was more to the Reform movement than the search for public acceptance. It was a revitalization of the faith. The need to bring harmony into Jewish civil and spiritual life was real. The foremost advocate of reform was Abraham Geiger, a noted scholar and critic who became chief rabbi at the synagogue of Breslau. He saw Judaism as a faith whose forms must not be dictated from the graves of antiquity, but as a vital, living creed. Thus, the elimination of archaic ritual was justified. To the distress of the Orthodox rabbinate, prayers for the coming of the Messiah and the Jews' return of Zion were eliminated. Here the rationale was that German Jews must look upon Germany as their one and only homeland. Reform Judaism removed none of the ethical requirements from its doctrine. Righteousness and the struggle for social justice, two concepts rooted in the Torah, remained central in the Reform movement. The very success of the reformers widened the gap between the traditionalists and the modernists, and theological debates sometimes disintegrated into divisive quarrels.

IS ZIONISM THE ANSWER?

The desire of the German Jews to be treated as equals with their Christian neighbors was not shared by the Gentile world. No matter how sincerely the Jews proclaimed their patriotism, how eagerly they embraced German culture, how successfully they advanced German economic progress, anti-Semitism did not disappear. Although most German Jews continued to hope that time and education would work on their behalf, many Jews were forced to face the obvious. Most painful was the unwillingness of the German government to protect their legal rights during riotous anti-Semitic outbursts. One reaction, indeed an ancient one, was flight. Its modern equivalent—emigration— caused large numbers to enter New York harbor beneath the outstretched arm of the Statue of Liberty. By 1880, this country had opened its doors to 250,000 German-speaking Jews. They were literate, many had skills, and they were hard working. From the shores of the Atlantic to the Pacific, their contributions to the cultural and economic life of the United States have been recognized. Although statistically they were soon overshadowed by the influx of eastern European Jews, the mark they left on American Jewish institutions was indelible.

The majority of Jewish Germans remained in the Reich. They continued to anticipate their complete integration into the fabric of German life. Through their achievements they hoped to convince the government and their fellow citizens that indeed, they were an asset to the nation. Every friendly gesture on the part of the politically and socially powerful was hailed as evidence of their acceptance. But not all German Jews shared this optimism. A gradually increasing number believed that only a Jewish homeland could answer the so-called Jewish question.

Zionism was the movement which called for the re-establishment of a Jewish nation in the Holy Land. Its modern beginning was the work of eastern Jews. The czars of Russia mistreated their Jewish people for generations, and idealistic young men and women chose to exchange Russian despotism for a return to the ancient homeland. The life they chose in the Jewish colonies of Turkish Palestine and its barren and malaria-infested soil was backbreaking and dangerous. In western Europe, however, Zionism was in direct conflict with assimilationism and its appeal was very limited; that is, until the emergence of the remarkable Theodor Herzl.

Herzl, born in 1860 in Budapest, grew up in a home where Reform Judaism was practiced. He worked in Vienna as a writer and journalist, barely affected by his occasional brushes with anti-Semitism. His life was changed when he went to Paris to report on the trial of Captain Alfred Dreyfus. Here he was, in the cultural center of Europe, among the people who had declared equality and fraternity a national motto, and yet he found widespread hatred of Jews. Dreyfus's alleged guilt was transformed into shouts of "Death to the Jews." Herzl not only came face to face with an ancient problem, he was challenged to find solutions and devoted his life to their realization.

Herzl's Zionism centered around three concepts: anti-Semitism is a permanent, fixed condition; the Jews are a nation like any other but for the lack of a territorial homeland; and Palestine should become the national home of the Jewish people. Jews had been at the mercy or the caprice of Gentiles for nearly two thousand years and nowhere were Jews secure. Only through the reestablishment of a state could they ever achieve equality. Despite the fact that relatively few German Jews actually settled in the impoverished, neglected Turkish province, the Zionist movement won considerable ideological and financial support. The ZV, or *Zionistishe Vereinigung* ("Zionist Union"), combined individual organizational units into a national organization which gave a sense of dignity and inner strength to its supporters.

THE CV REACTION

The assimilationists protested vehemently. Their efforts had been directed toward convincing their Christian neighbors that Jews were citizens whose patriotic devotion could not be challenged. Now the Zionists asserted that integration into the national life of the Diaspora was at best implausible. This, they claimed, played into the hands of anti-Semites. Through their own union, the CV, or *Centralverein deutscher Staatsbuerger Juedisches Glaubens* ("Central Union of German Citizens of the Jewish Faith"), they exerted pressure on the German government to end all discrimination. The CV considered it a point of honor to combat anti-Semitism, not submissively, but as their right as German citizens. Its legal arm fought bias in the courts while its educational efforts stressed the timelessness and significance of Jewish values. Although fearful of political activity, the CV represented sixty thousand, or 12 percent, of German Jewry. Their work provided hope that the problem of *Germantum* versus *Judentum* would be resolved and soon Jews would feel comfortable in practicing their religion as fully accepted members of the German whole.

But anti-Semitism is not a rational emotion, nor is it susceptible to rational approaches. Heinrich Class's book, *Wenn Ich Kaiser Wer* ("If I were Emperor"), made that point with great success. Published in 1912, Class fanned the old fires of anti-Semitism and kindled new ones. He suggested the enactment of laws forbidding Jews from voting, removing them from public service, banning them from the armed forces, prohibiting them from owning land, and outlawing their service as directors in some institutions. He suggested that they should pay double the ordinary taxes. When the Nazis came to power, they found these suggestions positively inspirational for legislative actions.

EFFECT OF WORLD WAR I

The rift between the Zionists and the assimilationists was temporarily healed by the outbreak of the First World War. In an overwhelming paroxysm of patriotic fervor, all differences were buried, not only among Jews but other opposing parties. Groups who had proclaimed their international brotherhood suddenly rallied enthusiastically round their national flag. German socialists, for example, were infected with the same fever as French socialists when the killing began. German Jews donned the uniforms and fought side by side with their Christian neighbors. As long as German victories fed the national ego, anti-Semitism was given a respite, albeit a short one. When the war finally ended in 1918, four years of carnage had destroyed much more than lives, property, and empires. The optimism that human progress was the ordained destiny of Western man was invalidated on the battlefield. The generation born after the war found cynicism instead of hope, economic and political turmoil, and the triumph of hatred over goodwill. Alienation was the catchword and the good old days were recalled as having been much better than they actually were. In the bitterness over a lost war and the ensuing disorder and revolutions, the familiar scapegoat was quickly hauled to the surface.

GERMAN JEWS DURING THE WEIMAR YEARS

The Weimar constitution was the instrument of government from 1919 until 1933. It provided for a democratic republic, modeled in part after the English and American systems. Most German Jews, about 1 percent of a population of sixty million, supported the liberal, prorepublican parties. The Weimar years seemed like the best of times, but signals abounded that the worst of times was approaching. Jews graduated in increasing numbers from universities and entered professions and financial institutions. Forty-six percent were self-employed and the majority belonged to the middle class. Intermarriage with Christians reached an extraordinary 60 percent. The CV, claiming to speak for German Jewry, did not endorse political candidates and continued to work on its German-Jewish good neighbor policy.

The Weimar years were turbulent. The German people did not adapt well to the uncertainties and the unseemly abuse of freedom granted by the democratic government. Fanatics short-circuited the election process by assassinating government officials. Among the casualties was Walter Rathenau, the Jewish minister of foreign affairs. He was killed by men who thought his death would avenge the defeat of the German armies. Attempts to overthrow the government came from the extreme right and the left, yet for fifteen years the Republic survived. Governing coalitions were created, then dissolved; Socialists and Centrists tried to cope with mounting internal and external pressures.

This was also a period of startling contrasts. Never before had Germans enjoyed such freedom of expression, nor had they been subjected to such political and financial instability. It was an age of great artistic achievements in architecture (the *Bauhaus* School), in filmmaking, (Marlene Dietrich's *Blue Angel*), in modern art (Dadaism), and in literature (Erich Maria Remarque's *All Quiet on the Western Front*). The seamy side of the liberated spirit was seen in the cities. License translated into licentiousness. Excesses of every sort, from pornography to gross exhibition of opulence made headlines that disgusted the struggling majority of Germans. Advocates of tradition collided with these new currents and blamed the amorality of the decade on the excess of artistic and personal liberties. Some Jewish artists and playwrights were in the forefront of modern expression. Not unexpectedly, some Germans found it expedient to blame them for all the evils that had befallen the nation.

Officially and legally, Jews were granted complete equality by the Weimar constitution. The old bureaucracy was still in power, so that most officials had been left in place. This guaranteed that anti-Semitism would not fade from public life. Nor did hatred of Jews abate in the private sector. The fact that German Jews were represented in disproportionate numbers in areas most visible to public view, such as the entertainment industry, the press, the legal profession, and as owners of large department stores, energized the old antipathies. Hitler was not the only politician to realize the vote-getting power of anti-Semitism, he was, however, by far the most successful.

JEWISH REACTION BEFORE 1933

Why didn't the German Jews see Hitler's handwriting on the wall? Why did they not flee while there was still time? These questions are often asked but they are based on the wisdom of retrospect. For those living in the early thirties, the choices were not so clear.

German Jews loved their homeland and felt emotionally and culturally tied to it. Their attachment, no doubt, blurred their vision. Even though the increase of Nazi delegates in the Reichstag was worrisome, emigration was viewed as unnecessary by most German Jews. In the years preceding 1933, many political observers believed that Nazi anti-Semitic venom was merely a vote-getting tactic. If Hitler ever came to power, so ran the argument, such rhetoric would cease and certainly would never be enacted into law. It was unthinkable that any German government would revert to the tactics of medieval fanaticism. Although debates concerning the wisdom of emigrating echoed in every Jewish home, the general consensus was to sit tight, wait, don't panic. Not even in nightmares was it possible to imagine the events of the Holocaust. Yes, they suffered indignities at the hands of those hooligan Brownshirts, yes, there was destruction of property and even several murders. But these were illegal acts and the courts were bound to reestablish the rule of law. After all, this was Germany, a nation proud of its superior civilization.

Suppose a family decided to leave Germany. Where could they go? To places with unpronounceable names that one could hardly find on a map? What would happen to parents and grandparents who would not or could not leave? or the sickly ones whom no country wanted? What of the businesses, built up over many years, how can one just walk away? For the rich and the famous, doors opened wide, for the family of middle-class means or the Jewish poor, the choices were few or none. The Western world had not yet recovered from the Great Depression; every nation was struggling to keep its own unemployed from going under. It was not a time to welcome strangers into a country. Be strong, be patient, it will pass; such was the reassuring advice offered by Jewish newspapers. The leaders of the CV urged the Jews to react with dignity and self-respect, with helpfulness toward each other and with perseverance. Since these were the words the Jewish community wanted to hear, they were heeded.

Realists who carefully studied the Nazi leadership, the mood of the people, the indifference of other nations to the rise of Nazi power issued prophetic warnings.

Leave, they said, run for your lives. But few were willing to forsake their accustomed lives. Only the increasing Nazi terror after Hitler became chancellor awoke them to the danger at their doors. Then the scramble to find refuge left many thousands without a place to flee. Approximately half of the German Jews waited too long or could find no nation to accept them in time to save their lives.

ORGANIZATION FOR SURVIVAL

During the years before the start of the Second World War, German Jews organized themselves for mutual aid. First they were ousted from political life, then their economic bases were cut away, followed soon after by ostracism from cultural and educational participation. With each loss, the German Jews created their own organizations to try and fill the void. They closed ranks, supported one another, and tried to provide for the spiritual and economic needs of their people. Many discovered their religious heritage and the synagogues had never been so well attended. Despite great difficulties, national organizations provided for entertainment by Jewish artists which included some first-class musical and theatrical performances. Schools for Jewish children were set up and adult education classes were offered. Aid for the poor, free soup kitchens, and clothing were provided until the death trains took the final remnant to the east.

As long as the authorities permitted, and it was to the advantage of the Nazis to allow such self-help, technical and agricultural training programs were instituted for young people hoping to emigrate to Palestine. Jewish agencies furnished counselors to aid prospective emigrants wade through the morass of paperwork. Several children's transports left for England where British families cared for youngsters in their homes. While any Jewish businesses still functioned, agencies tried to find work for the unemployed. Sports competitions were organized in an effort to create an atmosphere of normalcy for the young people. Two Jewish newspapers kept their subscribers informed of the latest dictates of the government, urged the people to stay calm, and regrettably, asked them to remain optimistic.

The local religious congregations, the *Gemeinden* ("congregations"), bore the burden for some of these activities, but on the national scale the RV, the *Reichsvertretung der Deutschen Juden*, played the major role. Until he was arrested and sent to Theresienstadt concentration camp, the renowned liberal Rabbi Leo Baeck led the struggle to preserve a semblance of German-Jewish life. When the German Jews were impoverished, they received financial help from overseas, particularly from Jewish organizations in the United States. After December 7, 1941, when Germany declared war on the United States, such aid ceased. The isolation of European Jewry was nearly complete.

The fact that the Nazis made use of Jewish organizations to implement their own agenda has created a cloud over their efforts. This perplexing issue will be examined in Chapter 8. But without question, during the period between 1933 and 1940, Jewish organizations extended material and moral assistance to their co-religionists.

MASTER PLAN OR EXPEDIENCY?

The Nazi commitment to make Germany *Judenrein* is not questioned by serious students of the Holocaust. Events occurring even before Hitler launched World War II left no doubt that he wanted to purge Germany of its Jews. A persistent question, as yet unresolved, concerns the methods the Nazis planned to employ in order to achieve their purely Aryan state. Was genocide the aim from the inception of Nazi doctrine or would emigration have satisfied their objectives? Some historians, known as the Intentionalists, are convinced that the actual, physical destruction of the Jews was already outlined in *Mein Kampf*. Opposing this point of view are the Functionalists, whose research has lead them to conclude that the annihilation strategy evolved when the war in the east presented the opportunities for the *Endloesung*, the "Final Solution." The proponents of this view affirm that Hitler's creatures, Himmler most of all, initiated the mass murders because this was Hitler's implied or actual verbal order.

The controversy remains unresolved. We know that until the attack on Poland, Nazi policies followed a pattern that differed from the one adopted after 1939. During the earlier years, the killing of Jews was incidental to the tactic of making their lives so wretched that they would flee to any corner of the world. The laws enacted became progressively more brutal and were always accompanied by obscene propaganda campaigns. But there were no death camps. Not until the fall of Poland were the murder factories erected. The sequence of events which had begun with "you may not work among us," advanced to "you may not live among us," and escalated to "you may not live at all." In the lands conquered by Germany after 1939 this sequel of events was very much accelerated. Confiscation of property, expulsion from homes, and physical annihilation could, and often did, occur on a single day.

WHO IS A JEW?

Nazi genetic experts had great difficulty in deciding on a legal definition of who was to be considered a Jew. Serious people engaged in lengthy, weighty debates on the subject. Precisely to whom did the increasing number of anti-Jewish laws apply? Particularly perplexing was the status of the children of mixed marriages. Dr. Bernard Loesener of the Department of the Interior was a recognized expert on Jewish Affairs and he was instructed to clarify the issue. The Law for the Restoration of the Professional Civil Service, enacted in April of 1933, set forth the official definition: A person is a non-Aryan if his parents or grandparents were Jewish. This applied to children having one Jewish parent or one Jewish grandparent or if one parent or grandparent practiced the Jewish religion. In other words, *Jew* and *non-Aryan* were interchangeable terms and religion and ethnicity both were applied to prove racial status. Christians were regarded as Jews/non-Aryans if they had one or more Jewish ancestors. But this definition required further clarification. Did the prohibitions applicable to Jews have equal validity in the case of a Christian who had the misfortune of having one Jewish grandparent? Was the valuable German blood flowing in that individual to be squandered? In 1935, the question was taken up again and a new category was created, the *Mischling* ("one of mixed race"). The revision maintained that:

1. a full Jew had three or four Jewish grandparents;
2. a *Mischling* half-Jew had two Jewish grandparents, practiced Judaism, and was the child of a three-quarter Jew;
3. a *Mischling* of the first degree had two Jewish grandparents, but did not practice Judaism and was not married to a Jew;
4. a *Mischling* of the second degree had one Jewish grandparent.

It seems inconceivable to us here and now that officials and so-called scientists spent months working out this absurdity. But there was a deadly aspect to the application of these classifications. Although *Mischlinge* were designated non-Aryans and prohibited from many activities, most German *Mischlinge* survived the Holocaust. Wilhelm Stuckart, state secretary of the interior, made this bizarre observation to explain his opposition to the deportation of *Mischlinge*:

> I have always considered it dangerous biologically to introduce German blood into the enemy camp. The intelligence and excellent education of the half-Jews, linked to their ancestral Germanic heritage, make them natural leaders outside Germany and therefore very dangerous. I prefer to see the *Mischlinge* die a natural death inside Germany.

It must be noted that although all Jews were non-Aryans, not all non-Aryans were Jews. For example, children of Polish-Jewish parents were treated as fully Jewish; Poles did not belong to the Aryan race and their blood was not worth the salvage.

During the period between Hitler's rise to power and the events known as *Kristallnacht*, "the night of the broken glass", November 9, 1938, anti-Jewish laws were issued in spurts and stops. During each lull, many German Jews and their sympathizers—yes, there were some—hoped that the worst was over. That was until the next series of decrees were issued. The years 1933, 1935, and 1938 were particularly prolific. Jews were legally barred from enjoying the rights of German citizenship, they were deprived of their freedom to work, and they lost the privilege of owning property.

THE BOYCOTT

Hitler lost no time in proving that his government's anti-Jewish rhetoric should be taken seriously. By decree, April 1, 1933 was declared a day of boycott of all Jewish businesses. An Action Committee of the NSDAP coordinated the efforts "to teach the Jews a lesson." On April 1 and for several days thereafter, Jewish stores, institutions, industrial concerns, and offices found SA troopers stationed at their entrances. Customers or clients who tried to enter were stopped, harangued, and sometimes beaten. The message was clear: Don't deal with Jews. This measure was also useful in testing the reaction of Christian Germans and foreign nations. The behavior of Germans on this occasion foreshadowed the conduct they adopted throughout the regime. With few exceptions, they complied with the boycott. When prevented from entering they were confused, momentarily annoyed, and then retreated. No sense getting into trouble with the Brownshirts. Certainly, some Christians were privately angered, perhaps even ashamed. But the nation remained quiet and Hitler had his answer.

The foreign press, however, in editorials and news stories, clearly demonstrated its repugnance. The Nazi leaders rather adroitly turned this criticism to their advantage. Was this negative press from abroad not proof of the existence of a Jewish international conspiracy against the Gentile world? Did this not corroborate the thesis of *The Protocols of the Elders*? Jewish leaders were instructed to urge their counterparts in Europe and America to use every pressure to stop the adverse portrayal of Germany. Unless these "misrepresentations" ceased, German Jewish interests would suffer further. Although these admonitions were not taken at face value outside of the Reich, they initiated a dilemma that would confound non-German Jews and well-intentioned Christians for many years: Will our protests against the Nazi tactics harm or help the Jews? Will our efforts incite reprisals against the very victims we wish to aid? Or will our silence be interpreted as indifference and thus encourage further outrages?

In 1933, Jews were ousted from the civil service and the legal professions. The Orthodox community suffered a distressing blow when kosher butchering was outlawed. The ratio of Jews permitted in public schools and universities was reduced. Thousands lost their livelihood when banned from working or participating in the cultural and intellectual life of the nation such as the press, radio, the arts, and the sciences. Frightening scenes of terror and humiliation became commonplace, when for example, elderly men were forced to scrub sidewalks or the beards of religious scholars were cut amid the jeering laughter of the SA. The government frowned upon such free-lance operations which might undermine party discipline. It was useless to seek redress through the justice system, the courts were not interested in such cases. Nevertheless, it became clear that a systematic approach to the Jewish question was needed.

THE NUREMBERG LAWS

The so-called Nuremberg Laws of 1935 provided that Jews were no longer citizens of the Reich; they were intruders, unwelcome subjects. Further, the laws prohibited marriage and sexual relations between Jews and Gentiles. For a Jewish partner, such an offense was punishable by the death penalty. Employment of Aryan female servants under the age of forty-five in Jewish homes was forbidden. The edict also forbade Jews to serve in the armed forces. German Jews were shocked, the seriousness of their situation could no longer be denied. All the hopes of the assimilationists that German respect for justice would preserve them were finally dashed. Instead, the law had been turned into an instrument of persecution.

Although during the 1930s the Germans did not enact a uniform policy concerning the emigration of its unwanted subjects, they officially encouraged their exodus. A flight tax of 25 percent of the proposed emigrant's assets was collected and until the middle of the decade, it was possible to transfer some money out of the country. Two special banks were established which shifted Jewish assets to Palestinian banks in a rather elaborate scheme designed to meet the German need for foreign currency. Local authorities throughout the Reich were advised to permit, even to assist, in the flight of the Jews.

But no golden door opened to receive them. The lines in front of foreign legations grew longer but the number of visas issued remained inadequate. During 1933, the year the greatest number of refugees left the fatherland, 37,000 Jews escaped. Some families crossed the borders into neighboring countries where they were not permitted to work. Only the philanthropy of American Jews sustained many of these emigres. However, when the Nazis marched into Poland, France, Belgium, and Holland, many of these semi-legal arrivals were among the first to be given up by their host countries and were sent to concentration and death camps.

The Nuremberg laws were supplemented many times. Eventually, over four hundred edicts dealt especially with the "Jewish problem." Jews were forbidden from entering parks, zoos, hotels, theaters, sports events, or any public building. They could not sit on public benches or use public transport. The early restriction of the number of Jewish children permitted to attend public schools was amended several times until a complete ban was enforced. They could not own radios, furs, or woolen clothing. When food and clothing was rationed, Jews received ever-decreasing amounts of life's necessities, no meat, no milk, no eggs. The restrictions on business activities mounted until Christians and Jews could not work side by side in any establishment.

Ever reluctant to have any action appear illegal, the courts found that any employers who had long-term contracts with Jewish workers could abrogate the agreements because Jewishness was given the official interpretation of being the equivalent of death—thus the arrangement was null and void. The Nazification of the courts guaranteed that legal challenges would be decided in favor of the government; for example, when the drivers' licenses of Jews were canceled, appeals were attempted but failed in court. The decrees issued became increasingly Kafkaesque. Minor infractions were punished with long terms of incarceration in Dachau, Buchenwald, or Sachsenhausen concentration camps. Those fortunate prisoners who proved their ability and willingness to leave Germany at once were freed. Eventually, the Nuremberg laws were amended to include an array of dehumanizing and degrading prohibitions: A yellow star had to be worn when appearing outside the home; Jews could not own phones but neither could they use public telephones; curfews kept Jews off the streets when others shopped, food rations grew constantly smaller. How can one justify the ban against identifying badges for blind and deaf Jews, or the tearful delivery of all Jewish-owned pets, even birds in their cages?

JUDEN RAUS ("JEWS GET OUT")

Until the attack on Poland in September 1939, the Nazi government used every means at its disposal to force the Jews to leave. They had been deprived of their professional and economic standing; they were socially ostracized, and newspapers such as Julius Streicher's pornographic *Stuermer* were unrelenting in their attacks. There were arrests without charges and beatings in the streets. Each time there was a let-up, the Jews hoped that the worst was over. The year 1936 was often misinterpreted in this way. Because the Olympic Games were played in Germany and the government wanted to make a good impression on the hundreds of thousands of visitors, signs in stores warning that Jews would not be served disappeared temporarily; park benches no longer advertised that these seats were for Aryans only; even Goebbels and the press restrained their abusive rhetoric. But the lull merely forecast a more violent storm.

EMIGRATION AT AN IMPASSE

The persecution of German Jews shifted into high gear during 1938. That summer the *Kennkarte* was issued, an identification card with fingerprints and picture to be carried at all times. Males were required to add the middle name of Israel, females were ordered to affix Sara to their first names. The government argued that these internal passports helped the state control its enemies. Goering ("guns, not butter") had taken charge of preparing the national economy for the coming war. His control of the Four Year plan gave him enormous power. As long as he could claim to be acting in the interest of military preparedness, he could counteract decrees of every other agency of the Reich. He demanded that all present and future traitors must be neutralized before the nation could fight a foreign war. The category of potential opponents included all of the German Jews from age one to one hundred.

With increasing speed, the economic bases of Jewish life were cut away. Lawyers and physicians were forbidden to practice. Jewish doctors, some four thousand still remained, could treat Jewish patients but now were designated as orderlies. The expulsion of thousands of foreign Jews to their homelands was carried out with careless brutality. But to the Nazis it seemed that German Jews were in no hurry to leave the fatherland. The problem, of course, was not their reluctance to go, they could not find nations willing to grant them asylum. The lines of applicants in front of many embassy gates in Berlin circled several blocks, but the number of visas issued was severely limited. Fear of increasing unemployment coupled with anti-Jewish prejudice caused foreign legations to slam shut their doors. It is doubtful that they had any notion that emigration was not a matter of preference but of life and death.

Only between 150,000 to 170,000 German Jews, that is, one-third of the pre-Nazi number, had left by 1938. Goering decided to speed up the process by completely removing them from the national economic life. The method was not new, it was called Aryanization and involved the forced sale of Jewish businesses and property to Aryans. The price was always set at a fraction of the actual value. But even that amount was not received by the sellers; special bank accounts were set up which doled out a small sum every month. In case of emigration, the remaining money was confiscated by the government. The rationale for this action was based on a legal interpretation which stated that all Jewish wealth was acquired by defrauding Aryans. Since their assets were acquired illegally, the state was entitled to reclaim them.

Exactly what resources were still in the hands of the Jews? An accounting was ordered. Forms arrived at the homes of German and Austrian Jews (the *Anschluss,* or "union with Austria," had taken place in March) which required that they list everything of value in their possession. The detail called for was precise, including ownership of such items as silver candlesticks, paintings, radios, furs, and jewelry. When the time came to confiscate these belongings, the authorities knew exactly who had what. Only some plausible justification was needed to dispossess the Jews of everything. And that would be provided by a Polish teenager living in Paris.

KRISTALLNACHT POGROM

If any doubt remained concerning the intentions of the Nazis to make Germany *Judenrein* ("cleansed of Jews"), they were removed by the events generally called *Kristallnacht,* "the night of the broken glass." Neither Christian nor Jew could ever again claim that they did not realize the seriousness of the Jewish plight. The terror of the nights of November 9, 10, and beyond were played out in full view of the German people. The fact that the Gentiles hurried away from the scenes of widespread destruction, that they averted their eyes when SA bullies beat up old men, and that they turned a deaf ear to the cries of their neighbors is a page of German history that no rationalization can whitewash.

During October, the Gestapo executed an order to forcibly remove all Jews born in Poland, even those who had become citizens, from the Reich and ship them across the Polish border. Some 17,000 men, women, and children were placed into sealed railroad cars and transported across the frontier. The Poles, however, refused to accept them and attempted to drive them back into Germany. The misery of these exiles was self-evident and eventually, under pressure from Jewish organizations, the deportees were reluctantly admitted into Poland. But a young man, Herschel Grynzpan, knew only that the Nazis had deported his family from Hanover. He was living in Paris, hoping to emigrate to Palestine. Shocked and distraught, he bought a revolver. At the German embassy he was admitted to the office of a minor functionary, the Third Secretary Ernst vom Rath. Shouting that this was to avenge his people, he shot the German, who died the next day, November 9.

The Nazi Party leadership was gathered to commemorate the fifteenth anniversary of the Munich beer hall putsch when the sensational news of the murder reached them. Goebbels, with Hitler's approval, gave the signal that this incident was to serve as the excuse for a major pogrom. The *Gauleiters* and SA chiefs rushed to the telephones to order the destruction of Jewish businesses, homes, and communal institutions. Later, Goering and Himmler, fearful that this coup would advance Goebbels's standing with the *Fuehrer*, ordered their minions to participate in the rampage.

ECONOMIC DESTRUCTION

The pogrom has been called *Kristallnacht* because thousands of windows were smashed and the broken shards glittered in the streets like crystal. All of Germany's 275 synagogues were destroyed; those which did not burn were dynamited. Places of business owned by Jews were demolished by arson, ax, club, and crowbar.

In areas where many Jewish-owned shops were clustered together, the streets resembled a combat area. The destruction was carried out by the eerie light of burning buildings, the air was acrid from the smell and smoke of scorched cloth and wood; the sirens and bells of police cars and fire equipment added to the hellish image. Sidewalks were impassable with goods strewn everywhere, here wine from the liquor store ran like a red river on which floated puffs of feathers from the bedding store, there eyeglasses and radios, candy and typewriters were trampled underfoot. Regular police and firemen were under orders not to interfere except to protect the property of Aryans.

Each town and city had variations of the scenario as local commanders of the SA, the Gestapo, and the Nazi Party interpreted the orders to "teach the Jews a lesson" with their own ideas. In some cities, private homes were ransacked, furnishings thrown from windows, and Jews were beaten. Where the SA was encouraged to give vent to frenzy, murders were committed, one hundred Jewish men were killed and an uncounted number injured. In other areas, words such as JEWS DIE were smeared on steps and doors of homes. Some Jewish schools were torched, others left alone. Placards were hung from many destroyed shops which read: THIS IS THE PEOPLE'S REVENGE FOR THE MURDER OF VOM RATH, DEATH TO INTERNATIONAL JEWRY. The Nazis tried hard to convince the German public that this pogrom was a spontaneous riot, caused by the wrath of the people. Never was spontaneity so well planned and systematically organized. In forty-eight hours a total of 7,500 businesses were demolished. The public at large did its best not to see, hear, or know anything and rarely participated in the attacks. Looting was forbidden and here again, local circumstances determined the observance or disregard of that order.

MASS ARRESTS

The *Judenaktion* of *Kristallnacht* was not restricted to the destruction of commercial establishments. For two days and nights the Gestapo, the internal security police known as the SD *(Sicherheitsdienst)*, and regular police combed the country in search of Jewish men between the ages of sixteen and sixty. With prepared lists of names and addresses, they swarmed the villages, towns, and cities. Streets, bus stations, and railroad terminals were turned into tragic theater as men were pulled from screaming families. Many of the arrests were accompanied by beatings although very few of the men resisted. For the most part they were completely bewildered: They asked: "What have I done?" "Where are you taking me?" but were answered with curses. Suicides reached a new peak.

There were no indictments, no trials. The crime committed by Herschel Grynz-pan required retribution from all the Reich's Jews. Thirty thousand men were shipped to concentration camps. Officially, they were removed from German society to prevent the German people from venting their "justified" revenge upon them. The camps Goering had set up were filled to capacity. Depending on the region, the men were sent to Dachau, Buchenwald, or Sachsenhausen. There the prisoners were marched in circles, stood endlessly at attention in order to be counted, did calisthenics, and tormented themselves with fearful pictures of the fate of their families. Eight hundred of them did not survive the hardships of the beatings and the stress of their "protective custody." In contrast to later incarcerations, these prisoners were released. First to go home were men who could prove that their emigration was imminent. Later, others returned who claimed that they were in the process of looking for a country of refuge. Obviously, at that point, that meant everyone.

A CASE IN POINT: BREMEN

On the fiftieth anniversary of *Kristallnacht* the city of Bremen commissioned an investigation into the events of November 9 and 10. The result of this research was intended to be used as teaching material in their schools. The following are some excerpts from that document:

> In Bremen . . . resided about 900 Jews whose homes were scattered all over town. When, during the night of November 9 to the 10 the order to "let loose" arrived at SA headquarters, the first reaction was to reach for the so-called Jews list. In Bremen this had been prepared as early as 1935. The list was copied and distributed that same night to the secondary SA facilities located in various districts.
> . . . SA troopers were summoned. They roamed the city without giving a thought to the nature of their orders and dutifully performed their mission.
> The results were recorded in the police archives. For example: In 17 Jewish businesses and residences windows were demolished, and, in part, furniture and shop fittings were destroyed.
> . . . "With total success we completed the incineration of the Synagogue on Garten Street and we also destroyed the living quarters of the Rabbi. We were also successful in laying waste the chapel in the cemetery and damaged the grave stones. The visitation to the old age home at . . . was carried out by particularly diligent SA men. Here windows were broken, doors splintered, mirrors shattered, the old people were stomped on and driven from the premises."

Two women and three men were murdered during the pogrom in Bremen. When this news reached the SA commander, the killers were told that they had gone too far. However, the men were exonerated when they claimed that they were following orders. But someone remembered after the end of the war, when they were brought to justice and sentenced to long prison terms.

THE AFTERMATH

No matter how blatantly the Goebbels press corps tried to assure the German public that the pogrom was an impulsive reaction by an enraged nation, the public response was negative. Too many people had seen and recognized the men with the torches and axes and knew they had come from the ranks of organized Nazis. A larger complaint concerned the terrible waste of perfectly usable goods. What purpose was served by the destruction of so much property? The cost of replacing the windows alone drew millions of foreign exchange marks from Germany and kept the Belgian glass factories running at full speed for many months. Were there not many Germans who could have made good use of the furniture, the clothing, the very buildings that had been rendered useless?

Within the party hierarchy, the nights of violence and vandalism against the Jews reverberated at the highest level. Goebbels had obviously tried to take charge of the Jewish policy and that was not to be tolerated. Goering and Hitler, still in Munich, inspected the damage in that city and the *Reichsmarschall* convinced the *Fuehrer* that such outbursts must not be tolerated. As a result, the conduct of Jewish affairs was assigned to Goering and Himmler and the ambitious Goebbels was not permitted to meddle again. On November 12, Goering convened a meeting to review the recent events and discuss the future management of the Jewish problem. The principal functionaries were Himmler's emissary Heydrich, Economics Minister Funk, Justice Minister Guertner, a representative from the foreign ministry, and a member of the insurance industry. Goebbels was also invited but received no thanks for his role. In fact, when Goering was finished denouncing the pointless destruction, the propaganda minister made no rebuttal.

The representative from the insurance companies association estimated the losses at 25,000,000 marks. (3,000,000 marks for broken glass). Goering directed that the insurance companies must pay the claims but since the Reich had suffered the real damage, the money was to go into the national treasury. The immense cleanup of the streets was the responsibility of the Jews. Goering then ordered Minister Funk to create legislation which would once and for all drive Jews from all economic participation in Germany. The Aryanization of businesses which had been more or less voluntary was made compulsory. In addition, as retribution for the crime committed by Grynzpan, the German Jews were fined the enormous sum of one billion marks. At the very time that the greatest demands for aid were made upon the Jewish community, when food, clothing and housing were needed desperately, its funds were expropriated and German Jews became paupers.

During the debate, Heydrich was complimented on the success of his methods in driving the Jews from Austria. Heydrich's reply augured ill for the future: Despite all his efforts, the exodus of the Jews was still entirely too slow. At the present rate it would take years to get rid of them all.

The foreign press of the Western world reported the events in their respective newspapers. In headlines and editorials Germany was condemned. Ambassadors from many nations delivered protests to the German Foreign Ministry. The law faculties of ninety-seven universities remonstrated against such racial-political terrorism. Pope Pius XI issued a rather vague statement of sympathy for the victims. Franklin D. Roosevelt recalled the American ambassador and declared that he found the actions of *Kristallnacht* to be utterly abhorrent. An attempt to boycott German goods from coming into the United States was not effective enough to deter future atrocities. The Nazis were convinced that they would be not be attacked with any weapon stronger than words. And words could never harm them. A League of Nations commission on refugees had met at Evian in October without reaching any conclusions; no doors were opened to admit the thousands of potential German Jewish refugees. Hitler interpreted this lack of action correctly: No one would actually *do* anything to help the Jews.

Yet somehow, after the November catastrophe, one hundred thousand German Jews managed to escape. They fled to Shanghai, South America, Africa, Asia, and places they could hardly find on a map. Seven thousand boys and girls were taken in by English families but a similar rescue attempt by the United States was held up by the State Department and the children perished. With the large red *J* (*Jude*) stamped on their passports, with an allotment of about twenty-five dollars per person, and with a Nazi official watching when they packed their suitcases, German Jews knew they must flee to anywhere. They had nothing left but their lives and now nothing mattered but escape.

Chapter 7

Hitler's War

When historians discuss the causes of wars, they often use the term *multiple causation*; only rarely is war the result of a single determining factor. But it is accurate to call World War II Hitler's war. He planned it, directed it, and worst of all, he wanted it. The theory that both world wars were really one single event divided by a twenty-year truce denigrates the essential role of the *Fuehrer*. It was his power, his leadership, his dream for Germany that plunged the world into its most devastating conflict. Two passions dominated Hitler's mental world: hatred for the Jews and the domination of Europe. German conquests provided an immense geographical expanse which fueled Hitler's zeal to wipe the Jews off the face of the earth. His victories enabled the SS to annihilate Jews from the Pyrenees to the Russian steppes, from the shores of the North and Baltic Seas to the Mediterranean. Tragically, when Hitler's two compulsions—the search for Lebensraum and his hatred of Jews—became German policy, the cost in human lives is estimated at 55,000,000 with the Holocaust accounting for 6,000,000.

The opinion that the Treaty of Versailles, concluded at the end of the First World War, inevitably caused the second one ignores the demonstrated willingness of the victors to moderate certain aspects of the treaty during the 1920s. No rationale exists to support the hypothesis that further adjustments could not have been realized. The fact that in 1918 the Germans forced a treaty on the Russians at Brest-Litovsk which was vastly more punitive than the provisions at Versailles makes the German demand for fairness ring hollow. Unless one believes that all historical events are ordained by a force beyond human power, Hitler must bear the major responsibility for turning Europe into a charnel house. It must be understood, however, that several domestic and foreign conditions had to preexist, both of which Hitler exploited brilliantly. The victorious Allies had lost their fervor to uphold the treaty and the German people accepted the half-truths spewed from the Nazi press. When the war erupted, the Western nations were unprepared and many Germans had become convinced that no other honorable alternative existed.

HITLER'S FOREIGN POLICY IDEOLOGY

The theories on which Hitler based his program sprang from his interpretation of several social, philosophical, and psychological hypotheses. From social Darwinism he concluded that all life is a struggle for survival, not merely for individuals, but for nations as well. The state whose people are fittest, that is, strongest, is by natural selection ordained to subjugate lesser races. From among the forerunners of racial theories he chose a Frenchman, Joseph Arthur Comte de Gobineau, author of the four volume *Essay on the Inequality of the Races* as his mentor. Gobineau asserted that only Aryans are creative and the purity of the race must be guarded as scrupulously as life itself. On the lowest rung of that racial hierarchy were the Jews, who were usurpers and contaminators. Also, the misinterpretation of Nietzsche was useful in order to authenticate the Nazi superman ideal. This Nordic demigod was not limited by the usual, ordinary moral values; he was above and beyond the fetters of civilized society. Since life equals struggle, then war is the final test, the true measure of greatness. The achievement of national grandeur cannot be subject to petty notions of integrity; the end always justifies the means; only winning matters, not the fairness or foulness of the fight.

LEBENSRAUM

There was never any secrecy regarding Hitler's foreign policy plans. He had outlined his intentions in *Mein Kampf* and in many speeches. Briefly and simply he was convinced that Germany, by virtue of its superior Aryan *Volk* and its dense population must seek space to live, that is, Lebensraum. This expansion was not to consist of colonies but was to be found in the broad and underpopulated regions of Europe's eastern lands. Possession of large areas of farmland was basic to the development of German hegemony in Europe. The Slavic inhabitants, inheritors of inferior racial qualities, must be forced to give way to the Germans and driven from their soil. Many would be killed and the survivors could be used to toil for their German masters.

The desirability and certainty of armed conflict gave some cohesion to Nazi foreign affairs. The making and breaking of treaties which seems ostensibly contradictory, was actually within the policy perimeters set by the *Fuehrer*. Hitler, who seldom took any interest in the details of domestic affairs, was personally involved in the implementation of his worldwide goals. On his very first week in office, he summoned his top generals and told them of his vision to conquer eastern Europe. Since the Revolution of 1917, so the Nazis claimed, the Soviet Union was ruled by Jews-Bolsheviks. (In Hitler's mind, *Jews* and *Bolsheviks* were interchangeable terms.) Russia was ripe for the taking, since its former tsarist/Germanic leadership had been replaced by a racially flawed dictatorship. The need for eastern territories would unavoidably lead to war. For the moment, Germany required a period of peace to prepare, since both the military and civilian populations must be made ready. This would be accomplished through diplomacy abroad and economic self-sufficiency at home. Dr. Goebbels's best efforts would do the rest.

Hitler's domestic policies become clearer when viewed as components of his foreign strategy. Schemes such as the proposed settlement of SS men and their families in the Ukraine, the preparation of the youth to bear arms or bear children, the so-called euthanasia killings of those deemed mentally and/or physically unfit, Doctor Mengele's bogus research in Auschwitz which sought to increase the number of twins born to German mothers, the brutal and wasteful treatment of defeated peoples, all are parts of Hitler's comprehensive scheme. Even the Holocaust, that is, the destruction of the racially most dangerous people in Europe, was seen by the Nazis as a major aspect in the creation of the brave new Nazi world. During the last several years of Hitler's regime, however, the killing of Jews became even more central than his need to win that war.

THE INTERNATIONAL ATMOSPHERE

The withdrawal of the United States from the international arena in the decades between the two great wars left France and England in the position of leadership of the Western world. It was a mantle both nations wore with poor grace. The war had weakened them, their people were disillusioned that victory had brought them no appreciable rewards. French and English politicians could not present a united front against the rising fascist states of Italy and Germany. Fear of communism at home and of the Soviet Union abroad dominated their policies and wishful thinking colored their perception of Hitler and Mussolini.

France feared a revival of German aggression above all other considerations. But it lacked the power to play the heavyweight in international affairs. The Third French Republic had suffered great human and economic losses during the war and her political party system was unable to operate as a cohesive whole. Extremists from the right and left could not reconcile their differences and crisis followed crisis. France wanted a Germany economically strong enough to make reparation payments but too weak to become a threat. Obviously, these were conflicting aims. Traditionally, France had relied on Russia to prevent German expansionism, but the Communist Revolution had deprived France of that counterbalance to German ambition. French diplomacy tried to compensate by concluding alliances with the newly established eastern nations: Poland, Czechoslovakia, Romania, and Yugoslavia. These, however, were small, struggling nations. The French derived little satisfaction from these treaties and decided to build an elaborate defense line along its German frontier. The Maginot line gave Frenchmen a false sense of safety that would be costly beyond all expectations.

The British hoped to maintain control over their empire despite the increasingly independent stance of their dominions. They had no desire to enhance French ambition to play the European superpower. The war had turned many Britons into pacifists and military expenditures were unpopular. Unemployment figures were high, and disillusionment with the lack of spoils from victory was rife. The British lion wanted to sleep without interference from the continent.

EARLY NAZI DIPLOMACY

Hitler inherited a number of international obligations from the Weimar Republic. Most significant was the Treaty of Versailles which had transferred considerable German territory to Poland and France, had forced the Republic to cede all colonies, had demilitarized the Rhineland and had reduced the German army to one hundred thousand volunteers. Of the huge reparations assessment, however, only a small portion was ever collected. Among Allied statesmen, doubts were voiced concerning the fairness of the treaty. German protestations that the treaty was a *Diktat*, coerced from a prostrate people, were no longer dismissed out of hand. The Locarno Pacts of 1925 removed the French armies from the Rhineland in return for German guarantees to respect the French and Belgium frontiers. In 1926, Germany was admitted into the League of Nations, ending its pariah status. League membership also denoted that Germany was now pledged to uphold the organization's peace-keeping responsibility. In 1928, the Weimar Republic was one of twenty-three nations to sign the Kellogg-Briand agreement that bound the signatories to the outlawing of war as an instrument of national policy. If Hitler had been satisfied to govern Germany in peaceful coexistence with its neighbors, further revisions of the Versailles provisions would have been feasible. But conciliation was not a road Hitler wanted to travel.

When Hitler became chancellor, the first order of business was to secure his own and his party's internal power. Within two years all political and most individual opposition had been eradicated and he was the unchallenged master of Germany. Now the *Fuehrer's* foreign ambitions could be given maximum attention. Hitler, however, was ever careful to preserve the image of the diligent caretaker of the people. The great sacrifices he would demand from the German people in the coming war must be made willingly. It was essential that Germans identify their well-being, their future, with the dreams and wishes of the *Fuehrer*. Thus, the most basic expectations of the Germans had to be met. Hitler often pointed to the promises he had kept; the reduction of unemployment, the restoration of law and order in the streets, the rebuilding of the infrastructure, and the restoration of German respect amid the family of nations.

THE PEACEFUL FACADE

Until Germany was militarily strong, Hitler assumed a circumspect attitude in foreign affairs. He spoke of his desire for peace with great conviction while plans to rearm Germany were progressing in secret. He claimed that all he sought was equality with other European nations. He retained conservative ministers in his foreign, defense, and state departments. Not until 1938 was the subservient Nazi Joachim von Ribbentrop given the official title of minister for foreign affairs. Hitler shrewdly offered to disband Germany's military completely, that is, as soon as its neighbors did the same. The offer was a sham; he knew very well that this proposal would not be accepted. But the appearance of peaceful intentions was maintained. Hitler skillfully fostered the perception that he was a sensible, trustworthy person whose wish to revise certain of the Versailles provisions was understandable. He was also well aware that the democratic nations of Europe feared the Communist Parties within their countries as well as the Soviet government which fostered and assisted them. Since the Nazi Party was the implacable enemy of the Soviet Union, it was tempting to overlook the alarming features of Hitler's policies, to act discreetly with the *Fuehrer* in order to prevent a possible rapprochement between Germany and Russia. Even when Hitler withdrew Germany from the League of Nations and from the Geneva Disarmament Conference, no alarm bells were sounded in London or Paris. After all, so ran the argument of the appeasers, *Herr* Hitler had to satisfy German public opinion, and that was the nature of politics.

THE NONAGGRESSION PACT WITH POLAND

In 1934, Hitler signed a treaty with Poland in which the two countries promised to maintain peace with one another for ten years. The pact startled the Western world. The Weimar government, in its search for allies, had sought good relations with the Soviet Union. How could Germany befriend Poland, the nation which was created out of deep cuts into western Russia and eastern Germany? The Treaty of Versailles had separated East Prussia from the rest of Germany and every German believed the loss of the Polish corridor was a scandal to be rectified in time. Thus, Poland had two neighbors who resented its very existence; Germany and Russia yearned to regain their lost territories. Adding to Polish insecurity was the lack of geographic barriers along its borders; Poland's flat terrain left it open to invasion from east and west. Naturally, the nonaggression pact with Germany was welcomed by Polish diplomats.

The treaty also sent a clear message to the Soviet Union that the era of the Weimar policy of cooperation was over. Evidently, the anti-Soviet propaganda coming from Goebbels's press should have been taken seriously. Russia would have to look for friends elsewhere. The truth that Hitler had no intention of abiding by the Polish concord, that he had no intention of honoring the agreement was simply incomprehensible to the world of the 1930s. Hitler was buying time in order to advance his military and psychological preparations for the war to come. Poland, of course, was invaded in 1939, and became the first victim of his obsession for eastern Lebensraum.

INERTIA IN FRANCE AND ENGLAND

During the years between 1933 and the outbreak of the war, Hitler tested the diplomatic waters again and again. How far could he go in ignoring the Versailles covenant before the former Allies would stop him? His foreign policy decisions required a careful reading of the resolve of France and England. Would they go to war to prevent the resurgence of a powerful Germany? Would the restoration of military conscription, ordered in 1935, give rise to alarm? The inadequate responses to the contravention of the Versailles Treaty revealed the ineffectiveness of the League of Nations. At this point, Germany was weak and Hitler masqueraded as a champion of peace, a reasonable man who demanded only justice for his people. Behind the facade, the Nazis were forging a mighty military machine. Only when his soldiers were the best-trained, best-equipped in Europe would Hitler's goals become clear. By fright or by fight he would achieve his great Thousand Year Reich.

Any decisive action by France and England would have delayed, perhaps halted the Nazi thrust. France wanted treaty compliance from Germany, but without English support its voice was muted. England hoped to return to its traditional isolation from the quarrels of Europe. Great Britain needed time and peace to recover from the effects of the Great War. Its dominions were loosening their ties to the mother country; trade dislocations and budget crises required resolution, labor unrest beset the government and the people. Great Britain hoped to safeguard its island by means of a naval agreement whereby the German navy was to remain at one-third the size of the English Navy although German submarines were permitted to constitute 60 percent of their English counterparts. France was alarmed. Alone in its demand for German compliance with the Versailles Treaty, it concluded a defensive alliance with the Soviet Union in 1935. Each would support the other in case of German aggression.

The maintenance of peace by common action, so optimistically pledged by the League of Nations, proved an empty promise. France and England, the backbone of the League, did not have the necessary spine to prevent the rise of renewed German aggression. International cooperation collapsed in the face of domestic problems. The United States, never a member of the League, could exert only limited influence. Hitler was free to pursue his goals.

BLOODLESS VICTORIES

Hitler's foreign policy reflected the inertia of the nations which were strong enough to oppose him. Each victory he achieved without resorting to war encouraged him to pursue further adventures. Germany's neighbors were unwilling to read the danger signs and today, with the advantage of hindsight, we are perplexed by this blindness. In the 1930s, however, the opinion was widely held that the German people would not support a war if some of their reasonable objectives were unopposed. Thus, tacit permission to abrogate certain provisions of the Versailles agreement seemed fair.

The Treaty of Versailles barred any German military presence in the Rhineland and in the highly industrialized Ruhr region near the French border. Most Germans found that prohibition insulting to their national honor. When Hitler moved troops into the forbidden zone in 1936, the League of Nations protested with words not action. Predictably, Hitler's popularity increased greatly. In the same year, Germany officially withdrew from the League and from the Locarno Pacts. These treaties had been signed by

Germany, France, Czechoslovakia, and Poland in 1925 to ensure peaceful adjudication of disputes. Italy and England had agreed to act as guarantors of the settlement. Once again, German conduct, so clearly in contrast with Hitler's peace-loving oratory, did not arouse serious concern among the Western nations.

The Spanish Civil War served as a proving ground for Hitler's soldiers, tactics, and weaponry. The fascist General Francisco Franco was engaged in a brutal war against the leftist republican government forces. Both Mussolini and Hitler sent him massive aid. While England and France declared their neutrality, German troops tested themselves and their armaments. The joint venture of the two dictators strengthened their mutual connection. In 1939, the Rome-Berlin axis was formed when they signed a formal alliance of aid and friendship. Both dictators could now proceed with new confidence in enacting their grandiose plans.

AUSTRIAN FIASCO AND VICTORY

Hitler, Austrian by birth, wanted to unify his actual and adopted homelands. The annexation was referred to as the *Anschluss*. Hitler first attempted to gain control over Austria in 1934. The German Nazi Party supported a growing number of Austrian Nazis and incited them to attempt a coup d'état against the government of Chancellor Engelbert Dollfuss. When the Austrian SS engaged in a political reign of terror, Dollfuss, a right-wing dictator in his own right, responded with tactics of mayhem and murder. Then the Austrian Nazis broke into his office and shot him in the throat. In the manner of a B gangster movie, the Nazis refused to allow him any medical attention and Dollfuss bled to death on the sofa of his office. But the plot to topple the government failed anyhow. The loyal Austrian Army under the leadership of Dr. Kurt von Schuschnigg, then the minister of justice, routed the Nazis. Meanwhile, Mussolini had his mobilized troops on the Italian-Austrian border to prevent the fall of the legitimate Austrian government. Hitler had to acknowledge that the *Anschluss* would have to wait.

Schuschnigg became chancellor and remained in office until 1938 when German troops marched into Austria and consummated the *Anschluss*. By then Mussolini's neutrality was assured, while the politicians of France and England continued to delude themselves that this act, although forbidden by the Versailles Treaty, would finally satisfy Germany. Great numbers of Austrians greeted the *Fuehrer* in an ecstasy of jubilation as he entered Vienna. Schuschnigg was sent to a concentration camp where, astonishingly, he survived and outlived Hitler by more than thirty years.

THE SUDETEN GERMANS

The pre-World War I Austrian Empire had been allied with Germany. When the Central Powers were defeated, its hegemony was broken up. Hungary, Yugoslavia, and Czechoslovakia became independent and Austria was left as a small, landlocked, German-speaking country. Among the newly established nations, Czechoslovakia was the showpiece of success. Its parliamentary democracy functioned well, Czech industry was balanced with Slovak agriculture, and the solid leadership of its president, Thomas Masaryk, enabled the young republic to thrive. Its greatest difficulties were the result of the ethnic diversity within its borders, fourteen million people composed of Czechs, Slovaks, Germans, Moravians, Hungarians, Austrians, Poles and Ruthenians. Among these, the German minority caused the most severe problems. More than three million so-called Sudeten Germans lived in the northwestern mountainous regions. They would have preferred to have been incorporated into the Reich. Although the government in Prague tried to accommodate their grievances, they remained dissatisfied.

A Bohemian politician named Konrad Heinlein founded the *Sudeten Deutsche Partei* which, he claimed, sought regional independence. Essentially, his ideology mirrored that of the Nazis. His relationship with Berlin was a matter of give and take; Heinlein took substantial financial support and he gave Hitler the excuse to demand the annexation of the Sudetenland. Heinlein's organization represented 60 percent of the Sudeten Germans and his deputies in Prague were instructed to be totally uncooperative. On orders from Hitler, they demanded virtual autonomy for their region; expecting, perhaps hoping, to be refused.

Encouraged by the easy success of the Austrian annexation, Hitler had decided to take over the Sudetenland. In February of 1938, Hitler tested international reaction by sending troops to the border. The Czechoslovakian government responded by massing a well-trained well-equipped army of four hundred thousand along the disputed area. When France and the Soviet Union indicated their willingness to uphold their treaty obligations and support Czechoslovakia in case of attack, the Germans were called back. But the British Prime minister Neville Chamberlain missed this final opportunity to put an end to Hitler's plans. He would not commit British aid to save the Czechs. Without English assurances, Czechoslovakia was doomed.

The execution of Hitler's plan to attach the Sudetenland to the Reich and subjugate the rest of the Czech nation was set for October, 1938. Heinlein was ordered to step up his agitation, to demand nothing less than autonomy. The Prague government under Eduard Benês tried desperately to prevent the dismemberment of the nation and offered Heinlein a semi-autonomous state, modeled after the Swiss cantons. But Hitler did not want concessions, he wanted the dissection of Czechoslovakia.

For the Benês government, the loss of the northwestern area spelled disaster. The mountains provided the country with a natural defense line and the loss of the region would seriously damage the viability of Czech industry. The survival of the republic was supposedly safeguarded by treaties with France, the Soviet Union, and England. The question was: Would these promises be kept in the face of German demands? The response of the British was the decisive one; France and the Soviets would not act alone to protect Czechoslovakia. As Heinlein and his Nazis created chaos, the Benês government tried to cope with the disorders by invoking martial law. On the twelfth of September, Hitler made a speech in which he accused the Benês government of atrocities against the German minority. Germany, he shouted, would not stand by while such crimes were committed. Europe was faced with a full-blown diplomatic crisis.

APPEASEMENT AT MUNICH

The dread of war impelled the British Prime Minister Chamberlain to go directly to Hitler. As an English gentleman, he was going to speak to his German counterpart and by a shake of hands secure tranquillity in Europe. He made the first airplane trip of his life to meet with Hitler in his mountain retreat at Berchtesgaden. Hitler's demands were unaltered: the *Fuehrer* wanted immediate possession of the Sudetenland or there would be war. Chamberlain, after consultation with his divided cabinet and the French Premier Edouard Daladier (but not with Benês), informed the Prague government that it must cede the areas inhabited by Germans. The Czechs had no choice but to accept the ultimatum. Believing he was the bearer of good news, Chamberlain returned to Hitler with the Czech reply. But instead of gratitude, Hitler was furious. He had decided to raise the stakes and now presented the British prime minister with a map which indicated new territorial demands. Chamberlain agreed to submit the map to the Benês government and the French. Paris responded with equivocation but Prague replied with a determined no. Millions of people all over Europe remained glued to their radios, hoping for peace but fearing war.

Benito Mussolini suggested the convening of a four-power conference to ease the

Adolf Hitler and Prime Minister Neville Chamberlain in Munich, 1938. (Courtesy AP/Wide World Photos.)

tension. Chamberlain, Daladier, Hitler, and Mussolini met on September 29 in Munich. Neither Czechoslovakia nor the Soviet Union were invited despite the fact that any decision would affect their vital interests. In the long run they may well have been grateful for that affront; future generations could not blame them for participating in the ensuing shameful events.

The Munich Conference has become a metaphor for appeasement. It was there that Czech independence was handed to Hitler in the vain hope that this sacrifice would assure peace. Once again, Hitler raised that hoped-for prospect when he declared that the Sudetenland was his final demand. Whether or not he was actually believed hardly matters, the truth was revealed soon enough: first, the League of Nations was a paper tiger; second, France and England were militarily unprepared, and third, Hitler had been utterly misjudged.

The Munich pact stipulated cession of the larger area demanded by Germany. This in effect left Czechoslovakia defenseless. Slovakia was given federated status; Poland and Hungary annexed small border districts. Benês resigned and the proud achievement of Versailles, a prosperous, democratic Czechoslovakia, was doomed. Nonetheless, upon his return to England, Chamberlain waved a copy of the agreement and told his countrymen that he had brought them "peace in our time." The gift of prophecy, however, belonged to Winston Churchill who warned that this was not the end but only the beginning of the reckoning, the first sip of the bitter cup to come.

Munich was a great success for Hitler and encouraged him to proceed toward further adventures. His generals had been fearful of military confrontations, but he had judged the irresolution of the West correctly. It is possible that at this time he began to be convinced of his infallibility. An ironic footnote to these events was the fact that a group of German officers under the leadership of its chief of the general staff, General Franz Halder, had plotted to remove Hitler by a coup d'état. When Chamberlain appeared in Munich, hat in hand, the planned resistance within the officer corps, which included several of its highest ranking members, was aborted.

THE CZECH FINALE

The dismemberment of the Czechs' territorial remnant was accomplished in the following spring. Hitler ordered the president of the truncated republic, Emil Hácha, to Berlin. The scenes enacted at that meeting concluded the Czech drama. Hácha begged Hitler to allow his people a national life. Hitler responded with threats that for every Czech battalion there was a German division ready to march. Czechoslovakia, he warned, was about to be invaded, with or without Hácha's consent. How much blood it would cost the Czech people was entirely up to Hácha. Unless his signature was affixed to the prepared document inviting the German troops to restore order in his country, squadrons of bombers would raze Prague. Hácha, who suffered from a heart ailment, fainted. Hitler's doctor revived him. Hácha pleaded for permission to telephone his cabinet but was refused. Finally, at four in the morning, he signed the document (see Map 7–1).

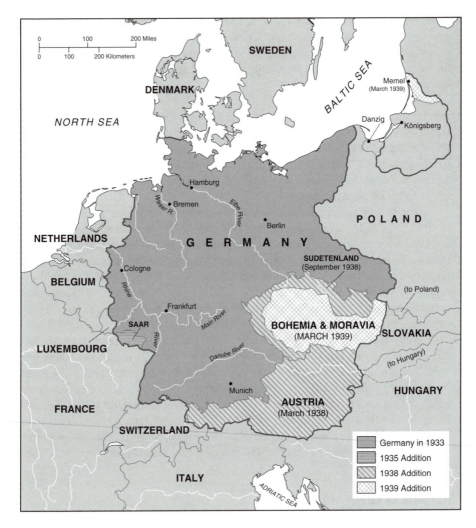

Map 7–1 *Germany's Expansion, 1933–1939* (From Jackson J. Spielvogel, *Hitler and Nazi Germany: A History, 2E.* Upper Saddle River, NJ: Prentice Hall, 1996.)

German troops marched into Czechoslovakia unopposed. This, however, was Hitler's last cheap victory. From here on, the German people would have to pay a price for his foreign adventures. France and England, even the Soviet Union, began to make military preparations. No longer was it debatable if Hitler would strike again, the question was merely where and when. During the summer of 1939 the world had its answer. The German propaganda ministry directed its full attention to the alleged suffering of the German minority living in Poland. There was an ominously familiar ring to the claims of atrocities committed against hapless Germans. The next victim of Hitler's aggression had been identified.

THE STARTLING HITLER-STALIN PACT

From its inception, Nazi doctrine had emphasized its total opposition to communism. The Goebbels's press, following Hitler's view, used the denigrating label of Bolshevism and often hyphenated the word with Judaism to indicate the symbiotic relationship between Jews and Communists. Nazism combined three essential concepts into one *Weltanschauung*: Communism represented an evil form of social organization; Jews, due to their racial defects, were destroyers and parasites; the Soviet Union, ruled by Communist-Jews, was the proper arena for German expansion. Thus, the annihilation of a hated regime and a hated people, and the conquest of needed territory dovetailed neatly into a single doctrine. Hitler had consistently denounced Stalin as the enemy of civilization, while Stalin referred to him as the Nazi beast. No wonder the Western world was astonished when an agreement between the Soviet Union and Germany was signed on August 23, 1939.

The two foreign ministers, Joachim von Ribbentrop and Vyacheslav Molotov, had worked out an accord which stipulated that for ten years neither country would interfere with the other in case of war. That much, at any rate, was revealed to the public. There was also a secret protocol which provided for the division of Poland and gave Stalin a free hand in the Baltic states. These arrangements were disclosed only after the Polish defeat by German armies. When one considers the fact that neither dictator had any scruples concerning the means permissible for the achievement of political goals, then the Berlin-Moscow entente was not nearly as bizarre as it seemed at first glance.

Stalin's intentions were probably twofold. The Munich pact of the previous year had caused consternation in Moscow. Was it possible that the four signatories in Munich might combine their forces against Russia? The Soviet government had been diplomatically rebuffed by the Western democracies and its isolation caused grave concern. The treaty with Germany relieved the anxiety concerning a combined Western assault. A second reason for the alliance was Russia's need for time to build up its military power. It is doubtful that Stalin did not expect an eventual German offensive against his nation. Both Hitler and Stalin used the agreement to develop agendas that were hidden from the public. If the conquest of Poland was merely the first step for further Lebensraum in Russia, clearly Stalin needed breathing space to prepare his country's defenses.

Hitler, on the other hand, dreaded the possibility of a two-front war. With Russia neutralized, he could conquer Poland quickly and easily and, should it became necessary, then turn his attention to the western front. He was hoping, though not certain, that the appeasement mentality of Munich would continue and that he could wage a little war against Poland alone. Should, however, France and England wish to spill their blood for the Poles, he would teach them a lesson in warfare but on one front at a time. There had been no change of the basic plan; Russia with its vast farmlands, its wealth in oil, and other natural resources was the proper place for planting the roots of the Thousand Year Reich.

The world was holding its breath and Hitler did not keep the anxious millions waiting very long. As always, he sought a justification for his actions. Preliminary to the attack on Poland a piece of absurd drama was enacted. The Poles must seem to be the aggressors for purposes of domestic and foreign propaganda. Himmler's aide, Reinhard Heydrich, chief of the Gestapo, simulated a raid on the small radio station in the German town of Gleiwitz, one mile from the Polish border. SS troopers, dressed in Polish uniforms, staged the fictitious attack. As "proof" of Poland's treachery, a dead body, dressed as a German civilian, was left behind. The victim, an inmate from a concentration camp, was shot to give the scene reality. With cameras rolling, this "evidence" was presented to an incredulous public. Hitler, whose armies had already massed at the Polish border, declared war on Poland on September 1, 1939. Within two days France and England honored their defensive treaties with Poland and declared war on Germany. World War II began with a farce but it ended in tragedy.

THE WAR AT A GLANCE

This account is not the place to detail the strategies, the battle plans, the new techniques introduced in this, the most devastating war in history. A few generalities have to suffice in order to explain the international configuration of the six million Holocaust victims. Our interest, therefore, is confined to the European arena of the conflict (see Map 7–2, p. 146). The Pacific and African operations, although vital in the defeat of the Germans and their Japanese ally, need no discourse here.

The two opposing groups became known as the Axis and Allied powers. Germany and its original partner, Italy, were more or less reluctantly joined by Hungary, Romania, Bulgaria, and Finland. Militarily, Germany played the major role. The alliance of Poland, France, and England developed into the Allied powers which eventually included the Soviet Union, the United States, Canada, Australia, New Zealand, and most of the remaining Western world. Spain maintained its official neutrality but had close ties to Germany. Sweden, Switzerland, Portugal, Ireland, and Turkey were able to stay out of the conflict because Hitler decided not to involve them.

During the first two years of the war, Germany was astonishingly successful. Its military tactics, the blitzkrieg, utilized mobility to an extent hitherto unknown in the manuals of any general staff. Hitler recognized that in manpower and resources his enemies were superior in the long run, that is, if they were given the time to utilize their potential strength. Thus, speed was the essential factor. German mechanized columns appeared deep in enemy territory long before their opponents thought it possible. The German offensive was usually initiated by heavy bombing; first the enemy air force and then communication and transportation systems were destroyed. These attacks were followed by dive-bombing of hostile troop concentrations to inflict heavy casualties and create chaos. Before recovery was possible, assaults by all types of mobile artillery, from light tanks to motorcycle companies, caused further losses and heightened the confusion. Heavy tanks secured the rear and prevented escape and reorganization. It is curious indeed that this method of warfare so successfully used by the Germans was first suggested in 1934 by a French colonel named Charles de Gaulle. But his superior officers rejected this strategy.

The war lasted six years. In the European theater of operations it ended on VE (victory in Europe) Day, May 8, 1945. It is impossible to measure its cost accurately.

Worldwide, the dead numbered between 40 and 55 million. The devastation and military expenditures were estimated at the incomprehensible figure of $2 trillion. This conflict changed forever the conduct of warfare. To a much greater degree than 1914–1918, it was global, involving four continents. Aerial bombardment brought death to cities and their civilian, noncombatant populations. The introduction of atomic weapons threatened the existence of all life on earth.

Even before the restoration of peace, many people living in the old colonial empires experienced an awakening of their nationalism. New countries were forged out of former colonies whose struggles to maintain liberty and economic viability continue to this day. Map makers drew new boundaries as political decisions uprooted millions. The German use of slave labor had displaced seven million people. Many did not want to return to their communist-dominated or war-torn homelands and roamed across Europe wondering where to rebuild their lives. The aftermath of the war presented the world with a new set of political, social, and economic problems. The United States and Russia emerged as rival cold-war superpowers. A new peace-keeping organization was created, and since hope does spring eternal, the world prays the United Nations may be able to accomplish its grand mission.

The war made possible the genocide of European Jewry. German victories enabled the Nazis to find, trap, and kill their victims. Even in areas where German occupation was of short duration such as in Italy and Hungary, Nazi organizational skills and fanaticism assured the annihilation of hundreds of thousands of Jews. It seems absurd to call killers dedicated, but the label does apply. Complete dedication to their task was required to identify, round up, isolate, and massacre so many people in so many countries. The war was also provided a cover for the extent and ruthlessness of the genocide. Hitler did not want the German people to know what the euphemism "resettlement of Jews" really meant. The general upheaval of everyday life during wartime made it possible to keep the truth from large segments—though by no means all—of the Germans.

THE DEFEAT OF POLAND

The war against Poland was over in a month. The blitzkrieg strategies caught the Polish army in a huge vise between the Baltic and Slovakia. Polish armed forces, including horse cavalry, tried bravely and pathetically to defend their country against tank units. Warsaw was bombarded relentlessly and held out for four weeks. The Soviets invaded Poland from the east to claim their share in accordance with the Molotov-Ribbentrop pact. The statistics of men killed in action speak for themselves: German losses were 11,000; Polish losses were 120,000 of which 70,000 were killed in battles against Germany and 50,000 against Russia. Although the French and English governments honored their treaty obligations and declared war on Germany, they were unable to supply any aid in time to prevent the fall of Poland. The campaign was over before they could ship arms or men.

The Germans occupied western and central Poland which contained a population of 20 million. In 1941, when Germany launched the Russian invasion, the eastern territory and its population of 12 million was quickly occupied by Germany. Jews and others who had fled from the Nazis thus were overwhelmed two years later.

Hitler had resolved to destroy Polish national life. He considered its Slavic inhabitants as racially undesirable and its farmlands suitable for Aryan expansion. To secure the subjugation of the defeated people, the annihilation of the entire Polish elite was "necessitated." With stunning ruthlessness, the aristocracy, military officers, political leaders, priests, and intelligentcia were purged from the nation. This, the Germans claimed, would eliminate any possibility of future anti-German resistance. The SS and Gestapo followed the armies in order to carry out this objective. The people of Poland were totally unprepared for such savagery. Their government fled to England, leaving behind chaos and despair. The Poles did not expect a merciful occupation, but nothing in modern history caused them to anticipate the deliberate murders of their most respected citizens.

Poland was cut in two. The western provinces, which the German called the *Ostgaue,* were annexed to the Reich. The largest of the four frontier districts was the named *Warthegau,* and these provinces were governed as if they were part of the nation. South-central Poland was referred to as the *General Government.* This large region became the private kingdom of Hitler's friend and lawyer, Hans Frank. Frank described his function as that of lord over so many slaves whose value was proportionate to their usefulness to Germany. Frank's residence was palatial, his power over life and death was essentially unlimited; his brutality and avarice second only to Goering's. Three major death camps were located in his territory and he often complained that the constant influx of Jews interfered with his administrative duties. Since the German army had a vital interest in maintaining its own control over Poland, disputes between the civilian *Gauleiters* and military commanders were frequent and spiteful.

HIMMLER'S VISION OF POLAND

Hans Frank, to his regret, did not own the Jews; Himmler's SS did. With yet another title to fit his increased authority, Himmler became executor of purification of the conquered lands. His assignment was extraordinarily ambitious. First, he was charged with the elimination or enslavement of the biologically undesirable population. Second, any Aryan elements in the population needed to be identified and preserved. Third, the lands formerly occupied by the removed or diminished native population were to be Germanized. Agricultural settlements of SS families were established on such land. Thus, the soil would be tied to the Reich forever. Like warrior knights from the Middle Ages, a new nobility would be created as a first step toward securing Lebensraum in the east. The serfs to toil on the estates for their German masters would, of course, be the Poles.

The cruelty of the occupation forces in the eastern occupied territories has been documented beyond question. Hitler's order had been simple enough; he wanted Poland Germanized in ten years. Polish people are often denounced for their indifference to the suffering of the Jews among them during the Holocaust years. While anti-Semitism was wide-spread, it is also true that many Polish individuals hid and saved their Jewish neighbors. The complaint that many were apathetic, even gleeful about the Jewish genocide must be understood from two perspectives. First, the government and the priesthood of Poland had a history of promoting anti-Semitism in church and school. Second, the brutality of the German occupation policy deprived the native population of their emotional and economic resources. Not only was the Polish elite doomed, but the Nazis rated all Polish people as having almost no value. The Germans provided them with a corrupt administration which was indifferent to their most basic needs. To make matters worse, Himmler was granted a free hand to interfere in the civilian bureaucracy under the aegis of his mandate to keep Poland secure. In effect, he terrorized the defeated people.

Without an orderly, functioning government, the population was at the mercy of individual, often competing, officials. Alleviation from starvation and the winter cold was not considered a function of the occupying looters of Polish food, goods, and treasures. The chaos of conflicting orders from the SS, the police, the *Gauleiters*, officers of the German army, and native officials serving with the remnants of Polish agencies caused terrible confusion. The Nazis had no wish to resolve this anarchy. They expected that a bewildered, rudderless, and fearful population would advance the process of turning a civilized society into numb and docile chattel.

It is not an exaggeration to speak of the enslavement of Polish workers. Men and women were treated as a renewable commodity. They were shipped here or there, to work on farms, in mines, or in factories. Almost a million farmers were uprooted to make way for the Germanization of the land. Workers who were deported to the Reich had a better chance of survival than their families at home, at least they were given some food. But hunger, cold, disease, and execution for real or imagined acts of sabotage took an appalling toll on Polish civilians. The fact that some Polish men and women came together in secret, usually in the forests, and formed resistance groups under such conditions is all the more remarkable. The sinister, almost unbelievable, crime against humanity called *lebensborn* was carried out with particular viciousness in Poland. Initiated by Himmler, "racially acceptable," that is, blond, blue-eyed children were kidnapped from their parents and sent to German couples for adoption. Several of the occupied countries were subject to this abomination which encompassed several hundred thousand children. If the Nazis kept records indicating the specific fate of the *lebensborn* children, they have not been found. Even now there are aged mothers and fathers searching for a trace of their lost boys and girls.

When the bloodletting was over, after six years of German occupation, Poland lay in ruins and more than 17 percent of its population, some six million, were dead. Of this number, about half were Jews and half were Christians. Only the Jews of Europe suffered a higher percentage of civilian losses.

THE WAR IN THE WEST

The period from the fall of Poland until the following spring has been dubbed the "phony war," or *Sitzkrieg* ("sit-down war") because there was no activity on the western front. Hitler hoped and failed to drive a wedge between the French-English alliance and his generals advised against a winter campaign. In the spring, the Germans struck again. In April, without the formality of a declaration of war, the Germans conquered Denmark in one day, while Norway held out for nearly a month. The admiralty had urged this campaign in order to secure submarine bases in the war against England. On May 10, the blitzkrieg armies marched into France. By invading the poorly prepared Low Countries, they outflanked the Maginot line. Holland asked for an armistice in five days, Belgium lasted three weeks. The combined armies of Britain and France were unable to stop the German advance. Only the "miracle of Dunkirk" saved the Allies from complete disaster. This miracle was actually a retreat. British ships rescued 215,000 of their own and 120,000 French soldiers from the northern beaches of France. In June, Paris was surrendered to prevent its destruction. A demoralized, defeatist French government under Marshall Henri Petain wanted peace at whatever cost. The official capitulation of France was consummated on June 22, 1940. On that day, at the exact spot in the forest of Compiegne where, on November 11, 1918 Germany had acknowledged its defeat, an ecstatic Hitler turned the tables on France. It was probably the moment of his greatest triumph. At this point, Mussolini added a further jewel to Hitler's crown; with France prostrate, he opted to join Hitler's war. Franklin Delano Roosevelt called this action a stab in the back and the phrase has stuck.

Hitler's terms were harsh. Alsace and Lorraine were annexed. The large northern sector, including Paris, was placed under military governance although Nazi politicians could not keep their hands off and frequently interfered. The French people were compelled to pay for the cost of the occupation. German aims, quite simply, were to exploit the conquered people and their products to the fullest. By implied and direct terror, the possibility of any opposition to the occupation forces was to be prevented. German ruthlessness in trying to wipe out the French underground resistance organizations cost thousands of French men and women their lives.

The central and southern two-fifths of France were permitted to form a puppet state. The once-vaunted hero, Marshall Petain, now became a German pawn. He often claimed that his Vichy administration saved many lives, however, the problem of collaboration with the enemy continues to haunt the French. When the war ended, Petain was tried and spent the rest of his life in prison. His Vice Premier, Pierre Lavalle, was an outright collaborator of the Nazis. He allowed his country to be looted, made no objection when slave laborers were forced to work in the Reich, and even tried to raise a French army to fight alongside the Germans. In his desire to please his Nazi masters, he not only complied with, but tried to anticipate their wishes. His role in the deportation of French Jews was essential (see Chapter 9). Lavalle too was tried by his countrymen and met his death by firing squad in 1945.

The Jews living in France were not all French. Tens of thousands were refugees from other Nazi-occupied lands. Many were illegal residents, thus their number cannot be precisely determined. The prewar native Jewish population was about three hundred thousand with perhaps an equal number of emigrès at the time of the fall of France. Paris was the magnet; in 1940 it is estimated that more than half of its Jews were from Poland, Czechoslovakia, and Germany. The conquest of Holland and Belgium caused a renewed influx. The possibility of a sudden and disastrous French defeat was totally unforeseen. As in all the conquered countries, foreign Jews were the first to be sacrificed to Nazi demands.

The Nazis had no master plan for the administration of their conquests. None of the defeated peoples were given a systematic, businesslike government. All were exploited but the degree of severity differed. An overlapping of imposed military, civilian and native authority was common. In Norway, the native Nazi Vidkun Quisling (his name is now synonymous with *traitor*) served as the puppet prime minister but shared power with the equally hated *Gauleiter* Josef Terboven. Denmark was permitted to keep its democratic institutions as long as the government cooperated with the Germans. When that cooperation was sabotaged by an active Danish resistance organization, Reich Commissioner Werner Best and the German Army appeared in Copenhagen. Although the German administration of Holland and Belgium differed in theory, the reality of daily life varied little. Belgium was governed as a military district and Holland by Nazi civilians under Artur Seyss-Inquart. Everywhere, native resources and manpower were diverted to benefit Germany; art treasures were looted from public and private collections. The small size of the Low Countries made it very difficult to escape from the constant German surveillance. Nonetheless, underground resistance fighters did organize and harassed the despised conquerors. The Nazis did not view the western Europeans with the same disdain reserved for Slavs and Jews. Generally, the French and northern Europeans did not suffer to the same degree as the eastern victims although they experienced shortages of everything and lived in a state of constant anxiety.

GREAT BRITAIN ALONE

Only the English remained to deprive Hitler of total victory. That stubborn island people, lead by Winston Churchill, refused to see the futility of resistance. Did they not realize that fate had ordained that Nazism must triumph? Although the English stood alone, they spurned Hitler's compromise peace offers. The attempt to provoke a pro-peace sentiment by inflicting heavy losses at sea also misfired. German submarines could not stop all of the vitally needed shipments from reaching the island. To starve out the English would be a slow process and Hitler was impatient. A quick conquest was essential because a prolonged war might bring Russia and the United States into the conflict. The *Fuehrer* decided to invade Great Britain. As soon as the German air force won dominance, the assault, Operation *Seeloewe* ("Sea Lion"), would begin. Goering promised that his *Luftwaffe* was equal to the task, but the RAF (Royal Air Force) could not be blasted from the skies. Even the relentless aerial bombing of English cities never achieved the necessary air superiority for the Germans. This, in Churchill's words, was Britain's finest hour. Hitler's invasion plans were canceled.

The German attack against the Soviet Union and the entrance of the United States into the war after the Japanese attack on Pearl Harbor on December 7, 1941, changed the balance of power in favor of the Allies. A free England allowed the Allies to bring the war to the Continent and stage the famous D-Day invasion of 1944, and from there on to victory in the streets of Berlin.

THE BALKAN CONNECTION

The failure to force Britain to the peace table created new problems for Hitler. Germany did not have the raw materials necessary for an extended war. Gasoline propelled its blitzkrieg and Germany had none. Oil-rich Romania and its Balkan neighbors Hungary and Bulgaria had been cajoled and threatened into cooperating with Nazi interests. Hitler would have preferred not to expend any military manpower in the Balkans and continue to dominate the area politically and economically. But there he came into conflict with his ally and erstwhile mentor, Benito Mussolini. The Italians looked upon southeastern Europe as their sphere of influence. They had invaded and conquered the small Adriatic nation of Albania and now coveted Greece.

Greece, however, was not Ethiopia or Albania. With the aid of British forces the Greeks routed the Italians. Germany had to divert armies to rescue *Il Duce* from humiliating defeat as well as safeguard the Romanian oil supplies. The combined Greek and English forces were beaten, even the island of Crete was occupied by Germans. It became necessary to secure Bulgaria and Yugoslavia as well. The cost of controlling the Balkans was an ongoing liability, particularly due to the persistent hostility from Yugoslav guerrillas. The Balkan diversion caused a fateful two-month delay in the attack on the Soviets; just how fateful would become clear when German armies found themselves fighting the Russian winter and the Soviet soldiers.

OPERATION BARBAROSSA

On June 22, 1941, two years after Hitler and Stalin had signed their ten-year nonaggression pact, Hitler attacked the Soviet Union. Thus, the two-front war he so greatly feared was now initiated. The knowledge that England was in no position to land troops on the shores of continental Europe and the expectation of a quick victory convinced the *Fuehrer* that he was not actually fighting on two fronts. The official pretext for the war was so thin that Goebbels need not have bothered to contrive it. The actual motivation was rooted in past hatred and present circumstances.

Hitler was unalterably convinced that German lebensraum was destined to be on Russian soil. His abhorrence of communism never abated. It was only a matter of time before ideology would be translated into attack. Hitler feared that the protracted English war would allow for a linkage between Russia, the United States, and England; it would be better to strike against the Soviets before this could happen. Furthermore, Mussolini's attack on Greece had brought English troops to the Balkans, threatening Germany's oil supply. The time was ripe. Hitler activated *Fall Barbarossa*, the code name for the Russian invasion. He anticipated victory before the onset of winter. The Soviet armies, Hitler claimed, were dominated by Jews and Bolsheviks and would offer little resistance.

Hitler was well aware that Japan and the United States were on a collision course. He encouraged the Japanese attack on the United States because he believed that a war in the Pacific would prevent American forces from playing a role in Europe. Russia, according to plan, would be crushed in a few months. At that point, even with some aid from overseas, England would be forced to surrender. Germany then

would be able to dictate peace terms. The motherland would have it all; raw materials, lebensraum, and slave workers to fulfill the destiny of Hitler's vision of the New Order, a German Empire that would dominate the subjugated nations of Europe.

Hitler miscalculated fatally. Although German divisions penetrated deep into the Soviet Union, they were unable to take either Leningrad (St. Petersburg) or Moscow. Unprepared, without winter clothing, the cold took its toll among the German soldiers. The western front bogged down along a line reaching from the outskirts of Leningrad to the eastern fringes of Moscow and stretched south to the gates of Stalingrad (Volgograd). The Battle of Stalingrad, considered a turning point of the war, stopped the German offensive and by the fall of 1942 German troops were on the defensive. Hitler had convinced himself that he was a military genius, and took personal command of the armed forces. No doubt, he had some military talent, however, when his strategies failed, he insisted that cowardice and treachery among the generals, not his orders, were to blame. His refusal to permit troops to retreat, even when in an untenable position, was particularly costly. In the spring of 1942, however, Allied victory was still far from certain. The Germans took the entire Crimean Peninsula, General Erwin Rommel, the Desert Fox, campaigned successfully in Africa, and the German U-boat fleet inflicted heavy losses on Allied shipping.

The people inhabiting these vast conquests had to endure the terrible ordeal of Nazi occupation. As in Poland, absurd racial theories determined policy. Where cooperation might have been achieved, enemies were created. Surely, this was the case in the Ukraine where at first the Germans were welcomed as liberators. But that goodwill evaporated when it became clear that the Germans viewed the Ukrainians with utter disdain. The Baltic states, too, might have collaborated, instead, German severity nullified that possibility. Soviet officers, and of course Jews, were singled out for the infamous "special treatment." Millions were enslaved, starved, and murdered outright. The German administration of the conquered regions was a botched operation. The authority of diverse Nazi officials, the military, the SS, and the private empires carved out by Goering, Himmler, and Albert Speer of the Armaments Ministry collided amid bewildering confusion. Disregard for the needs of the native population was the only point of unanimity. Over three-and-a-half million Russian soldiers were taken prisoner during the first months of the war. They were labeled subhuman in the German press and treated as if that were true. The Nazis were unprepared to accommodate so many POWs and instituted a deliberate policy of mass starvation in concentration camps and arbitrary shootings in the fields and woods of Russia. Only when German labor shortages became extreme were the survivors used as slave laborers. At the end of the war, the Soviet Union had lost 20 million of its people. This staggering number was greater than the combined losses of all other participants in the war.

THE TURNING OF THE TIDE

It is impossible to know with certainty why Hitler declared war on the United States just after the Pearl Harbor attack. The fact that he had concluded a tripartite agreement of mutual aid with Italy and Japan was not a decisive issue; Hitler honored his signature quite selectively. Perhaps he believed that President Roosevelt was bound to

Map 7–2 *Military Operations of World War II: The German Offensives, 1939-1942* (From Jackson J. Spielvogel, *Hitler and Nazi Germany: A History, 2E.* Upper Saddle River, NJ: Prentice Hall, 1996.)

enter the conflict in any case, or that the United States presented little danger because the Americans would be unable to fight in the Pacific as well as in the Atlantic theater of operations. He may have believed that Europe would be prostrate at his feet before the hated Roosevelt could interfere. How little he understood the Americans; obviously, he did not grasp that such a declaration rallied the American people to a resolute, unified stand against the Germans.

Hitler was right when he stated that Germany could not win a long war. When the quick success of the earlier campaigns could not be duplicated after 1942, Allied victory was simply a matter of time. The courage and perseverance of Britain and Russia afforded the United States the necessary breathing space to draw upon its great human and material resources. On the seas, in the air, and on the ground the combined effort of the Allies overwhelmed the Germans. The contributions of the United States were essential. Not only did the U.S. send soldiers and sailors, armaments and medical supplies, but also vitally needed quantities of food. The psychological effect of the American commitment is difficult to measure, but surely inspired renewed courage to the weary, embattled people throughout Europe. Nonetheless, victory was not cheaply won. To the last day of the war, Hitler's armies inflicted heavy losses, even when the final outcome was no longer in doubt.

Allied forces, under the leadership of General Dwight D. Eisenhower, attacked Germany in a huge pincer movement with Berlin at the center. Russian armies moved westward along a vast front from the Baltic Sea in the north to Bulgaria in the south. They pushed through Poland, took the Balkan countries and continued their offensive toward the north and west. In the winter of 1944 they were poised on the German border.

The Western Allies invaded Sicily in 1943, and struggled up the Italian boot against heavily defended German installations. Sick of the war, King Victor Emanuel expressed the wishes of his people when he dismissed Mussolini and hoped to make peace. For all intents and purposes, Italian troops were no longer a factor after the summer of 1943. Rome and Florence were taken in 1944. Italian partisan fighters had imprisoned *Il Duce*. He was freed in a daring German helicopter rescue mission, but in April 1945, Italian anti-Fascists captured and executed him. The Allied armies reached northern Italy, where they remained deadlocked with German divisions until the end of the war.

The successful landing on D-Day, June 6, 1944, gave the Soviets the second front for which they had so long and so urgently pressed. From Normandy, American, British, Commonwealth, and Free French troops fought their way eastward while others moved north from the Mediterranean. The German armies still numbered 10 million men who suffered as well as inflicted heavy casualties. Hitler hoped to halt the

Air raid on Berlin during WWII. (Courtesy UPI/Bettmann.)

western assault at the fortifications on Germany's Western frontier (Siegfried line), a defense installation running opposite the Maginot line. But the fortifications could not check the advance of the Allies into the Reich itself. German cities were bombed relentlessly and as the rubble piled up, German civilians experienced the horror their *Fuehrer* had unleashed on so many other nations.

Hitler was still directing operations from one of his several underground bunkers. In July 1944, a group of Army and civilian anti-Nazis attempted to assassinate him. Hitler's fury and revenge were maniacal; accusations, some true, some false, condemned men to death by methods of execution that Spanish Inquisitors would have envied.

As Allied soldiers entered Berlin, Hitler—in his bunker beneath the Chancellery garden—continued to direct armies which no longer existed. His disdain for the German people was obvious when he ordered the devastation of everything the enemy might use. If these orders had been carried out, the destruction of the Reich would have been total. Hitler, irrational, perhaps insane, saw treason everywhere; his generals, even Goering and Himmler could no longer be trusted. Worst of all, the German people preferred peace to death, thus proving their weakness and their unworthiness. Afraid of falling into Russian hands, he shot himself on April 30, 1945. According to his instructions, his body was burned. Goebbels had also remained in the Berlin bunker and had not wavered in his loyalty. He poisoned his six children and then he and his wife committed suicide. One week later, Hitler's designated successor, Admiral Karl Doenitz, surrendered unconditionally to emissaries of the British, French, Soviet, and American forces.

The legacy of the twelve years of Hitler's dictatorship cannot be evaluated in the context of this text. Suffice it to say that from the ashes of the Third Reich a vastly different world was wrought. Every aspect of human life, psychological, military, economic, political, religious, and philosophical, was permanently and deeply affected. There was so much suffering, so many losses, such upheaval, even the balm of time cannot erase the scars. And yet, veterans of many battles, men well versed in the cruelty of war, testified that nothing in their experience equaled the horror they felt upon entering a concentration camp. There they saw the absolute evil that man can do to man.

Chapter 8

From Ideology to Isolation

In the study of the Holocaust, it is not possible to overstate the importance of the dehumanization process. The effort was double-edged; the victims were to accept their own denigration and SS personnel were to act on the belief that Jews were not really human. Memoirs of survivors and reports from concentration camp guards lead to the conclusion that the psychological bombardments were more successful with the perpetrators than with the victims. Starved and dirty, without family, without livelihood, without clothes, hair, or shoes, without their very names, the vast majority of the victims behaved within the perimeters of ethical conduct. That, however, cannot be said of the executioners. It was not difficult for the officials who generated the paperwork leading to the mass killings to distance themselves from actuality; so many "pieces" to be delivered and "treated." The men who dealt with actual individuals marked for death needed to be convinced that they were engaged in a cleansing operation, that they were ridding the world of a lethal infection. Himmler talked about their great and difficult service many times. The fact that very few of the SS troopers who were engaged in the mass murders requested changes of assignment (which were granted), leaves no question about the success of the educational techniques of the Nazis.

Language played an important role in the dehumanization process. A prime example is the designation Final Solution (*Endloesung*) to characterize the Nazis' program for annihilating the Jews. The objective of "purifying" the Reich by purging it of Jews was clearly fixed in Nazi doctrine from the beginning. In due course, Nazi conquests exported the *Judenrein* concept to most of the European continent. Historians are not certain just when Hitler decided to translate his desire to erase Jews from the face of the earth into actuality. Possibly, this was his plan from the start of his political career. Even his early speeches and his opus, *Mein Kampf*, are replete with expressions of violent anti-Semitism. Some historians, the Intentionalists, believe that genocide was always the blueprint, always the intent. An opposing view is held by the Functionalists, who see the death factories as the result of an evolutionary process. Circumstances, particularly the confusion of wartime conditions, the large number of eastern Jews who came under Nazi hegemony, and the general indifference of the world to the fate of the Jews resulted in a step-by-step acceleration of persecution. In view of the fact that the Nazis tried to promote emigration during the prewar years, (the aborted Lublin reservation and Madacascar colony plans were cases in point), this observer is more comfortable with the Functionalists. But emigrants must become immigrants and the borders were closed to all but a few hundred thousand refugees. In any case, the question concerning the origin of the Final Solution is not of central importance in this account.

WHAT DID THE GERMAN PEOPLE KNOW?

It is not possible to ascertain how many German civilians were aware of the existence and functions of the death camps. Obviously, many knew. First of all, there were the participants in the process and their friends and relatives. Others who had access to the truth included members of the regular *Wehrmacht* who assisted in roundups, even in shootings. Certainly, large numbers of bureaucrats were involved in expediting this enormous and complicated undertaking. Railroads were rerouted, financial institutions received and disbursed goods and funds taken from the Jews, and thousands of businessmen benefited from the Aryanization process. Employees in the Health Ministry were frequently concerned with ghetto and concentration camp epidemics; diplomats from the Foreign Affairs section had to be apprised in order to respond to questions from abroad; manufacturers of poison gas and crematoria had to suspect the ultimate uses of their products. Recipients of used clothing from which the Jewish star had recently been removed surely must have wondered or perhaps knew what happened to the original owners. As the Jews disappeared from their neighborhoods, many Germans guessed but did not face the truth about the meaning of the official explanation: "relocation."

It is noteworthy that the German government tried to prevent any knowledge of the genocide from reaching its citizens. Participants in the slaughter swore an oath to keep their terrible secrets. Does this indicate that despite years of intensive anti-Jewish propaganda, Nazi officials did not believe that ordinary Germans would condone their actions? Himmler frequently spoke of his mission to annihilate the Jews in almost religious terms, but only to his own minions. Hitler, quite literally with his dying breath, consoled himself that he had at least been victorious in the destruction of the Jews. But no public announcement ever set forth what actually happened to the Jews. Thus, it is not possible to discern how many Germans realized that the human cargo of the trains moving to Poland carried men, women, and children who were condemned to die. The German people, by and large, preferred to remain in the dark; they had so many problems of their own. The war had taken sons and husbands from their midst; destruction by Allied bombing affected millions of families, and no doubt prompted an attitude of indifference to other people's problems. Dreadful rumors were whispered, but it was easier to deny their possible truth than to deal with yet another emotional burden.

AN OVERVIEW

Before detailing the mechanics of the Holocaust, it is useful to glean a general understanding of the framework of the operation. Although there were differences in place and time, once the decision was made to solve the Jewish problem by means of total eradication, the road to the gas chambers was but the final step in a series of recognizable, preparatory actions. The ideological basis, that is, the paranoid hatred of Jews, had been government policy since 1933. The agents to carry out the genocide, the SS, had the training, the will, the arms, and the official instructions to commit the mass murders. The *Fuehrer* needed no approval for his actions. No parliament, no court of justice, no political opposition had survived to challenge the crimes of the state. The voice of the people was stilled, the churches, with minor exceptions, were submissive to secular authority, and the killing mechanisms and techniques either already existed or were devised without difficulty.

The first step toward annihilation was to ascertain how many Jews lived in a designated region. American students, accustomed to religious anonymity, are often puzzled about the ability of the Nazis to identify their victims. During the 1940s, it was not difficult to uncover the professed faith of European nationals. Not only did most official statistics indicate religion, but ordinary documents such as licenses, insurance policies, passports, applications for jobs, school records, membership in organizations, and so on commonly recorded one's religious beliefs. The registers of Jewish congregations and associations were confiscated as a matter of course wherever the Germans required them. Thus, it was not difficult to discover the number of Jews, their addresses, their occupations, and even the status of their bank accounts. While the *Mischlinge* were accorded special consideration in the Reich, such refinement was rarely applied in the conquered areas.

The removal of Jews from the economic life usually followed the process of identification. In Germany, this procedure took several years but it was accomplished rapidly in the conquered territories. Through directives for Aryanization and by forcible expulsion, Jews were deprived of their businesses and professional livelihoods. The looting of all their possessions was usually the prelude to their murders.

The removal of Jews to ghettos was another step on the path to destruction. This isolation and centralization simplified the future disposition of the Jewish population. Concentrating the Jews of an entire area in designated neighborhoods within specific Polish cities served several purposes. Their physical removal from their homes facilitated the expropriation process; property left behind was declared abandoned and acquired by this or that German agency. Ghettos were easily controlled; the Jewish councils, the *Judenraete,* were useful in running the routine affairs in the ghetto. Little manpower was required to prevent possible escapes and smuggling from such confined, enclosed areas. Jews from the western and southern European regions of German occupation were sent to the Polish ghettos. In due time, these

Jewish centers simplified transport to the death camps. Lastly, conditions within the ghettos also served to reduce the number of Jews by means of starvation and rampant disease.

The final phase of the Holocaust was the outright killing process. At first, the SS squads, the *Einsatzgruppen*, used guns. When shooting was deemed too slow and such direct contact with the victims regarded as psychologically undesirable (for the shooters), new methods had to be found. After a brief experiment using carbon monoxide gas generated from the exhaust of vehicles, the death factory was initiated. Instead of the killers rounding up the victims, the victims were brought to the killing centers. Railroads transported Jewish families to Poland from all of the Nazi-dominated lands. Some trains terminated within ghettos, others proceeded directly to the gas chambers. Within three years all the ghettos were liquidated; its teeming thousands killed by the lethal fumes of a shower room in a death camp.

TYPES AND AIMS OF CONCENTRATION CAMPS

The term *concentration camp* has several interpretations and thus requires clarification. The original, official German explanation had stated that their purpose was the re-education of the political opposition. Antisocial inmates were to be turned into useful citizens. Under the guise of placing troublemakers into "protective custody for the restoration of law and order," the government had the legal right to imprison suspects without trial. The earliest major camps, Dachau, Buchenwald, and Sachsenhausen imprisoned dissidents such as labor union leaders, communists, socialists, members of the clergy, pacifists, and others. Jews were always among the victims, but in the early months after Hitler came to power they did not comprise the majority.

The original educational intent was never put into practice and the sham was dropped. Concentration camps were huge prisons where so-called enemies of the state served sentences at the pleasure of several agencies entrusted with the security of the regime. The system expanded rapidly and developed three distinguishable types. Some sites combined several functions within the same compound. Best-known are the death camps of Treblinka, Chelmo, Maidanek, Belzec, and Auschwitz-Birkenau, the killing centers which carried out genocide. Here the great majority of prisoners were murdered upon arrival by one of several methods.

It can be argued that the second group of some twenty concentration camps were designed to serve the killing process as well. Here death came more slowly as the result of catastrophic living conditions. These installations were attached to work sites and the prisoners were forced to perform heavy labor. Most of the victims survived for a few weeks, some for a few months. The number of work-related camps was constantly augmented, largest among these were Gross-Rosen, Ravensbrueck, Stutthof, Bergen-Belsen, and Theresienstadt in Austria. Jews predominated among the prisoners in most of these camps.

A third type of mass-detention facilities were designated as labor camps. The inmates were for the most part non-Jewish men and women who had been rounded up in the conquered nations. Their work was usually connected to military requirements.

Some of the factories and mines exploited the skills of both Jews and of Gentiles. In such facilities, the Jews were quartered separately, received less food, and suffered greater brutality. A vast network of hundreds of satellite installations was created which enslaved millions of workers throughout Germany and its conquered territories. Buchenwald alone had 134 subcamps. The Germans treated their slave workers as a renewable labor supply whose welfare was of no concern to the state. Often toiling below the surface of the earth, men and women saw no daylight, lacked even the most rudimentary hygienic facilities, and received starvation rations. Inevitably, the death toll was high. When the Reich collapsed, they became the displaced persons of Europe, trying to find loved ones, some fearful of returning to communist-dominated homelands, many suffering ill health and deep psychological scars. Their number, estimated at seven million, staggers the imagination and presented a serious problem to the Allied occupying forces at the end of the war.

THE SS: STATE WITHIN THE STATE?

The SS was an elite political army. Since no equivalent force exists in this country, it is not possible to compare it to anything familiar to American students. In discipline, the SS imitated the military, in ideology it was trained to follow the *Fuehrer* with fanatical loyalty. Depending on the specialty of the unit, the SS was empowered to act as police, as judge, jury, and executioner, as spy and counterspy, as future Aryan settlers in the eastern lebensraum conquests, as enforcers of political correctness, and as liquidators of all people deemed unworthy of life.

The popular image of the neat Germans, devotees of cleanliness and orderliness, was not borne out by Hitler's method of governing the country. As was noted earlier, the newsreels, depicting the perfect cadence of goose-stepping boots, hid the haphazard style of the *Fuehrer's* governance. Like a medieval liege lord, he preferred to have his vassals vie with one another for their realms as long as their loyalty to him did not waver. It is also a commonly held notion that Heinrich Himmler's domain ran with the precision of a fine clock. This perception too failed to withstand the scrutiny of historical research. While it was clear that the source of Himmler's power came directly from Hitler, no clear line connected the *treue* Heinrich's authority to his own group commanders. Himmler imitated his *Fuehrer's* formula and gave his subordinates ambiguous, often overlapping, areas of control. As his authority doubled and redoubled, the most aggressive of his department chiefs accumulated the greatest force in their hands. To the sorrow of millions, they competed in their efforts to impress Himmler with the fierce thoroughness of their search for supposed enemies of the Reich.

HIMMLER'S DOMAIN

SS stands for *Schutzstaffel*, or "Defense Echelon," also called the Black Order. From the small band of handsome men selected to guard the *Fuehrer*, Himmler carved out an empire of power and fear. As the circles of SS responsibilities widened, so did the number of collateral organizations. All of the Reich's policing power was amassed by the office of the Reich Security Main Office (RSHA) under Himmler. The general SS, the parent organization, was constantly culled of men to serve in one of the auxiliary groups. First among the additional duties was party security. Ferreting out heretics within the Nazi party was the job of the SD, (*Sicherheitsdienst* or "Security Service"). These units under Reinhard Heydrich were augmented until they numbered one hundred thousand and were responsible for total internal security. Heydrich was a technocrat par excellence. A man without friends, he had been cashiered from the navy for womanizing, an insult he never forgot. His raw ambition and coldblooded pragmatism were exactly what was needed by the SS. Himmler relied on him to find the practical means to implement his vague visions of an Aryanized Europe. Although Heydrich had no particular hatred for the Jews, this indifference did not diminish his effectiveness in the management of their destruction. A specialist in terror with an insatiable hunger for power, he had the bearing, the blond appearance, and the arrogance of the very model Aryan superman. His meteoric career ended in 1942 when Czech resistance fighters killed him with grenades thrown under his car. Hitler and Himmler reacted to that assassination with a fury that cost 860 Czechs their lives. The entire Czech village of Lidice was destroyed on the unproven charge that the assassins had been sheltered there.

The *Totenkopfverbaende* ("Death's-head Units") were SS specialists empowered to guard and administer the concentration camps. The name was derived from the emblem on their uniforms, a human skull. In 1934, Himmler appointed a convicted political terrorist, Theodor Eicke, to the post of inspector of concentration camps. Eicke had served as a commander at Dachau and went about his task with uncompromising hatred for the inmates. He scrapped the pretense that the camps were rehabilitation centers and changed their function to institutions of punishment. Eicke's directives were clear and brutal, encompassing such details as solitary confinement, the use of beatings, and so forth. He instructed volunteers who aspired to join his organization that pity for the enemy was an unworthy emotion for an SS man.

In 1936, in a successful power struggle with Goering, Himmler acquired control over the regular German police, called *Ordo* (*Ordnungspolizei*). Its members were uniformed and did such ordinary police work as regulating traffic and patrolling the streets. However, when the need arose, Himmler did not hesitate to simply incorporate entire squads into the SS. The same sort of unwelcome adoption coerced the Equestrian Association into the SS. In fact, Hitler awarded honorary SS command titles to men who had no connection to the SS. Thus, the notion that all of Himmler's men were totally imbued with Nazi ideology is open to question.

The secret state police (*Geheime Staatspolizei* or "Gestapo") had been spun off from the SD and became the Nazi party's most powerful organ for ferreting out political dissenters. Its very name was whispered with dread; the use of torture in interrogation was routine, escape was all but impossible, appeals from Gestapo verdicts were futile, and the normal limits of common law or common humanity did not apply. A network of informers called *Spitzels*, tattled on their neighbors, even concerning such offenses as telling an anti-Nazi joke. Wherever German conquests brought Nazi rule, the Gestapo followed to investigate, sometimes to conduct show trials in its own courts, to imprison, and to execute. Fear was intentionally fostered as an effective weapon to discourage potential insubordination. The *Kripo,(Kriminalpolizei)* or criminal police, was also attached to Himmler's security forces. Its units often participated in the annihilation of Jews. Their role in executing the Final Solution was rationalized by a fine legal point: Being a Jew was in itself a crime and all Jewish property was the result of criminal activity, thus the criminal police were rightfully involved in the elimination of this element.

The *Einsatzgruppen*, also called *Sonderkommandos* ("Special Mobile Task Forces") played a particularly dreadful role in the *Endloesung*. Himmler's trusted disciple Heydrich selected them from his SD troops. They were told that their task would be heavy indeed but no details were revealed. Their number never exceeded 3,000, and how so few men were able to murder between 1,500,000 and 2,000,000 human beings will be discussed in the next chapter.

Another branch of the SS was the *Waffen* SS, or military arm of the organization. Hitler was never convinced that the officers of the regular army were completely loyal to him, whereas the special units of the *Waffen* SS could be trusted. Early recruits were thoroughly indoctrinated with Nazi ideology; they combined the skills of the regular soldier with the fanaticism of the true believer in Hitler's vision. First used in the Russian campaign, later in France, they earned a reputation for courage in battle and open disdain for the native population. They served under their own officers but were attached to regiments of the regular army. As might be expected, animosity between their units and the *Wehrmacht* was a common problem.

The *Waffen* SS was partially successful in its effort to attract large numbers of non-Germans into its ranks. At the end of the war an astounding one million men had joined their regiments, about half of these were foreigners designated as "racial Germans" and "foreign Aryans." As the war dragged on, the requirements of total commitment to Hitler and training in Nazi ideology were often shortened or ignored. Men who hoped for military glory and quick advancement which was not available to them in the regular army constituted a large segment of the *Waffen* SS. After the war, they may have regretted that the runic SS symbol had been tattooed on the undersides of their arms.

Clearly, Himmler had created a visible and an invisible empire. As the functions and the personnel of secret police, regular police, and *Waffen* SS expanded, Himmler was in the best position to execute the Final Solution of the Jewish problem. This was a plum coveted by others, including the Foreign Office, Internal Affairs Ministry, the Propaganda Agency, and the Economic Ministry, but Himmler had the *Fuehrer's* confidence and that resolved the matter. The Black Order, with all its various competing yet interlocking branches, became the instrument of destruction in Hitler's war against the Jews.

THE SS: MEMBERSHIP AND TRAINING

Himmler's troops were a fluid, constantly changing aggregation of units rather than a centralized, stable, monolithic organization. Commanders changed, functions of troops were altered, methods of recruitment and training were adjusted to fit new circumstances, and competing chiefs of the various subgroups rose and fell in power. Only Himmler's authority and absolute obedience to his orders remained unchallenged. Although the SS began as a well-trained, carefully selected corps of the Aryan elite, during the war it incorporated whole organizations en masse and membership qualifications became less stringent. With the caveat that the internal gyrations of the SS cannot be followed in the limited space of this text, we will view its role as it affected the Holocaust.

Not until Germany was defeated did the world (and that includes most Germans) discover the full design of the secret realm of the SS. Himmler had adamantly refused to share with anyone, including other Reich ministries, any information about his Black Order. Even the methods used in his training schools, the so-called Adolf Hitler Schools, were wrapped in secrecy. The criteria for enlistment, however, had to be made common knowledge in order to attract the desired types.

WHO SERVED IN THE SS?

How comforting it would be to say that the storm troop units were composed of sadists, misfits, and the assorted flotsam and jetsam of human society. Then, we could separate the rest of humanity and ourselves from their acts of brutality and retreat into the solace that such deeds were not committed by normal people, not by the likes of us. But such consolation cannot be granted. Himmler's men, no doubt, included a small percentage of psychological misfits, neurotics, even psychotics, but they numbered approximately 5 percent of the total. The great majority were so ordinary, they were, in the words of Hannah Arendt, author of *The Origins of Totalitarianism*, banal, commonplace. Nor did researchers find any common denominators among the mass murderers. Yes, many were very ambitious, eager for advancement and recognition, but such generalizations are true of most careerists. Nothing in the Blackshirts' family backgrounds—upbringing, education, or religious affiliation—suggested their future willingness to commit unprecedented crimes against humanity. The fact that they were exposed to extensive propaganda manipulation which included the dehumanization of the victims and bombastic assurances concerning their sacred mission does not provide a satisfactory answer. Perhaps some future social scientific research will furnish more convincing clues to the riddle of the anatomy of an SS man.

Basically, the SS was a volunteer organization. The credentials for its officers resembled those of the *Wehrmacht*. Among Himmler's most cherished recruits were the sons of the old aristocracy. Their upbringing had accustomed them to taking command and expecting obedience. They carried themselves with the proud bearing, some might say overbearing manner, which Himmler demanded. No doubt the carefully fostered notion that the SS represented Germany's new elite, appealed to their arrogance. Among the Black Order's senior officers, more than half came from families whose surnames began with the vaunted *von*.

The upper middle class, that is, successful professional, industrial, and business families, also contributed sons to the SS. These were not the ne'er-do-wells, indeed the number of academic degrees among this group is surprising. Many were lawyers, some were physicians, and others were economic and technical specialists. Their recruitment often began in the Hitler Youth movement and was based on recommendations from their troop leaders. These were the technocrats, young men who saw career opportunities no other endeavor could offer. Their chances in the regular army were not nearly as promising; in the *Reichswehr,* tradition played an important role in the selection of officer candidates, while the SS promoted all qualified candidates.

Most of the noncommissioned SS volunteers came from the farms. The revival of primogeniture left younger sons of small landowners free to seek their fortune in the prestigious Black Order. If they performed exceptionally well, they might be given the opportunity to enter SS officer training school. The respect, even awe, afforded the smart black uniform and the secrecy surrounding many of their functions, created an aura many young men found hard to resist. It was, of course, necessary to meet the requirements: a well-proportioned body, Nordic-type features and coloring, excellent physical condition, and a hard-to-define authoritative bearing. Certificates, such as, baptismal and marriage records had to prove the candidates Aryan ancestry going back to the year 1800. The future Aryan lords who would colonize the eastern lebensraum must look splendid and act masterful.

An applicant's minimum age was eighteen. His initial training lasted six months. The rigorous physical demands were equaled by intensely emotional commitments. Midnight oath-taking, torchlight ceremonies, ideological drumming and repetitions— the indoctrination resembled that of a cult. Upon completion of this phase, the novice swore to Hitler his personal loyalty unto death. Next, he was obliged to fulfill his *Landjahr,* or labor service, requirement. German youths between the ages of nineteen and twenty-five were required to work without pay for one year wherever the authorities chose to send them. Most common were assignments on farms where men worked in the fields and women did household chores. At the end of that duty, the hopeful SS trooper owed yet another obligation to the state, his military training. If his record in the army was good, his inauguration into the SS brotherhood was finally at hand. In yet another impressive ceremony, he swore that he would not marry without the approval of the *SS Reichsfuehrer.* In other words, his future wife had to pass the racial purity muster, and her appearance had to be judged worthy to bear an SS man's children. As might have been noted, there were no intellectual requirements at all.

THE ISOLATION OF GERMAN JEWS

The forced relocation of Jews into closed-off quarters was an intermediate step between expulsion from their homes and the Final Solution. It was Himmler's responsibility to set up ghettos in conquered Poland, mainly in Hans Frank's General Government. Cities with rail junctions were preferred locations. The Intentionalists see this move as a planned preliminary step leading to the death camps; Functionalists hold the view that confining the Jews was a stopgap measure pending further expulsions or resettlements, possibly to the French island of Madagascar. The potential establishment of a Jewish colony was a subject under discussion among Nazis dealing with the Jewish question in 1940. Meanwhile, Adolf Eichmann who headed the Jewish Emigration Service for the SS, was spinning his own dream of a Jewish reserve in Poland, to be called Nisco and governed by him, of course.

The physical separation of Jews from the rest of the population had been under way in the greater Reich, that is, Germany, Austria, and Czechoslovakia, for some time before the invasion of Poland. Evictions of Jews from their residences were legalized by the imaginative stratagem that since Jews were not members of the German people's community, the *Volksgemeinschaft*, they could not be members of the residential community, the *Hausgemeinschaft*. The removal of Jewish families to assigned locations was added to the responsibilities of the Gestapo.

The wall-enclosed or fenced-in ghettos instituted in Poland were not established within the Reich. German Jews, including those who lived in villages or small towns, were allocated specific houses within larger cities. The doors of apartments into which the Jews were forced to move were marked with a star, black print on white paper. In 1942, it was decided that German Jews over six years of age must wear on their chests a six-pointed star the size of the palm of a hand, with the word *JUDE* written in black on yellow background. It is difficult to conceive of serious bureaucrats attending numerous meetings to decide on the size of the lettering and the age of the youngest children to be labeled.

The confinement of German Jews within the Reich was an interim measure. Their expulsion from the sacred soil of the motherland was never in doubt, only the method and timing had to be chosen. In due time they would join their fellow Jews in eastern concentration and death camps. Mass deportations of Berlin's Jews began in 1941. Most were shipped in cattle cars to the Lodz ghetto. There they shared the life and death of its inhabitants. But the German experience gave the Nazis the model of procedures to be applied in conquered Poland. The guidelines had been fixed, the legal rationalization had been approved. Since the Germans were indifferent to Polish assessment of their actions, anti-Jewish laws were implemented more quickly, more cruelly, and more openly.

The German pattern was valuable in controlling the ghetto population through councils of elders, the *Judenraete*. German Jewry had traditionally regulated its own religious, educational, and welfare needs. Under the stress of Nazi attacks, the great majority of religious congregations had formed a centralized umbrella organization which eventually was called the RV, the *Reichsvertretung*, (the "national representative agency"). Its renowned leader was the Reform Rabbi Leo Baeck, a man with outstanding credentials, a scholar, World War I army chaplain, and leader of Berlin's Jewish community. We can glimpse his character by his refusal to leave Germany while there was time. When he was arrested in 1943 and sent to the Teresienstadt concentration camp he served as the head of the Council of Elders there. He survived the camp and until his death in 1956 he continued to play a prominent role in Jewish affairs. Although his stature was singular, his role as head of the *Judenrat* was imitated in all the ghettos. Rabbi Baeck shared with his Polish counterparts the hopeless task of trying to balance the needs of his people with the increasingly brutal orders of the

Nazi masters. His moral courage, his dedication, and his hope that a Jewish administration was preferable to a German one cannot be doubted. But the results were such that in the future, grave doubt would be raised concerning the role of the *Judenraete*. The SS used them to do much of their work, thus they functioned as agents of their own destruction.

PURGING THE JEWS FROM WESTERN POLAND

The conquest of Poland brought 2,000,000 Jews under German rule. That number was increased again when Germany attacked the Soviet Union in 1941. More than 1,500,000 Jews, many of whom had fled western Poland earlier, now came under Nazi control. Poland's military defeat was accomplished so quickly, neither the government in Warsaw nor the villagers on their farms could comprehend the debacle. Polish Jewry had no illusions about the Germans, but they had no idea that plans for their complete destruction were under consideration.

As early as September 19, 1939, Heydrich met with *Wehrmacht* personnel to explain the policy of cleansing Poland of its Jews, its intelligentsia, clergy, and aristocracy. But there was to be an end to the amateurish improvisations by the SS. Activities by single or small groups of Nazis, such as beatings, shootings, kidnapping, for forced labor, arson, collections of ransom for release of prominent men in the community, public humiliations, and various methods of torture, all such unofficial conduct was to be replaced by a unified, properly organized approach. Since the army hoped to stay aloof—brutality against civilians was bad for discipline and morale—the SS took on the responsibility to enforce the *Fuehrer's* wishes. Heydrich availed himself of the ultimate technocrat, Adolf Eichmann. He was the man to implement the expulsion and relocation of millions of people, a task to challenge even his proven talents.

The Germans had incorporated three districts in western Poland into the German nation. The Jews living in the newly created *Gaue* of greater Germany were to be purged from their towns and villages at once. Hitler had ordered the "cleansing" of the area. The region of Wartheland, and the enlarged East Prussian and Silesian provinces and greater Danzig were to become *Judenrein*. Himmler wanted this massive uprooting of hundreds of communities completed within three months, a goal that even his best effort could not effect.

The new eastern boundary of Poland, previously established by the Ribbentrop-Molotov treaty with the Soviet Union, was along the river Bug. The first expulsions from that region consisted of forcing the Jewish families across the river into Soviet territory. The brutality of this action was exemplified by the fate of the Jews of Chelm. Of the 1,800 deportees, 400 survived. Hundreds were gunned down, and many drowned when forced to swim across the Bug. In some areas, Soviet soldiers on the east bank would not permit them to come ashore, causing the hapless victims to run that gauntlet twice. Six months after the defeat of Poland, 78,000 Polish Jews had been driven eastward. Although their experiences were horrifying, those who made their way to the Russian interior comprised the largest number of Polish Jews to survive the war.

THE DEPORTATIONS

The logistics of Jewish deportations were organized by Eichmann. He viewed the initial trial runs within Poland as experimental, since soon the railroads would carry Jews from southern, central, and western Europe to Hans Frank's General Government. The deportations during the winter of 1939–1940 were instructive in such matters as how to procure the rolling stock from the railway authority, how to set up intermediate camps, and how to coordinate the various authorities involved in the mass exodus. A timetable had to be developed and the expellees needed to be assembled at selected points. The Jews had to be registered and searched for contraband articles; an accounting had to be prepared of the properties left behind, and arrangements had to be made for their disposal. Eichmann found that negotiation with the Ministry of Transport required considerable skill. It was never a simple matter to secure the necessary rolling stock. The SS was compelled to pay for the transportation of the Jews, usually with funds collected by the Jewish elders from their communities. Cost was based on the number of "pieces" a train carried. How the "pieces" arrived did not matter, the same fee was paid whether they reached their destination dead or alive.

Eichmann wanted the deportations to progress with a minimum of strain on the SS. Stratagems of deception duped many victims to willingly gather at or near railroad stations. They were told that the German policy called for resettlement in the east, no harm would come to them, families would be permitted to stay together, and the early arrivals would be in the best positions to establish their new lives. The local Jewish elders were persuaded to encourage their neighbors to make their exodus as trouble-free as possible. Resistance to German orders would endanger the whole community.

Survivors of the Holocaust shudder as they remember their transport to the camps. Each train was made up of freight and cattle cars and was expected to carry a total of one thousand Jews. Filling the cars was accomplished by violent pushing until every inch was occupied and there was no room to sit down. A single pail in the corner soon overflowed with human waste. The humiliation of men and women attending to their bodily needs in public was a foretaste of the dehumanization process intentionally designed by the Nazis. People who died on the trains had no space to fall down. There were cases of mothers giving birth in cars so packed they had to squat. Thirst made people delirious, hunger caused fainting and madness. Worst of all was the overwhelming need for a breath of air. The trains were sealed and many cars had no ventilation.

Initially, deportees were permitted to bring some food and water, even a few zlotys (Polish money), and forty-four pounds of luggage, but these concessions were canceled as conditions grew increasingly harsh. Families who had traveled just a few days barely recognized each other when they tumbled from the cars upon arrival. Dirty, disoriented, physically weakened, trembling with fear for themselves and loved ones, they were often incapable of absorbing the events that had engulfed them so suddenly. Their confusion seemed to infuriate the SS and they were met with blows and curses. When Jews were shipped from all the lands in Europe where the swastika had triumphed, the very trains became adjuncts to the killing process.

CREATING OF GHETTOS

The first deportations from the Polish areas annexed by Germany were organized in the final days of the Polish campaign. But merely shifting the Jews from one place to another did not solve the greater Jewish problem for Himmler. Until a decision was made concerning the future handling of the millions of undesirables now under German jurisdiction, an interim solution was needed. Taking a page from the history of the Middle Ages, the Nazis decided to create ghettos in the major cities of Poland. The five major ghettos were located in Warsaw, Lodz, Cracow, Lublin, and Lvov. Initially, only Polish Jews were confined, but ghettoization was soon extended to include other Jewish nationals. German Jews were added in 1940. During the same year, the conquests in the west expanded Himmler's responsibilities to include France, Holland, Belgium, Denmark, and Norway. All areas were ordered to become *Judenrein*. Hitler's later campaigns in southern and southeastern Europe brought additional trainloads of Jews to Poland from the Balkan countries and Italy. The great majority of these victims, however, did not interrupt their final journey by a stay in Polish ghettos but went directly to the concentration and death camps.

Heydrich was an efficient administrator. Even before the Poles surrendered, he began to expel Jews from western Poland. As a rule, they were given no time to prepare for the exodus from villages and small towns where their ancestors had lived for hundreds of years. In some instances, they were permitted fifteen minutes to pack some belongings. Those who had relatives in the territories not scheduled for annexation to the Reich were urged to leave on their own. The rest were forced to depart on foot or by train to cities designated by the Germans. The bulk of their possessions were left behind and declared abandoned property. As such, it was subject to immediate confiscation. Goering, personally and as the chief of the Four Year Plan, was the main beneficiary of this plunder.

Most Polish Jews were poor and the booty was disappointing. The physical boundaries of the ghettos were usually enclosed by walls or high fences. Gates were locked at night and guarded, thus escape was nearly impossible. Those who did manage to get to the Gentile side needed papers, food, and money to survive and it was difficult to procure any one of these vital items. The SS controlled every facet of ghetto life with very little direct contact with its population and a minimum of manpower. For their survival, the inhabitants were totally dependent on supplies from the outside. Food and water, electricity and waste disposal, medicines and telephones, postal service and cemetery space were supplied or withheld at will by the Nazis. The size of the ghettos, the number of blocks, houses, and available rooms were determined by SS decrees. Frequent reduction in space allotted for the ghetto caused constant anxiety. Overcrowding was intense. Occupancy of seven persons per room was common and was exacerbated by the continuous influx of refugees from all over Europe. The death rate from starvation was in direct ratio to the insufficient food rations and lack of medical supplies. No matter how well-meaning the *Judenrat* administrators, nothing could change the fact that the fate of the Jews was in the hands of their enemies.

LIFE IN THE GHETTOS

The Nazis placed the burden of ghetto management on the Jewish council of elders, the *Judenraete*. The use of established leadership within a community had worked well in the Reich and was readily transplanted to Poland. Not only did that arrangement minimize the need for Nazi personnel, there were additional advantages. Instead of hating the almost invisible Germans as life grew inexorably more brutal, the ghetto dwellers were likely to blame their own leaders. The lack of even the most basic necessities was more easily ascribed to the Jewish elder in charge of distributing goods than to a faceless German authority. Thus, hostility which might develop into resistance was

The Star of David attached to the top of this street car indicates it is in use for residents of Warsaw's Ghetto. (Courtesy Bettmann.)

deflected from the real oppressors, the SS. Furthermore, when prominent Jews urged their fellow victims to obey, to be hopeful, to remain peaceful, the possibility of overt defiance was greatly diminished. Finally, the Jewish councils were a convenient target for blackmail. At the slightest sign of noncompliance, the threat of killing the ghetto leaders more often than not brought about prompt submission.

The SS and/or Gestapo commanders had offices within the ghetto but cared only that their orders were obeyed promptly and efficiently. How the elders regulated the day-to-day routine of ghetto life was of little or no concern. Thus, every one of the more than twenty Polish ghettos had its own individuality. The differences depended on such variables as the personality of the German commander, or the influence exerted by the army officer in charge of the military district. Even the ghetto's geographic location could ease or worsen the suffering. In addition, the styles of leadership among the heads of the *Judenraete* varied significantly. At one extreme were the autocrats with messianic complexes who claimed that God had willed them to save their communities. At the opposite end were the ghettos organized to represent, as much as circumstances permitted, the will of the majority. Those leaders who knew or guessed that their labors mattered little—since all would soon be dead—struggled to retain their sanity. Human failings and decency, all were exemplified in ghetto life and administration. Perhaps the most common complaint against the leadership was favoritism. The elders were often in the position of sparing their own family and friends some particular depredation, providing for a better room, an extra ration, an excuse from the heaviest labor, or arranging a delay in boarding the train that eventually took them all to no man's land. The bitterness engendered by unfair practices of Jews toward other Jews was pointedly intense.

GENERAL FEATURES

Despite the diversity among ghettos, a number of common characteristics were discernible. All Jews were held responsible for the infractions of individuals. Punishment was meted out to the collective community; this was an effective method of maintaining mastery over large numbers of people. All Jews were subjected to curfews, all were compelled to wear identifying markings, a star on an armband or pinned to the chest or back. All men and women were liable to report for forced labor. The Germans set quotas for the numbers of the workers which were demanded each day. Every ghetto was overcrowded, inevitably causing the spread of communicable diseases. Typhus was the most recurrent plague but various illnesses which were induced by malnutrition and poor sanitation decimated the population. The greatest suffering was caused by hunger. Each month starvation killed an increased number of people. Children and the elderly died first, but the lack of food felled even the once strong and hale. In winter, the shortage of fuel contributed to death by hypothermia; people died in their beds, in the street, at the workplace. Any ghetto resident could be shot down or beaten to death by a German without any cause whatever. Such incidents were common and heightened the atmosphere of unremitting anxiety. The more prominent members of a community were a favorite target of torture and murder for trumped-up reasons or no reasons at all.

Fear permeated the air of the ghetto. No one knew with certainty what the Nazis planned to do and rumors replaced information. Each day created another round of hope and despair: Jews with skills could work and live; no, the SS was enraged at *Wehrmacht* interference and for spite would kill everyone; resettlement in the east would begin soon; no, only a fiery death awaited those who left the ghetto; the war was going badly for the Germans and the Jews would be liberated; oh, no, defeat at the front would merely incite the SS to further outrages. In this atmosphere, every emotion, envy, selfishness, and contentiousness, as well as generosity, sacrifice, and altruism was magnified. There were quarrels about food, water, and coal, about medicines and the best place to wait in line at the soup kitchens. Endless discussions concerning the value of work permits and the price of anything available on the black market occupied the idle hours. The wildest rumors found acceptance as people were desperate to get through just one more day.

The number of successful escapes from the ghetto was pitifully small. Getting over the wall, through the sewer pipes, or under the fence was merely the first step; finding a place to hide and survive was much more difficult. The Polish countryside was nearly always hostile. Jews who spoke Polish imperfectly, whose faces looked Semitic rather then Slavic, who were too weak to work or too disoriented to think clearly were lost. It must be remembered that providing food and shelter for a Jew was a capital offense during the German occupation. Such charity could endanger the lives of an entire well-meaning family. Despite all difficulties ghetto children added significantly to the food supply. Even little ones managed to get to the Gentile side. They brought back vegetables bought or stolen from Polish farmers. Some German guards opted not to see the children, others beat them terribly or shot them for a couple of beets or potatoes.

FUNCTIONS OF THE *JUDENRAETE*

For as long as possible, which was three years at most, the elders attempted to give ghetto life a semblance of normalcy. Bureaucracies were established to provide schools, hospitals, and orphanages. Officials in charge of sanitation faced the impossible task of preventing human waste from causing deadly contamination. Fire brigades were organized to prevent the slum dwellings from burning to the ground. While it was still possible to receive packages or money, mainly from American Jewish institutions, the *Raete* distributed these donations. For the most part, the elders were forced to tax everything imaginable to raise the money required to carry out their functions. Where the Germans permitted production of goods needed by their army, a small portion of the item's value might be made available to the councils.

A Jewish police force, the *Kapos*, not only kept public order but counted out the daily columns of slave laborers who worked in various installations outside the ghetto. *Kapos* attracted the worst elements in a community, their brutality earned them a loathing that sometimes exceeded hatred for the Germans. Factory work was much

Jews in front of a well in the Ghetto of Lublin. (Courtesy AP/Wide World Photos.)

sought after. Compared to digging antitank ditches and road repair, the work was bearable. The Germans always made money from their captives, even when they allotted the *Judenraete* a portion of the payment they collected for "their" Jews. Work, which often meant larger food rations, was equated with life itself. The notion that those who contributed to the German war effort would survive lingered to the very end. But there was never enough work, particularly when the SS forbade laborers to go to the Gentile side. Without a source of supplies from the outside, no large-scale manufacturing was possible within the confines of the ghettos.

There was always a brisk street-corner business of buying and selling personal belongings. The greatest demand was for food, followed by the need for warm clothing and heating materials. After the Nazis requisitioned such items as furs, woolens, leather goods, bedding, acute suffering resulted during the harsh Polish winters. Even when the *Judenraete* made an effort to parcel out available supplies with fairness, it was never possible to be completely impartial.

The number of ghetto dwellers changed constantly due to decimation by deaths and increases from the influx of non-Polish Jews. The newcomers were not always gracefully accepted. When the ghettos were first established there were considerable differences in the economic standing of the population. In the end, nearly all were paupers although a gap between the have-somethings and the have-nothings remained. The councils tried, with some success, to feed their people by requisitioning the food supply which the Germans permitted into the ghetto and doling it out in soup kitchens.

When the Nazis decided to reduce the number of Jews by starvation, the nutritional value of the soup could not sustain life. Those families that had been able to hide something of value found a flourishing black market where a pearl might buy a piece of smuggled horse meat.

While the ghettos existed, every attempt was made to imitate the world that had been left behind. Although suicide rates increased and some people escaped into insanity when unable to cope with the sights of dead bodies in the streets, of beggars in rags and children too weak to cry, the great majority fought hard to retain their humanity. They sought and found solace through participation in a variety of cultural and religious activities. Actors performed in makeshift theaters; political parties continued to argue Zionist, socialist, and other issues; debating societies disputed philosophy and religion; musicians gathered to play and sing for their own pleasure and that of others. The devout prayed to God and asked for his merciful intervention. Although the Germans forbade the establishment of schools, many teachers gathered pupils in their rooms and hoped to give the children some hours of normalcy. Newspapers were secretly authored, copied, and avidly read. Books had never been more precious. Men, women, and children kept diaries to bear witness to their suffering. In prose, poetry, and with pictures, they described what they saw and felt, and hoped that the world would remember them. Some of their manuscripts and a number of drawings and photographs survived the liquidation of the ghettos and allow us to marvel at the vigor of the intellectual energy of ghetto life. The people of the book were indeed sustained by their ancient heritage until death.

THE LODZ GHETTO, CASE IN POINT

In 1941, the process of confining Polish Jewry in ghettos was well underway. By August of 1944, the last major ghetto, Lodz, had been emptied. At the Wannsee Conference of January 20, 1942, the Nazi hierarchy in charge of the Jewish question decided that mass murder was the solution. The earlier concentration of European Jews in ghettos eased the execution of the final step: The Jews themselves would provide much of the required paperwork, and most expediently, the personnel to collect the victims and load the trains. In terms of history, the period of ghettoization was brief, but in relation to the Holocaust it provided an important link. It is estimated that one-fifth of Polish Jewry died due to ghetto conditions, that is, before the Final Solution was implemented in the death camps. It is also defensible to state that ghettos allowed the *Endloesung* to proceed with momentous speed.

The chief of the Lodz council was named Mordekhai Chaim Rumkowski, a childless widower, formerly the director of an orphanage. His dictatorial administration was well intentioned at best, self-serving at worst, and bizarre for sure. One must presume that he developed megalomania; he was certain only he could save "his" Jews. His willingness to lead the community during the trauma of Nazi occupation was explicable only in terms of his mission: God had appointed him to do His work. The original members of his council, who may have been unwilling to accept his authoritarian style, were murdered following a summons to appear before the Nazis. There-after, his *Judenrat* was composed of people who had no previous standing in the community and who did not try to curb Rumkowski's excesses.

The Lodz ghetto existed for four years and four months, longer than any other. It was sealed off in April 1940 and its 160,000 people endured the same misery of star-vation, illness, and helpless anxiety suffered by all the other Polish Jews. Compared to other ghettos, however, Lodz had several, albeit temporary, advantages. The enclosed area contained some farmland where a little food could be grown; the overcrowding reached 5.8 persons per room, not over 7 as in other ghettos. Rumkowski preached the doctrine that hard work for the Germans would keep the Jews alive. That shred of hope was as vital as food, until, in the end, the truth of their impending death could no longer be denied.

Surely, Rumkowski realized the impossibility of serving two contradictory pur-poses: saving his people on the one hand, and assisting the Germans who planned to kill them on the other. His authority was always a gift from his Nazi masters, to be granted or withdrawn at will or whim. The SS chief charged with the supervision of the Lodz ghetto was named Hans Biebow. It served his object to have a strong admin-istration within the ghetto, to have one man responsible for carrying out his orders. Biebow had no objections to enriching the SS coffers at the expense of those who had to work at a feverish pace to manufacture clothing within the ghetto. He wanted calm and orderliness and never even hinted at the eventual dissolution of the ghetto.

Rumkowski, the "king of the Lodz Jews," had almost no previous administrative experience, yet he organized ghetto life with ruthlessness and skill. He developed not only police, welfare, hospital, judicial, educational, and religious departments, but he turned the ghetto into a giant workshop. Among the Jews of Lodz were a large num-ber of skilled workers, many of whom had been involved in the flourishing textile man-ufacture of the region. There were also cabinet makers, tailors, shoemakers, tinsmiths, and others. Food rations and work production were linked and Rumkowski permitted no interference with his design: Work and we shall live. He printed ghetto money with his picture, issued orders above his personal seal, appeared at public functions with his retinue, and bestowed regal favors upon petitioners. Many Lodz workers had been unionized and continued to identify with their associations. When they organized a strike in order to win some concessions to ease their terrible working conditions, Rumkowski refused to back down. He brooked no tampering with his authority and hunger drove the workers back to their ten-hour work days at starvation rations.

During the 1941–1942 winter, the ragged thousands in the Lodz ghetto were stunned to receive their first order of evacuation. It was merely the beginning, the last such demand came in August of 1944. The Nazis told Rumkowski to ready ten thou-sand men, women, and children for "resettlement." The Jews did not know that this was a death warrant, to be carried out in the gas chambers of Chelmo. Rumkowski decreed that this consignment should be selected from among the "undesirables" of the ghetto residents. In effect, that meant the expulsion of those who had run afoul of the admin-istration (perhaps for the theft of a potato) along with their families. Those who refused to present themselves for deportation received no food rations. If Rumkowski had any illusions that the Germans would be satisfied with one trainload, he learned the truth within a month. Nearly one thousand Jews per day made the heart-wrenching trip to the rail station. As Germans repeated their demands to reduce the ghetto population, the next group to be pushed out were the people who were unable to do productive work. The unemployed from age ten and up were shoved into the waiting freight cars. When that category had been exhausted, non-Polish Jews who had been shipped in from other parts of Europe were placed on the death list.

The order for new selections coincided with the arrival of a group of Jews from Wartheland. They knew about the installations of mass murder and removed any doubt that "resettlement" was the euphemism for death. When the Nazis instructed Rumkowski to transport the sick, the ten thousand children under age ten, and all men and women over sixty-five, the terror experienced by the population cannot be described. Now that the truth could no longer be denied, who would be willing to shove the victims into their freight cars? For a promise that their own children would be saved, amid screams and curses of helpless parents and children, the *Kapos* tried to complete their dreadful task, but Germans, aided by collaborators from the Baltic states and the Ukraine, had to finish the savage roundup.

Rumkowski's authority disappeared along with his Jews. He kept a few of his welfare programs operating and hoped the worst was over. Perhaps he thought he had saved the remnant. During the summer of 1944 some 76,000 Jews continued to work and survive in the Lodz ghetto. But as the German armies retreated across Russia, the eradication of Poland's second largest ghetto was ordered. The men and women who had endured for so long and hoped so fervently to live until Germany's defeat were consigned to the chimneys of Auschwitz-Birkenau. Among the last to go was Mordekhai Rumkowski.

THE WARSAW GHETTO, ANOTHER CASE IN POINT

The Warsaw ghetto was the largest. For a time, about a half million Jews, from Warsaw, from the surrounding countryside, and from Germany and Austria were imprisoned within its ten-foot-high walls. It was organized in October of 1940, about a year after the defeat of Poland. One month later it was sealed off and the twenty-two entrances to the outside world were closed. Five hundred thousand people had been pushed into an area of approximately three and one-half square miles. Only by realizing that between seven and thirteen people lived in every single room of the approximately 1,500 buildings is it possible to comprehend the overcrowding. Whatever the suffering in other ghettos, it was duplicated and intensified in Warsaw. It must also be remembered that the Polish capital had undergone extensive bombardments and much of it lay in rubble.

As was true in all ghettos, only those who worked as slave laborers were issued food rations. The allotment was so meager, less than two hundred calories per day, that only smuggling prevented immediate mass starvation. The Germans did not permit any nutritious foods such as fruits, fresh vegetables, meat, milk, or fish into the ghetto. Packages sent from the outside were confiscated and safe drinking water was at a premium. Malnutrition made the population susceptible to epidemics which raked across the city with regularity.

The Warsaw ghetto was under the internal administration of twenty-four members of a council of elders headed by the widely respected engineer Adam Czerniakow. His meticulous diary survived the war and gives convincing evidence of his earnest desire to provide a fair administration. He hoped to preserve Jewish lives and act as a buffer between the SS and his people. From the onset, these goals were unattainable. To the Nazis, he was merely a useful instrument of management and eventually an aid in the accomplishment of genocide. If he hoped that his people would understand his dilemma, he was largely disappointed. He was blamed for every shortage, every cruelty ordered by his masters. The actions of the *Kapos,* who enforced German demands, were placed at his door. Occasionally he stood up to the SS, even winning some minor point, but in reality, he was unable to alter German intentions, not even by a day.

Czerniakow tried to be impartial in the distribution of allotments of food, fuel, and services; but there was never enough and the afflicted people reproached him angrily. Just as the Nazis predicted, the *Judenrat* was blamed for the misery of ghetto life. The elders struggled to keep the Warsaw ghetto calm. They supported various institutions designed to alleviate some of the suffering by sponsoring intellectual, educational, and recreational activities. Clandestine unofficial organizations were equally important in easing the stress of an unnatural existence. Among their self-help activities were efforts to make themselves valued and valuable in the eyes of the Nazis. All types of merchandise were in short supply and the Jews turned to manufacturing. Ghetto craftsmen literally made something from almost nothing, rags and junk were transformed into useful items. They produced clothing, bed linen, shoes, cutlery, pots and pans, paper, and toys. The vitality necessary to forge such enterprises under such circumstances was in itself a triumph. The workers hoped that the German army would realize that it was to their advantage to authorize ghetto production. For nearly a year, the Germans permitted the flow of some raw materials into the ghetto. During the exchange of goods from the Jewish to the Polish part of Warsaw, it was possible to smuggle in some food. Aside from this quasi-legal trade, an illegal underground system of manufacture and exchange developed. With luck or pluck, by means of black market ventures or corruption, some Jews actually, though only momentarily, became rich. They lived with reckless abandon, ate in restaurants and smoked cigarettes in cafes. The gap between these few and the starving masses created unbearable tension.

In 1942, Himmler ordered the liquidation of all ghettos; liquidation was the SS euphemism for mass murder. The entire process was to be completed by the end of the year, though actually, it was not completed until the summer of 1944. The Warsaw ghetto, imprisoning at that point an estimated 350,000 people, was among the first to hear the tolling of that bell. In July 1942, the Nazis began to demand that the *Judenrat* provide "settlers" for the journey to the east. The death camp Treblinka was the usual destination of the Warsaw Jews. The weak and helpless were the first to be dragged to the *Umschlagplatz,* the transfer place of assembly for the deportees. The SS promised that volunteers for the "resettlement" would find better conditions; they distributed pre-

Nazis rounding up Jewish men, women, and children during the destruction of the Jewish Ghetto in Warsaw, 1943. (Courtesy Bettmann.)

cious rations of bread and jam to those who willingly reported to the train station. When the supply of volunteers ran out, *Kapos* forced their fellow Jews into the freight cars. The Warsaw ghetto police, numbering about 1,700 was under the leadership of a hated apostate, Jozef Szerynski who handled the roundup with brutal competence. It should be noted that the *Kapos* had been promised that their own families would be exempt from deportation. That they apparently believed that lie underscores the human eagerness for self-deception when faced with dire choices. Nearly all of the *Kapos* and their families were sent to Treblinka in September 1942, on Yom Kippur, the Day of Atonement.

On July 23, 1942, Adam Czerniakow shot himself. He had been asked to hand over the children and could not do it. He knew where the trains were going and he could do nothing to stop them. The debate, whether he should have used his gun to kill Germans, whether he should have rallied the people into rebellion, is pointless. His note said that he "could no longer bear all this." We do not know, nor can we ever know, his true state of mind when he made his decision. His death changed nothing. The expulsions continued. The Nazis called in auxiliary forces composed of some eight hundred Ukranians, Lithuanians, and Letts who were eager to participate in the *Aktion*. The Polish historian Emanuel Ringelblum, whose chronicles were discovered after the war, recorded events with laconic accuracy: Yesterday so many disappeared, today, so many more. He lamented the fact that the Jews had not offered active resistance when their number was greater. In his estimation, a mere fifty SS men directed the entire evacuation of the ghetto.

One week after the liquidation order was issued, about 65,000 Warsaw Jews had been sent to their death. Each train was loaded with a cargo of 7,000 screaming, crying, silent, praying, terrified human beings. The march of Korczak's orphans was an unforgettable sight. The internationally renowned educator and pediatrician Janusz Korczak had cared for many foundlings. When offered the opportunity to escape, he refused. With two little ones in his arms, he and his staff led their charges, dressed in their Sabbath best, singing and carrying banners, to the *Umschlagplatz*. Even the Germans were stunned. When people were afraid to leave their rooms, the Germans and their accomplices encircled specific streets, stormed the houses, and drove out the inhabitants. By end of the summer, 300,000 men, women, and children had been forced out of the ghetto.

The remnant of the Warsaw ghetto population, approximately 65,000, was largely made up of young people. They continued to work in the several factories still operating. Perhaps because their more cautious elders were no longer among them, the idea of forcibly resisting the Nazis became a movement, a reality, a declaration of war against their murderers. Here the most significant of the armed struggles between Nazis and Jews was fought before, inevitably, the Warsaw ghetto was razed and turned into ashes and its inhabitants lost to the world (see Chapter 10).

Chapter 9

The Genocide

At the core of the Holocaust was the ideology of hatred: Hitler's conviction that the Jews were the enemy of Germany in particular and of the world in general. The translation of this dogma into genocide was accomplished by a dutiful bureaucracy, by modern technology, and by troops of disciplined and well-trained killers. The entire process was dependent on the prerequisite of a totalitarian government which controlled a nation of people who were compliant or irresolute or believed that they were not responsible for their actions if ordered by their leaders. The answer to "can it happen again?" is contingent on the presence of similar conditions, especially under cover of wartime confusion. The possibility exists, including a recurrence in parts of the Western world.

There is no doubt about the methods used by the Nazis to annihilate millions. There is, however, a constant adjustment about the numbers involved. It might be disturbing to students to find that statistics can differ from one source to another. The reasons for these discrepancies are due to the fact that there are still warehouses full of Nazi documents that have not been evaluated by historians and the analysis of these, as well as already available material, continues. We may never have an exact count of the victims but that has no bearing on the essence of Holocaust history.

THE WANNSEE DECISION

This infamous meeting of January 20, 1942, in a lovely villa outside of Berlin confirmed a process which actually had begun earlier. The result of the conference was the official adoption of the Final Solution (a euphemism for total destruction) of all Jews within Germany's grasp. During the invasion of the Soviet Union which began in June, 1941, mobile murder squads, the *Einsatzgruppen,* had followed the German armies eastward and systematically shot hundreds of thousands of Jews. At Wannsee, members of the German bureaucracy involved with the "Jewish problem" were asked to agree to the official course of action already underway.

The conferees, gathered in Wannsee's pleasant surroundings, were responding to orders that Hermann Goering had issued to Reinhard Heydrich six months prior to the meeting. Heydrich, chief of the SD, had been charged with the formulation of a "comprehensive plan for a final solution of the Jewish question." The meeting was convened to allow him to present his strategy and give the members of the group an opportunity to discuss and approve his outline.

Fourteen officials, representing ministries and the military, were convened. The Eastern Gauleiter Dr. Meyer; the Chief of the East Ministry, Dr. Leibrandt; the Minister of the Interior, Dr. Stuckart; State Secretary of the Four Year Plan, Neumann; State Secretary of Justice, Dr. Freisler; State Secretary of the Polish General Government, Dr. Buhler; Foreign Office Under State Secretary, Luther; Brigadier General SS, Klopfer; Ministerial Director Kritzinger of the Chancellery; General SS, Hoffmann; Lieutenant Colonel SS, Eichmann; Brigadier General SS, Dr. Schoengarth from the Polish General Government, and Major SS, Dr. Lange who was stationed in Latvia. The list is of particular interest because seven of the representatives were academics with doctorates.

As plenipotentiary for the Final Solution, Heydrich chaired the meeting. He began with a review of various measures which had been tried previously and failed to make German territories *Judenrein*. The *Fuehrer* had authorized the evacuation of all Jews to Poland where they would be used as slave laborers. Heydrich then reverted to the official double talk when he stated that it was expected that many would die of natural causes. If the survivors tried to rebuild Jewish life, they would be dealt with accordingly. The assembled delegates knew the true meaning of these words—they were a death sentence for millions. Overwork, hunger, and disease would certainly diminish the number of Jews, the remnant would receive "special treatment." Apparently, there was no discussion on this momentous decision, agreement was reached without difficulty. Only the possibility of reclassifying the *Mischlinge* was debated but no changes were approved. The meeting then adjourned for lunch.

MOBILE KILLING SQUADS: AIMS

The original concept of mobile terror units dated back to the annexation of Austria and Czechoslovakia where they played a minor role in the "pacification" of the region. During and after the Polish conquest, terror squads were active in the decimation of the Polish elite, and in a rather haphazard way, in the killing of Jews. In the western theater of operations—France, the Low Countries, Denmark, and Norway—the army did not permit SS intrusion, much to Himmler's distress. In the campaign against the Soviet Union, however, Himmler was given nearly complete freedom to conduct waves of organized massacres that have no counterparts in history.

Heydrich had begun to prepare for major *Aktionen* in May, 1941. He assembled three thousand men, picked from every organization under Himmler's authority, and told them that "real men" were needed for a task of special difficulty but of enormous

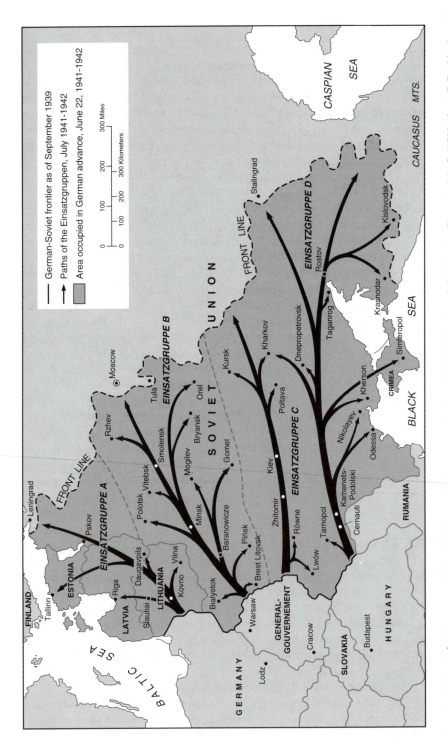

Map 9–1 The Einsatzgruppen, 1941–1942 (From *The War Against the Jews 1933–1945*, by Lucy S. Davidowicz. Text copyright © 1975 by Lucy S. Davidowicz, maps by Vincent Kotschar, copyright © 1975 by Henry Holt and Co., Inc. Reprinted by permission of Henry Holt and Co., Inc.)

importance. Their duty was to be performed in the east, not a place to which volunteers were likely to flock. No specifics regarding their mission were revealed until after weeks of intensive indoctrination. Even then, references to their actual objectives were oblique, cloaked in euphemisms like "political criminals" requiring "special treatment"; "eradication of typhus carriers"; and "the Bolshevik menace."

The official assignment of the *Einsatzgruppen* was to follow the German army into the Soviet Union and protect its rear from attack by partisans and saboteurs. In actuality, their mission was the slaughter of innocent civilians on a hitherto unprecedented scale. The *Einsatzgruppen* shot between one and a half and two million Jews as well as many hundreds of thousands of non-Jews within a period of less then two years. Among the Gentile victims, the number of Russian prisoners of war was particularly high. The standard legal cover for these execution was a small hyphen Hitler placed between two words so that they became one: *Jew-Bolshevik*. All Jews, per se, were indicted as communists; consequently they were dangerous subversives. Since Jewish children, even the unborn, were genetically destined to become mortal enemies of Germany, they too were under a death sentence. When that accusation wore thin, several commanders of the mobile squads told their men that the killings were necessary to prevent typhus, or some other epidemic. These incredible rationalizations seemed to satisfy the ever-present need for legal authority for the commission of heinous crimes.

Nearly all the German generals of the regular army accepted the presence of the *Einsatzgruppen* as long as they did not interfere with regular army activities. After the war, the military claimed that it had no hand in the dreadful work of the mobile killing units, but the facts do not bear out those assertions. The records show that in some regions there was considerable cooperation between the *Einsatzgruppen* and the *Wehrmacht* in rounding up victims, even in the actual shootings. The military, as a matter of policy, turned all captured Jewish prisoners of war over to the SS for immediate execution. When Colonel-General Johannes Blaskowitz and Admiral Canaris, the chief of the *Abwehr* (German military counterintelligence organization), protested to their superiors in Berlin about the savagery of the SS, they were told not to interject themselves into an area outside their competence.

ORGANIZATION

The commanders of the mobile killing squads came from the German middle class. Most were professional men, lawyers, doctors, intellectuals, and even a minister of the Protestant church. Their troops were not dissimilar to their counterparts in other SS organizations. The *Einsatzgruppen* were organized into four units: Group A, the largest with 990 men, went north to the Baltic states; B operated in the north-central region of Russia; C worked in the south in the vicinity of Kiev; and D, the smallest, with a strength of 500, advanced behind the most southern German army in the Crimea (see Map 9–1). Each battalion was augmented by auxiliary troops of native eastern Europeans. Among these were ethnic Germans who lived in Poland. A large contingent of volunteers came from the Baltic States, and Romania and the Ukraine were well represented. The murder of sixty thousand Jews in Odessa, which shocked even the Germans, was the grisly work of Romanians. These men knew exactly what their functions would be when they signed on, and their deliberate, often enthusiastic participation in these crimes defies rational analysis.

BOLTS FROM THE BLUE

As the German invasion of the summer of 1941 penetrated deep into Russia, the people in the conquered regions were totally unprepared for the fate that awaited them. They had no idea that Hitler was poised to wage another war—unconnected to combat between belligerents—against many Slavic and all the Jewish civilians. Marked for annihilation were all Communist Party functionaries, the political leadership of captured towns and villages, and most numerous, the Jews. The Soviet government had not warned the Russian people that this invasion was not to be compared to the Kaiser's in 1914. In fact, some Soviet citizens who despised Stalin and suffered under the harshness of his regime actually welcomed the invading troops as liberators. Even the Jews had no idea what to expect at the hands of the Nazis. But the illusion that the Germans would adhere to the accepted rules of warfare did not last long. The ruthlessness of the invaders and their contempt for the defeated population became evident very quickly.

As the first wave of killers swept behind the German armies into Russia, the Jews were easily deceived. They had no reason to question such comforting words as *resettlement, temporary relocation, moving out of the battle zones,* and such. When they were ordered to assemble in the town square, they obeyed; when told to march to the outskirts, they obeyed; when directed to climb aboard trucks, they obeyed. When the vehicles were filled and there was no room for some, they ran, hands outstretched, pleading to be lifted on board. Had anyone told them that they were about to be shot, it is unlikely that they would have believed it. What an outrageous idea! In many rural areas the Jews were the only skilled artisans. Germans valued hard workers. It was impossible to envision the madness of a government which would destroy its own advantage.

After the first wave of killings, rumors of the mass shootings flew ahead of the *Einsatzgruppen.* The roundup of the victims became more difficult and more brutal. Many Jews, perhaps one and a half million, fled eastward, deeper into the vastness of the Soviet Union. They comprised the bulk of Holocaust survivors from Nazi occupied areas. The Jewish component of the population in the conquered regions was estimated at three and a half million which included those in the region of eastern Poland that had been briefly ceded to the Soviet Union, those in the Baltic States, and the two million in the Soviet Union. Despite the fact that over 40 percent of the intended victims escaped, the numbers killed by the *Einsatzgruppen* were staggering. During the first five months of the operation it is estimated that half a million men, women, and children were executed. A second wave of killings was ordered to kill those who had evaded the first *Aktion.* When this was halted in the fall of 1942, the figure of one and one half million human beings murdered had been reached. These murders were not the result of bombs delivered from planes high above, or barrages of cannons fired in the heat of battle, these victims stood helplessly in front of their killers who shot them, one by one, by one, by one. . . .

METHODS OF MADNESS

The commanders of the *Einsatzgruppen* developed their own modus operandi in gathering the victims, by lying to them to keep calm and by the method of transportation they used to get them to the killing sites. Some wanted their victims kneeling, others standing when they were shot; some asked the Jews to hand over their valuables, others preferred that their houses remain intact until taken over by SS economic personnel. None of the killers were permitted to profit in any way from the death of the Jews. All property, now declared abandoned, became the possession of the SS organization. There is no need to detail these differences in execution because in essence the methods were similar. The description which follows is a composite of the testimonies given at the Nuremberg War Crimes Trial and other trials, the recollections of survivors, and accounts from members of the *Einsatzgruppen*. There are also German documents and corroboration from onlookers to attest that the killers usually proceeded in this sequence.

After the German army had rolled through a small Russian town, the inhabitants who had fled into nearby woods to escape the first onslaught filtered back to their homes. Even under German occupation, life took on a degree of normalcy since the battles were fought farther to the east. Depending on location, however, within days or weeks or months, a new and different enemy suddenly appeared. These Germans were dressed in black, not in the army gray. They were members of a unit from a mobile killing squad. The *Einsatzgruppen*, as they fanned across the countryside, were usually broken up into smaller units, *Einsatzkommandos,* and these were again subdivided into *Sonderkommandos* which often consisted of less than fifty men. The officer in command asked for the rabbi or the head of the town's Jewish council. Having no idea what to expect, the community leaders hurried into the presence of the Germans. The officer, in a casual manner, told them that all the Jews must assemble at once in the square. Within ten minutes, a roll call would be conducted by the German authorities in order to make plans for future resettlement of the Jews. Nothing to worry about, a mere formality; leave everything in your homes and make certain that everyone, even babies are present. Anyone failing to follow orders will be shot.

News of the SS's command spread very quickly. Some of the Jews had heard terrible rumors concerning such roll calls and were frightened. A few of the young people decided to hide despite parental admonition that it was best to comply. They slipped away, hoping to reach some of the partisan groups forming in the woods. The majority of the Jews suspended their individual judgment and followed the advice of their leaders: Authority must be obeyed. Clusters of families gathered in the marketplace. In minutes, several hundred Jews stood quietly before the Germans.

The black-shirted commander appeared. He was on horseback and looked very imposing. He told the Jews that there was a slight change in his plan; he would explain later. Everyone was to go to a hillside a few kilometers outside the town. Groups of one hundred must leave every ten minutes; some of his soldiers would go along. Those who were too weak to walk could go on the truck. The rabbi wanted to ask why this was necessary, but when he stepped forward, the soldiers pointed their guns at him and he stepped back. While some of the very old, the sick, and the very young were helped onto the truck, the first group left. Gentile neighbors watched them disappear from view. They wondered why the Germans had requisitioned a bulldozer. The noise of its motor could be heard, coming from beyond the hill. What could the Germans be digging?

When the Jewish families arrived at the knoll, they were met by another small squad of SS men, possibly ten or twenty. Their leader shouted at the families to hurry and get undressed. Get undressed? Surely, they did not understand. But when one of the soldiers began to tear the dress and underclothes off one of the women, there could be no doubt. The children were the first to become panic-stricken, some ran about wildly, others clung to their parents. The Germans were shouting, ordering the naked men, women, and children to line up in front of them, on the ridge atop the hill. When several children ran towards the woods, one of the soldiers raised his rifle and they fell dead. The Jews gasped, the mothers screamed, but the shooter merely reloaded. At that moment, many Jews realized that they were about to be killed. But even though their eyes told them the truth, their brains and hearts could not accept such a verdict. A shocked numbness seemed to roll across the crowd. Many faces lost all expression as they stood naked, with children in their arms, in a row in front of their killers. A beautiful young girl broke away, ran toward the Nazis. In Yiddish, she cried, "look at me, look at me, I am only sixteen. . . ." She never finished her sentence, and fell in a heap. That bullet animated the group. Old men tried to bless their children, mothers clutched their own and other peoples' offspring, wives and husbands attempted one last embrace, and some called upon God to help them. The men from the *Einsatzkommando* cursed and then the whole squad opened fire and the Jews plunged into the mass grave below.

Some people were shot but not killed. They lay among the dead and dying, trying to climb out of their grave. But a fresh hundred victims had arrived. Since they could hear the cries and terrible moans coming from below, they understood their fate quickly. That glazed look of disbelief swept across many faces, unable to comprehend an incomprehensible cataclysm. Some of the children and young people recovered their will to live and made for the woods. Once in a while, such an escape was successful. An old man with a flowing beard refused to take off his underwear. Religious Jews will not appear naked before their children. He was the first to be killed in his group.

The Germans counted their victims, that was Himmler's requirement and he would have remarked that this was a good *Aktion*, very little trouble. The newly dead and wounded fell upon those already in the ditch. There was a horrible clutching and grabbing among the injured to get to the top, to get air to breathe. Blood, so much blood, mixed with the bladder and bowel contents of the dead and dying. The ditch was heaving with bodies pushing and pulling. And the bodies kept piling up. Only a few, very few, escaped from such mass graves. Even if a victim had the strength to climb out of the pit, it required extraordinary survival instincts to hide when the Nazis brought back the bulldozers to cover up their gruesome work.

THE KILLERS

No matter how thoroughly the brains of the killers had been washed, like Lady Macbeth's damned spot, it was never enough. Their officers repeatedly reminded them that they were instruments of a great historic mission, but the words could not cancel the deeds. These were men with families, how could they separate their own cherished children from the ones they tossed into mass graves, some dead, some still living? Could they accept the burdens of savagery that Himmler placed upon them and remain sane? Even with an unlimited liquor supply at their disposal, could they ever return to a society in which murder is a punishable crime? One also has to wonder why so few of the men requested other duties. Such transfers were possible without penalty. Was fear of reassignment to the dreaded Russian front an overriding concern? Perhaps the recognition of accountability blurs after ten, or a hundred, or a thousand murders.

Himmler was aware of the problem and he was concerned. He toured the *Einsatzgruppen* often and tried to lift the morale of his men. He told them that he knew that theirs was a heavy task and somehow they must "overcome themselves." Did he mean that they must suspend their humanness? their feelings of pity and morality? even their ordinary intelligence? After all, how great a menace were the Jews when it was known that not a single member of any mobile unit was killed by a Jew? In August, 1941, Himmler witnessed an *Aktion*. It was a small massacre, merely two hundred Jews. The commander of the squad noted that Himmler was extremely nervous when the executions began. By the time they were over, the chief of the SS was near collapsing. He gathered himself enough to make one of his speeches, but the men had seen his reaction. The officer of the unit told Himmler that his men were finished as normal members of society. "What kind of followers are we training here? Either neurotics or savages!"

A better, faster method for killing Jews was urgently needed. The gas chambers were the eventual result of the search to spare emotional anguish—not for those about to be killed—but for the killers.

SOME GERMAN REACTIONS

Some of the German witnesses to the killings were revolted by the savagery of the SS. The disgust stemmed from two sources. First, the murder of Jewish craftsmen ruined the very industries from which the German war effort expected to benefit. Second, such massacres could not be kept secret, even though special squads were combing the country, digging up the bodies, burning them, and using special bone crushers to disguise the evidence. What would the people at home and the world say about the mass murders of civilians? A case in point was *Gauleiter* Wilhelm Kube, the political head of White (Russia) Ruthenia. Like many other dedicated Nazis, he despised the Jews but disapproved violently of the SS and its atrocities. He was furious that the *Einsatzgruppen* destroyed his work force and shamed the name of Germans. Furthermore, they crisscrossed his domain without reporting to him. In the strange world of Naziism, *Gauleiter* Kube, the anti-Semite, worked hard to save Jews. When he heard of planned shootings, he warned the potential victims; he protested to his superiors and found a sympathetic ear in the *Reichskommissar* for the *Ostland* Heinrich Lohse. Not only were the SS inflicting unnecessary savagery upon the Jews, the mass killings of ordinary Russian peasants was equally self-destructive for the orderly governing of Soviet lands. Kube had become a thorn in Himmler's side and while the *Reichsfuehrer* was considering ways to neutralize him, Soviet partisans solved his problem. In September of 1943 Kube's maid placed a lethal bomb under his bed. Himmler was delighted and called the assassination a blessing.

The use of the mobile killing units was coming to an end in any case. Himmler decided that gas would replace precious bullets and a more impersonal method of ridding Europe of its Jews would result in less trauma for his SS killers. Furthermore, it was not possible to restrict the number of witnesses when the executions took place in the open.

THE GAS VANS

At first, the *Einsatzgruppen* trapped the Jews where they lived, later the death camps reversed the arrangement and the victims were transported to the killing centers. Midway between these methods was a third course of action, a transitional one, the gas vans. Their use was relatively brief because they failed in two important respects: the numbers killed were too small compared to the effort expended and the vans did not alleviate the distress of the executioners.

The vans were introduced in Chelmo, a camp the Nazis had established north of Lodz. An old, isolated mansion had been converted into a killing site. Its commander started out with three gas vans which were specially equipped to asphyxiate the Jews of Lodz. Always reluctant to let anything of potential value escape them, the prisoners were told to undress. To avoid possible resistance to this order, they were assured that prior to resettlement a disinfecting procedure was required. No need to get upset, this was a matter of hygiene. The truck would take them to the de-lousing quarters. Later, the clothing was stored for possible use by Germans, although at the end of the war mountains of garments had accumulated.

Fifty or more men, women, and children were then ordered to climb aboard each van. They had no inkling that a hose had been attached to the exhaust pipe of the diesel motor so that the deadly carbon monoxide fumes emptied into the interior. If all went according to plan, the driver rode around for fifteen minutes to poison his cargo.

Jewish women selected for slave labor in Auschwitz-Birkenau. (Courtesy United States Holocaust Memorial Museum.)

Then he stopped near a pit where a group of Jews emptied the van. They removed any valuables not discovered earlier and buried the corpses. Only the promise that their lives would be spared could induce some Jews into the *Sonderkommando*, this ghastly special work detail. The bodies they handled were covered with bodily discharges, horribly distorted by the gas, and yet left strangely flexible, as if still alive. The Nazis, of course, did not keep their word; sooner or later the members of the charnel *Sonderkommando* joined the other corpses in the pit.

This, the Nazis decided, was not a good method. The locked-in victims realized what was happening and screamed, banged on the doors, pleaded, and caused the drivers great discomfort. Sometimes it took longer than the prescribed quarter-hour to complete the process. Also, gasoline was in short supply and needed for military purposes. And finally, with so many Jews to be killed, fifty or sixty at a time was simply too slow. At that rate it could take years to finish the operation.

THE DEATH FACTORIES

The solution to Himmler's problem—how to expedite the Final Solution—was found in the expertise of Criminal Police Inspector Christian Wirth. Since the abandonment of the so-called euthanasia killings in Germany, Wirth was at loose ends. He had

Map 9–2 *The German Partition of Poland, 1939/41–1945* (From *The War Against the Jews 1933–1945*, by Lucy S. Davidowicz. Text copyright © 1975 by Lucy S. Davidowicz, maps by Vincent Kotschar, copyright © 1975 by Henry Holt and Co., Inc. Reprinted by permission of Henry Holt and Co., Inc.)

been responsible for the installation of the ostensible bath houses in which "undesirables" handicapped Germans had been murdered by carbon monoxide. Himmler procured Wirth's services and he supervised the installation of gas chambers in most of the killing centers in Poland. But the Wirth method, which used carbon monoxide gas from fixed diesel engines, was soon superseded. The vermin-killing poison hydrogen cyanide, patented by I.G. Farben and known as Zyklon-B, created fumes which were more efficient. The blue crystals killed more quickly and were easily dispensed from the roof into openings in the ceilings above the shower rooms.

The production quotas at the death camps of Chelmo, Belzec, Sobibor, Majdanek, Treblinka, and Auschwitz-Birkenau (see Map 9–2) were measured in the numbers put to death. In the language of the reports submitted to SS headquarters in Berlin, certain criminals had received "special treatment." In a monstrous imitation of the world of ordinary manufacturers, there was competition among the death factories to see which could produce the highest number per day. Auschwitz-Birkenau, the largest of the facilities, could kill twelve thousand prisoners a day; a record of achievement no other camp commander could challenge. But then, no other facility could accommodate two thousand victims at one time and kill them in fifteen minutes or less. Indeed, the name *Auschwitz* well deserves to be a symbol of the Holocaust.

The machinery of destruction was in place. Now the ghettos were emptied and the trains from Nazi-occupied Europe began to roll toward the Polish countryside. Several officers of the *Wehrmacht* had made feeble attempts to save the Jews who worked in industry, but failed. Himmler, empowered by the *Fuehrer* himself, had total control. He found in SS Major-General Odilo Globocnik the right tool to take charge of all the death camps. Globocnik's unsavory character combined the hardness and cruelty that this work demanded. Under his supervision, the death factories of Majdanek, Sobibor, and Treblinka were built. When the killing stopped in 1945, the victims numbered approximately six million, of these, between one and a half and two million were children.

In the strange world of Nazi bookkeeping, the names of the prisoners who went directly to their deaths were not recorded, but detailed files were kept on the concentration and slave-labor camp inmates. Documentation from the fees the German railroad received for transporting Jews to the death camps as well as other sources allow an approximate count of the victims whose names were not registered. Present research suggests the following totals of Jews killed:

Chelmo	152,000
Belzec	600,000
Sobibor	250,000
Treblinka	700,000
Majdanek	125,000
Auschwitz	2,000,000

The number given for Auschwitz-Birkenau is a minimal figure, other estimates range as high as four million. Undoubtedly, nearly four million Jews died in the death camps. The victims of the *Einsatzgruppen*, and additional hundreds of thousands killed in the ghettos, and concentration and slave-labor camps result in the aggregate assessment of six million.

GAS CHAMBERS

The first gas chambers were installed by Wirth in the Belzec camp, located on the railway line between Lublin and Lvov. Considerable effort was made to conceal the true purpose of the structure in order to deceive the victims. Signs, such as THIS WAY TO THE DISINFECTION ROOM, and arrows pointing TO THE SHOWER BATH were designed to prevent panic. The diesel engine which fed the gas into a sealed chamber was activated as soon as the prisoners were locked in. Roughly thirty minutes later, the "special treatment" had been administered. Thus, mass murder had been made easier for the killers, as direct contact with the victims was minimal.

The men of the special *Totenkopfverbaende*, the concentration camp guard units, found it reassuring to regard themselves as faithful civil servants. Himmler visited often to tell them so; they were merely following orders and doing a very difficult but necessary job of destroying a dangerous pestilence. The guards at Chelmo, where many sick Jews were gassed, actually received bonus pay as if they were, in fact, killing people who suffered from infectious diseases. Although every concentration camp survivor witnessed and/or suffered many incidents of sadistic treatment by guards, the SS's official position discouraged private acts of degenerate behavior. A Commission of Special Inquiry investigated some of the most flagrant cases. Two hundred complaints resulted in convictions for corruption and unauthorized murder. Most infamous among the condemned was Karl Koch, commandant of Buchenwald and Lublin. He was given the death sentence for pursuing private wealth and for indulging his sadistic cravings. In the mad world of Naziism, only the state had the right to loot, torture, maim, and kill. It is safe to assume that even though the SS discouraged individual depravity, an unknown number of guards who were never indicted would have been judged criminally insane in any court of law.

THE MANY FORMS OF DECEPTION

The question "why did nearly all the condemned Jews go so quietly to their deaths?" is raised by many students during the study of Holocaust history. Although it is not possible to give a conclusive explanation, a response is in order. First, one must attempt to re-create the largely conservative, paternalistic society of eastern Jewry. For American students, secure in their homeland, reared in an atmosphere where critical thinking, even iconoclasm, is acceptable, this is a difficult leap. Aside from the lack of cultural incentives, there were historical and psychological barriers to Jewish resistance. As will be noted in the next chapter, in due time opposition did develop. The reason for the initial inertia may well be based on a combination of traditional, instinctive, and practical motivations.

Nothing in the history of the last thousand years had prepared Jews to fight for their lives. As strangers, more or less tolerated by reluctant host countries, they had relied on petitions, on the goodwill of a few friendly officials or kings, and on bribery as a means of survival. The past had taught them to absorb the blows of their enemies; strik-

Communal grave at the Bergen-Belsen concentration camp. (Courtesy UPI/Bettmann.)

ing back, even in self-defense, induced retaliation of catastrophic proportions against the entire community. Jewish boys sought to bring honor to their families by virtue of scholarship, not through physical strength and prowess. And always, after each disaster, the Jews rebuilt their lives and their society and thus they survived.

We, who study authenticated facts fifty years after the events, find it difficult to comprehend the Holocaust. How could the Jews in Treblinka or Belzec have grasped that they would die in minutes? The human psyche has limits of endurance. Self-deception or denial of reality relieves the psyche of its agony when all else fails. Thus, the instinct for life negated the truth about the strange, acrid smell in the air and the meaning of the ashes coming from the chimney. Some of the victims, so suddenly deprived of every aspect of their former lives, seemed to have turned into automatons. They were empty shells, going here, standing there, as if their minds had already ceased to function. Others, who had come from starvation-plagued ghettos or other concentration camps, similarly resembled the walking dead. Unable to assimilate the past, they could not comprehend the present.

The commanders of various death camps devised their own methods of keeping their installations running smoothly. Deceit and guile reinforced the prisoners' self-deception. In Auschwitz-Birkenau, the arriving trains were met by music from an orchestra; in Treblinka, flowers bloomed at the railway depot and the Jews were divided by trades to affirm the deception of their eventual resettlement. In the anterooms of the "showers," the Jews were told to tie their shoes together to prevent mix ups later and to remember the number of the peg on which they hung their clothing. The women were reassured that their hair would grow back, the shaving of heads was a sanitary measure, since lice brought typhus. They were urged to hold their babies close so none would get lost in the confusion.

The Jews complied. Actually, what could they have done, these rows of naked men and women, facing the SS with their loaded guns, their dogs and whips? Had the Germans not proven time and again that disobedience by one would cause the death of many? Who would dare to lift a hand, or try to run away when the retaliation would be so swift and so terrible? And finally, who among them had the energy of mind and body to resist? Many who knew that death was a certainty had but one wish: let it be over with, let it end.

THE *SONDERKOMMANDOS*

All the death camps were located on or near railroad lines. The Jews arrived first from Poland and Slovakia, then from Germany, the Low Countries, France, Greece, the Balkans, and finally Italy and Hungary. Death's-head SS units met the trains, augmented by detachments of Jewish prisoners, the *Sonderkommandos*. Many camps also employed auxiliary troops made up of volunteers from the local population. When the cars were unlocked, a putrid stench escaped from the interior. Depending on the length of the journey, the severity of the crowding, the degree of cold or heat endured, and the number of days spent without food and water, prisoners were in a state of partial or complete shock. They had no idea where they were, often the windowless cars had not allowed them to see the terrain through which they had passed. Rumors and fear, and sometimes darkness had added to the trauma of the journey.

Those who were able jumped from the train, the others were pushed out. New arrivals who could not control their hysteria were beaten or killed by the SS in order to preserve an orderly procession to the gas chambers. Every car had a number of dead propped up among the living. Members of the *Sonderkommandos* hauled them away and then hosed down the filthy wagons. They worked hard and fast, screaming at the prisoners, sometimes hitting them in order to impress the SS with their usefulness. They knew how easily they could be replaced and forced to join the line to the deadly showers. Many of the hundreds of men who had just arrived were willing to do this dreadful work in order to live a little longer. Death camps, as opposed to the slave-labor camps, required only small work forces. That meant that nearly all, and in many instances, every single person coming off a train was immediately dispatched to die. Women and children had virtually no chance of surviving death camp selections.

In some death camps, *Sonderkommandos* were replaced frequently, others allowed them to work for several months. The Nazis made use of these prisoners before and after the gassing. With German orderliness, barbers shaved the hair of the women, others cleaned and sorted the belongings of the dead, piling up eyeglasses, tons of hair, baby shoes, and crutches. The most fortunate inmates worked in the offices, preparing reams of paperwork and keeping accurate accounts for Himmler's comptrollers in Berlin. The most harrowing duty entailed the handling of corpses. First, the dead had to be removed from the gas chambers. These, too, had to be cleaned of human waste. Disposal of the corpses, however, could not take place until a final act of robbery and desecration was committed. Members of the *Sonderkommando* were required to pry open the jaws of the dead and remove any gold from their teeth, others searched for jewels that might have been hidden in any bodily orifices. Depending on the facilities of the camp, the corpses were turned into ashes in the ovens of the crematoria, or buried in mass graves, or soaked with gasoline and burned in pits.

Before the Holocaust ended, most of the camps had erected cremation facilities as a solution to the problem of disposing of so many hundreds of thousands of bodies. This method was also useful in destroying the evidence of the crimes. This issue became more important when the initial German victories in the Soviet Union turned into military reversals. During the last few months of the war, a frantic attempt was made to incinerate bodies of victims which earlier had been thrown into mass graves. But time ran out. It took six hours to burn a hundred paraffin-soaked bodies. There was never enough gasoline to speed the process. Advancing Russian troops encountered evidence of heaps of partially burnt corpses as they fought their way toward Germany.

AUSCHWITZ ORGANIZATION

Some 160 miles southwest of Warsaw, in a swampy marsh near the German border of upper Silesia, the Nazis established the largest and most complex of their many concentration camps. The demented world of Auschwitz gave full expression to the worst betrayal of humanity found in the annals of history. Because of its size, the completeness of its facilities, this camp merits a closer look. Its name is rightfully placed at the center of the genocide of European Jewry.

The concentration camp was established in 1940 as a place of incarceration for a large variety of people declared dangerous by the Nazis. The wrought iron legend over its main gate, *Arbeit macht frei* ("work gives freedom"), encapsulated the irony of a place where only death brought freedom. The barbed-wire fences were electrified, sentries with machine guns looked down upon the hapless masses day and night. From time to time, a few shots fired just for practice—killing a few prisoners—was woven into the daily routine. Two hundred dogs trained in tracking and killing were kenneled just behind the SS barracks. Auschwitz was the only camp where prisoners who survived their immediate destruction were branded with a number which was tattooed on the inside of their left forearm. Even before the addition of the slave-labor and death-camp facilities, the entire installation was designed to speed the "natural" reduction of prisoners. Hunger, cold, disease, terror tactics, and executions were the norm in this upside-down world. A full stomach, warmth, or kindness were rare exceptions.

The Nazis adopted techniques first established in the German concentration camps such as Dachau, Buchenwald, and Sachsenhausen. To keep SS personnel at a minimum, they used inmates to supervise other inmates. As the camp expanded, a hierarchy of prison guards developed. Positions such as Camp Elders, Block Elders, and Room Orderlies allowed the Nazis to run their concentration camps with relatively few guards. The term *Elders*, however, belies the type of inmates who held these posts. The SS preferred non-Jewish convicted criminals, mostly from Germany and some from the conquered countries for these appointments, but there were also a number of Jewish *Kapos* in the camps. Since it was their function to maintain rigid discipline, the most vicious among them were apt to be chosen.

A *Kapo* held the power of life and death over his prisoners even though the SS could execute him as indifferently as any other inmate. If a *Kapo* struck an inmate and marked his face by the blow, that man would not survive the next selection for the gas chambers. The *Kapo's* authority to make work assignments was equivalent to deciding if an already weak or ill man would or would not live another day. On the other hand, a choice job in the kitchen or in any enclosed structure extended some inmates' chance of survival. Obviously, many prisoners lived in constant fear and secret rage. Mastering these emotions, however, was vital in a place where three months was the average time a prisoner remained alive.

Although Jews made up the majority of men and women who died in Auschwitz, Gentiles, particularly Poles who had somehow run afoul of the Nazis, were numerous among the imprisoned. Also, there were Germans convicted of crimes ranging from robbery to antisocial behavior (such as unwillingness to work), Gypsies, whose fate was not decided for years, pacifists such as Seventh Day Adventists, and homosexuals. After June 1941, Soviet prisoners of war were kept there and hundreds of thousands were deliberately starved to death. In complete disregard of the international conventions regarding the treatment of POWs, they were also the first victims of the newly installed Zyklon-B gas experiments. Jews began to arrive en masse after the Wannsee Conference, first from nearby Poland and Silesia, later from the entire European continent. The great majority were immediately conveyed to the gassing facilities at Birkenau.

Auschwitz grew constantly between 1941 and 1944 until the map was dotted with names like Auschwitz I, (the main camp); Auschwitz II, (the Birkenau killing factory); Auschwitz III (Monowitz, the slave-labor camp for Buna, the IG Farben oil and rubber plants). Many other factories, including Siemens-Schuckert and Krupp, clustered nearby. Few Jewish arrivals, about 10 percent of the men, considerably fewer women, and none of the children and older generation were permitted to live and work. The imprisoned non-Jews fared better and comprised the majority of the slave workers until 1944 when the Hungarian Jews filled their thinning ranks. The pull between the Germans who wanted to use Jewish labor in war-related industries and the push from the Nazi fanatics who were bent on total annihilation was never quite resolved. The number of survivors, estimated at a maximum of a half million, compared to the six million who died, justified the Nazis' claim of victory in their war against the Jewish people.

CHEAPER THAN SLAVES

The industrial complex at Auschwitz encompassed several square miles. The IG Farben cartel, Germany's largest industrial enterprise, had established an extensive compound which included the Buna Werke for the manufacture of synthetic rubber, and a

Inmates in their barracks at the Buchenwald concentration camp. (Courtesy Bettmann.)

coal-based oil refinery. To save the workmen some strength, they were no longer marched the several miles from the main camp, but were housed and fed in barracks near the factories. In fact, they were leased chattel, replaced easily when worn out, for whom the SS received payment. Only toward the end of the war, when the need for workers became acute and the SS Economic and Administrative Department under Oswald Pohl was given authority over the inmates, did conditions improve slightly.

The workday usually started at three or four in the morning and lasted until late evening. Aside from laboring in the factories, quarries, and various road construction projects surrounding the camp, a number of Jews were employed in processing the products of death. Aside from the earlier mentioned operations of the *Sonderkommandos*, work details were assigned to the huge storage structures called "Canada" (a place of riches). Here prisoners counted, cleaned, sorted, and readied for shipment to Germany the enormous quantities of goods left behind by the murdered Jews. Depending on their former wealth, the dead were now robbed of everything from hair ribbons to diamonds sown into hems. Inmate accountants recorded every item, for as the Germans so often said: "*Ordnung muss sein!*" (There must be order). Members of the SS took personal advantage of the pool of talent at their disposal. Jewish tailors fashioned suits, coats, and uniforms for the SS and their families; former cobblers made them shoes and fine boots, jewelers created lovely pieces from the abundant amount of gold and precious stones. For most of the period of Auschwitz's existence, Rudolf Hoess was its commander. Whenever he wanted to impress visiting dignitaries, or amuse himself and his staff, he could count on the availability of talented musicians and actors to brighten their dreary life in the Polish wasteland.

HUNGER

The inmates of Auschwitz had less value than slaves. They cost nothing, the *Judenraete* had paid the price of their transportation to the camp. They were doomed at any rate and could be replaced at will. Intentionally, as well as to save food needed by Germans, inmates received starvation rations. Hunger, the sort one cannot even imagine, gnawed at the men and women relentlessly. While there was no general formula for survival in Auschwitz, and while every individual had to find his and her own strength to get through another day, the one common memory is hunger. Enduring terror, dehumanization, deprivation of the simplest human sanitary needs, and the fear for missing loved ones, each prisoner dealt with such suffering in ways unique to his and her personality. But hunger was the universal dimension, the single most remembered agony.

A thin soup with a few grams of black bread made of some substitute for grain was the main meal at midday. Mornings and evenings, a liquid called coffee and another piece of bread was doled out. Naturally, a forbidden trade developed. Prisoners who had the energy and will bought and sold any item that could eventually result in extra food. That required access to "Canada" where everything could be obtained, or to the machine shops or any place at all where theft might go unnoticed. A homemade tin cup for a cigarette, a cigarette for a vest, a vest for a piece of chocolate, a piece of chocolate for an apple. . . .

These were the "organizers"; they risked punishment, even death with their smuggling. They became experts, bartering item for item, but at the end of the chain was something edible. The "organizers" were akin to the *Prominenten*, the men and their female counterparts who by virtue of their luck and pluck maintained the outward aspects of their humanity. Often they bore low numbers on their arms, indicative of their early arrival and amazingly long survival in the camp. The men shaved, using the precious hot liquid at breakfast and dull knives, the women exchanged a meal for a comb or a toothbrush. They washed their clothes and put them on wet, even in winter. Sooner or later, the SS noticed them and considered them reliable. Sometimes they were rewarded with positions of some authority, or were permitted to work indoors, or given a Red Cross package. Such gifts were life-giving. Unlike the *Kapos*, the *Prominenten* were generally respected and often helpful to others. They set an example of how to remain civilized in a savage and brutal environment.

Not only the death camps in Poland, but all concentration camps were intended to reduce the number of inmates by "natural" means. There was, of course, nothing natural about five-hundred-calorie-a-day diets, lack of proper clothing, long hours of exhausting labor, beatings, or overcrowded barracks where two or three slept in the space for one. There was nothing natural about the institutionalized dehumanization designed to break the spirit. The SS knew that the will to survive was essential to survival and their dehumanization techniques were part and parcel of the genocide process. Don't let a prisoner wash, don't let him go to the latrine, curse him, never let him look at you, make him watch the hangings and shootings of his fellow prisoners, and soon his broken spirit will pull his body into the grave. In the language of the *Lager* (shortened from *Konzentrationslager*), the prisoners who had reached the end of their strength were called "Musselmen." It was easy to recognize them with their empty stare, their robot-like movements. They cowered, unseeing, unspeaking. They no longer washed nor picked the lice from their bodies. Waiting for death without impatience, without any visible emotion, they were sure to disappear at the next selection.

THE HUNGARIAN TRAGEDY

Hungary had been a more or less reluctant ally of the Nazi regime in order to fulfill its own goals of aggrandizement. With Hitler's approval Hungary had expanded its territory at the expense of Slovakia, Romania, and Yugoslavia. Although Hungarian troops were active on the Russian front, Germany found this ally lacking in commitment to the war. The Hungarian government under the Regent Nicholas Horthy had also resisted Nazi pressure to deliver its approximately 800,000 Jews into German captivity. Thus, this ancient and renowned Jewish community believed it had weathered the Holocaust; the Germans were losing the war and the Nazi nightmare would soon be over.

The situation, however, changed rapidly and tragically in 1944. Internal turmoil instigated by the extreme right weakened the Horthy government. The dilemma

The crematoria at Buchenwald. The remains in the oven are of women. (Courtesy AP/Wide World Photos.)

worsened when Hitler suspected that Horthy planned to negotiate a separate peace with the advancing Soviet Union. By kidnapping Horthy's son, the regent was forced to cede power to the pro-Nazi Arrow Cross fascists who took their orders from Berlin. For all intents and purposes Hungary was an occupied nation. The Jews had lost their protection.

Beginning in March of 1944, just eleven months before Budapest was captured by the Russian army, the Jews faced the terror of Eichmann. Using his well-established method, he began to set up ghettos, create *Judenraete,* and appoint SS personnel to confiscate properties "abandoned" by the Jews. Eichmann had long hoped to get his hands on this largest remnant of European Jewry and was well prepared for his task. With the eager aid of Arrow Cross police, the roundups and deportations began almost at once. The first thousands of victims came from the provinces at the periphery of the nation and the intent was to deport the Jews of Budapest as soon as these regions were *Judenrein.*

Without a possible shred of doubt, the Germans had lost the war. But the killing of Jews continued without letup. This belated attack did not go unnoticed by the international community. The American and British governments and the Pope raised their voices in protest. There was also the threat of punishment for Nazi crimes against civilians. But these efforts merely generated an interruption, not a cessation of the annihilation process. Hungarian Jews were sent to Auschwitz until the approach of Soviet armies closed it down. The confusion of the final battles between the Allies and Germany made it impossible to get the trains the SS so urgently demanded. Eichmann then organized treks to march north across Austria. This took place in the winter of 1944–1945 and the losses were enormous. Mauthausen concentration camp was made an interim destination, but by the end of the war Hungarian survivors were found in many German camps. With the Russians at the very gates of Budapest, Eichmann's zealousness for killing Jews never abated. Gas chambers, starvation, freezing, and illness killed thousands of Hungarian Jews every day. Their death toll, so close to the fall of the Third Reich, was a staggering 500,000. Only in the besieged city of Budapest did some 160,000 Jews survive.

SURVIVING IN A CONCENTRATION CAMP

Not the survivors, nor the psychiatrists, and certainly not the historians can unravel the secret of surviving in Auschwitz and its counterparts. The initial decisions at the railroad siding were based on a series of accidents. Were any workers needed from this shipment? Did the woman carry a child? Was she pregnant? Did Dr. Mengele or his fellow doctors not like a face, a body? Did the commander need a violinist for the camp orchestra? or an electrician? Did the prisoner look older or younger than approximately forty years? Such were the reasons for the arm or the riding crop to point to the right or the fatal left. There simply was no rational explanation why some lived beyond their first day.

But what of the inmates who lived to tell of the underworld of places like Auschwitz? Their memories and memoirs fill us with awe. Terrorized, emaciated, exhausted drudges, they endured. SS records indicated that they expected their slaves to work about three months. After that, they succumbed or became useless and were gassed. And yet some of the inmates, men and women who never cooperated with the murderers, who never did anything to betray their decency, survived; some for the astounding period of five years.

Why? How? Victor Frankl, himself a prisoner and a psychiatrist, believed that survival was connected to the successful search for a meaning to one's suffering. Physical strength, status of health, erstwhile occupation, all that meant nothing. If a prisoner could find a rationale for his agony, he might hold out against all odds. If he could discover a reason for enduring his suffering, then his mind and body might resist the welcome relief of death. It did not matter what inspired his resistance as long as it filled him with a passion to live. Perhaps he or she wanted to see the day of Germany's defeat, or take revenge against a tormentor, or bear witness to what happened here, or search for members of his family who might have escaped, or, because just one more time, he wanted to eat enough to feel full. The voices of many survivors point toward the need to live to fulfill some obligation: "I had to take care of my sister"; "I knew God had a purpose for me"; "If we all died, who would believe this ever happened?"

Recent studies indicated that women imprisoned in concentration camps had a better survival rate then men. Reared in the tradition of nurturers, women created artificial families in their bunkers. Small groups, perhaps four or five girls who may have come from the same town, or spoke the same dialect, or arrived on the train together, bonded with one another. They shared what little they had, tried to protect each other, and they talked, always, they talked. Often, an older woman would take on the role of mother; she comforted her girls, advised them, assured them that their menstrual periods would return once they ate properly, and yes, they would have husbands and children someday. Because they were always hungry, food was a prime topic of conversation. How carefully they described each detail in the preparation of a traditional Passover meal. Sometimes, they sang together, even laughed. The Orthodox remembered the Jewish holidays and tried to recall the appropriate prayers. And, of course, they often wept, but not alone. Custom and social conventions expected men to suffer in silence and without complaint. It was not manly to cry or seek help from a comrade. Thus, most of the men had to cope with isolation within the camp in addition to the abandonment by the world outside the barbed wire. Many women, on the other hand, found comfort in sharing their tears and their humanity in the most inhuman places on earth.

THE DOCTORS

In Auschwitz medical doctors did not practice medicine. They provided no treatment to the sick or injured, not even an aspirin for pain and fever. The only surgery performed was in connection with experiments so diabolical, that they dishonored the name of science. In all the slave-labor and concentration camps, doctors routinely condemned the men and women to death because they judged who was fit or unfit to work; in the death camps they were essentially participants in the murder of millions.

The plunge from healer to killer originated in Nazi ideology gone berserk. The doctrine of the Aryan super-German was given undeserved credibility by means of distortions called racial science. Biologists and medical doctors established a variety of criteria for the pure Nordic type: skin tones, bone structure, eye color, height, weight, and so on. A distortion of Darwin's theories led to the "purification" of Germany by eliminating its mentally and physically flawed population. In the Thousand Year Reich, only those declared fit according to government standards had the right to live. Nazi doctors determined who could live and who must die. They called this program euthanasia, but it was murder. In Hitler and Himmler's world, the annihilation of an entire biologically dangerous people, the Jews, was the next logical step. Medical personnel accepted their genocidal assignments and became willing instruments in the deaths of millions.

Doctors functioned in three areas related to the Holocaust. They dictated life or death for prisoners at the railroad sites and at the *Appells* ("roll calls," or "inspections"); they conducted medical experiments which were certain to kill their subjects; and they injected fatal phenol into the hearts of inmates in their hospitals.

The infamous Dr. Mengele enjoyed his role at the railroad siding. Dubbed "the Angel of Death," he volunteered to meet nearly all the trains. A handsome man, immaculate in his SS uniform, he pointed with his riding crop to the right or to the left; one line for the gas chambers, the other to labor barracks. Surviving the initial selection, however, guaranteed nothing; selections for death occurred continuously. Every morning, the prisoners stood at attention to be counted and recounted during the dreaded *Appell*. Black-clad SS doctors moved up and down the rows of men or women to supply fodder for the gas chambers. The weak, the ill, the bruised, the men or women who simply did not please the SS men, were ordered to join the lines leading to the deadly showers.

The medical experiments conducted at Auschwitz and several other camps were indescribably dreadful. The proclaimed aim was scientific research, the reality was pure horror. Ordinary language cannot portray the butchery and criminality of this group of German doctors nor can a rational mind comprehend them. The doctors practiced various types of male and female sterilization techniques; they competed to see how many hundreds of sterilization procedures a single doctor could perform in a day. They sought the limits of endurance and tested to what degree prisoners could endure high and low temperatures, deprivation of oxygen; the length of time required for artificially introduced infections to become fatal, and how soon a new mother's bound-up breasts would cause deadly fever. The doctors wanted to know how much and what type of torture would break a man and finally destroy him.

Dr. Mengele's experiments with twins were expected to yield information that would increase the number of multiple births for Aryan women. Few adults or children survived his manipulations of their bodies. He was also fascinated with dwarfs and hunchbacks and kept them in the hospital facilities until his experiments killed them. The Nazi racial and eugenic medical establishment in Berlin approved and welcomed the findings of camp doctors. After all, no other place on earth afforded such unlimited access to experimentation on people whose screams they did not hear.

Camp hospital facilities doubled as medical killing centers. Some Jewish and non-German doctors were permitted to assist the Nazis in the camps. Their efforts to do some healing, to help some patients should be noted, but overall they could not be effective.

When it was doubtful that a prisoner could return to work, when the hospital wards were too crowded, the phenol injections were ordered. Patients had no idea what it meant when a doctor or an orderly, needle in hand, told them to cross their arms over their eyes. Only when inmates were sure that their illness or exhaustion made them certain targets for the next selection did they venture into the hospital. There was always a chance they could survive if unnoticed, if allowed a few days rest and slightly better food. It was a risk taken only as a last resort.

CAMPS IN CENTRAL EUROPE

The death camps were located in Poland but the concentration camp system spread across central Europe from the borders of France and Holland into Austria and Czechoslovakia. Some of the sites confined permanent prisoners, others were used as stopovers for the eastward journey. Moving inmates from one camp to another was a common practice, some survivors could recall more than a dozen in their personal history. The map of Germany was dotted with *Lagers*, some huge, others holding a few hundred slave laborers for a nearby factory. The prison population always included Jews, but they were not necessarily in the majority. Only after the advance of the Soviet armies impelled the Nazis to march the inmates westward were the German camps deluged with the pathetic, dying remnant from Poland.

During the early years of the Third Reich, Dachau, Buchenwald, and Sachsenhausen were the destinations of political dissenters, trade union leaders, and members of religious organizations who opposed the Nazis. Most were held without trials and served sentences of indeterminate length. When the harshness of German rule over their foreign conquests created opposition, the Gestapo seized hundreds of thousands of accused resistance fighters. It was never clear why the Nazis shot some suspects immediately, while others were shipped to death camps and still others to concentration camps. The arrests of underground resisters required expansion of the number and size of *Lagers*. When the Nazis began to force foreign workers and prisoners of war into the German defense industry, many slave-labor camps—often indistinguishable from concentration camps—were constructed. In addition, there was an increase of German citizens who ran afoul of the secret police for such crimes as grumbling against the war and the nebulous offense of defeatism. Although only estimates are available, the total of prisoners numbered not in the hundreds of thousands, but in the millions. Nor will it ever be known how many died due to starvation, disease, despair, beatings, or shootings.

TERESIENSTADT AND RAVENSBRUCK

Every concentration camp had unique features due to its geography, its administration, its inmates and/or work requirements. Two of the *Lagers* were extraordinary and merit particular attention.

Teresienstadt (Terezin), located in the Bohemian section of Czechoslovakia, was established by Heydrich in 1941. It was organized to resemble a ghetto, with a council of elders and a chairman running the internal affairs of the Jewish community. Originally a military fortress, the site had stables, workshops, and a street of ramshackle houses. Teresienstadt was reputed to be the most humane camp in the constellation of German *Lagers*. Well-connected elderly German Jews, decorated Jewish war veterans, prominent scholars, and Jews married to Aryans paid with their life's savings for the "opportunity" to go there. The Germans had promised that some privileged few could live out their pleasant retirement years in lovely Bohemia. Once the Jews arrived and realized they had been deceived, they were unable to escape their prison/ghetto. The inmates who were permitted to remain in Teresienstadt had a fair chance of survival, but their numbers were small. It has been suggested that the Nazis considered some of these "residents" worth more alive than dead, to be used as possible pawns in exchange for German prisoners or for purposes of blackmail.

Teresienstadt had two faces. One looked like an impoverished but viable Jewish community of old people who sustained themselves by their own work in several cottage industries and through gifts from the Red Cross. Families lived together, the food was poor, but lectures and music nourished the soul. These inmates were not as cut off from the rest of the outside world as other camp prisoners. Here the SS dealt with the council rather than with individuals. Almost the entire group of Danish Jews who had not taken part in the great escape from Denmark (see Chapter 10) survived here due to the scrupulous vigilance of the Danish government. When the Nazis were pressured by the International Red Cross to permit an inspection of the camp, they grudgingly gave permission. The inspectors were treated to an elaborate charade. After an intensive cleanup, for one day, flowers appeared on the sidewalks, well-dressed people sipped tea in the afternoon, and children played around the well-stocked pushcarts of street vendors. The Red Cross representatives saw nothing of the suffering of the hidden camp and wrote a favorable report on their findings.

Teresienstadt, however, was a stopover for thousands of Jews on their way to Auschwitz and other camps. While waiting for transport east, they lived in over-crowded misery for weeks or months. There was no fuel to heat their stone-walled rooms, too little food, and the ever-present fear of where the next train would take them. The former Chief Rabbi of Germany, Leo Baeck, was among the prominent Jews kept in Teresienstadt. He knew what "resettlement" meant and resolved not to reveal the truth. One can only guess what that decision must have cost him. Many Jews from Prague, Berlin, and Vienna were routed through Teresienstadt to Auschwitz as well as the dreaded stone quarries at Mauthausen in Austria. Much of the work of organizing the transfers was handled by the Jewish council which hoped to save a remnant by coop-erating with the Nazis.

Ravensbruck, established in 1939, was a camp for women only. Before the influx of Jewish women at the approach of the Soviet armies, the majority of inmates were not Jewish. Like so many other concentration camps, it was located in a swampy, unhealthy area. The variety of inmates enslaved there represented not only the racial fanaticism of the Nazi mentality, but their well-founded fear that the world they con-quered did not share their totalitarian ideals. The fact that these prisoners were women, some just girls, was given no consideration.

The internal camp management was largely in the hands of German women who were convicted criminals. But its population was international. Prisoners included female Russian soldiers, nurses, Red Cross workers from everywhere in Europe, and resistance fighters, especially from France and Poland. The latter were subjected to medical experiments involving the transplanting of human bones. Their suffering resonated in the bodies of all inmates who tried to alleviate their pain by words and deeds of solidarity. The main industry employing the prisoners was somewhat strange in a country under bombardment on three fronts and from the air: the remodeling of the furs expropriated from Nazi victims. If nothing else, the wives of Nazi leaders would wear lovely fur coats.

It is probable that 50,000 women perished in the camp. The number would have been higher but for a last-minute rescue of 14,000 women in April of 1945. Himmler finally agreed to the entreaties of the Swedish diplomat Count Folke Bernadotte to permit their release. Himmler was then entertaining the illusion that the Allies would allow him to represent Germany in peace negotiations, thus his gesture of goodwill. At this late moment of the war and of the Holocaust a single day often made the difference between life and death.

THE DEATH MARCHES

The encirclement of Germany was almost complete in the late winter of 1944 and early spring of 1945. The Soviet armies rolled across the Polish plains, the Western Allies moved up from Italy and crossed into Germany from France. The gassings were stopped during November, 1944 as frantic efforts were exerted to cover up history's greatest crime. Huge shipments of goods taken from the dead were hurriedly sent to Germany, gas chambers and crematoria were blown up, and bodies were disinterred from mass graves and burned. Mountains of accumulated paperwork were thrown into the flames, but time was running out. Some of the inmates were able to hide vital Nazi records before the evacuations virtually emptied the death camps.

During the last several months of the Thousand Year Reich, the remaining prisoners, many of whom were recent arrivals from Hungary, presented a problem for the SS. The country was engulfed in fighting, it was a time of complete confusion, yet most of the concentration camp guards obeyed their final orders to march their prisoners to camps in central Germany. The roads were choked with fleeing Germans, there was no food or shelter, the SS had no instructions as to how they were expected to reach their first stopover at the Silesian camp of Gross Rosen. A final tragedy was the inevitable result. The roads on which starved, freezing, barely alive survivors were hurried along were littered with the dead and dying. Many were left where they fell, others were shot by the SS. Just a few hours from liberation, from food and medical care, from life itself, the Holocaust claimed them.

Chapter 10

Resistance and Rescue

In the context of opposition to the Nazis, the term *resistance* requires some definition. Does the word refer only to organized combat or does it include individual actions? Is the use of weapons implied or can it be of a nonviolent nature? Is it appropriate, as has been suggested, that survival itself qualifies as a form of resistance, since the Nazis sought the death of every Jew? Did not the Righteous Gentiles who saved Jews from certain death take a stand against Hitler? What of the Germans, from both military and civilian circles, who challenged the regime on several occasions when they attempted to assassinate Hitler? Surely, the men and women who fought the Nazis as members of partisan organizations were resistance soldiers. How should one characterize the workers in ghettos and in slave-labor camps who sabotaged the economic enterprises of the Nazis by producing flawed goods? Jewish writers risked their lives to publish forbidden newspapers; teachers defied the Gestapo when they secretly instructed their students. Illegal smuggling of food prevented the total collapse of ghetto life and was frequently carried out by children. The historian Emanuel Ringelblum and others resisted by collecting and preserving information on the fate of the Jews. Art and music as well as poetry expressed a defiance of Nazi decrees. Clearly, resistance had varied forms, so it is necessary to set the limits of its meaning within this text.

The main thrust of this history concerns the annihilation of the Jews. It is therefore proper to narrow the theme to actual clashes between Jews and their German oppressors. Although the annals of survivors are replete with extraordinary acts of heroism, such individual achievements did not change the course of the Nazis' war against the Jewish people. The dimensions of industrial sabotage are difficult to evaluate. German industrialists complained frequently about the low productivity of their forced laborers, but it is not possible to know if the cause was physical and emotional exhaustion or subversive action. It is easier to evaluate the impact on German aims due to organized Jewish resistance. Where men and women fought as members of guerrilla units, they inflicted measurable damage on German operations. The ability to procure or devise weapons was essential; without arms, without a hiding place and food supply, opposition was suicidal. When Jews died in hopeless actions which did no harm to the enemy, they actually advanced the Nazi goal of genocide. Later generations may admire the courage required to engage in self-destructive exploits because it counters the painful accusation that Jews went like sheep to their slaughter. But it is not the historian's duty to provide either consolation or provocation. The facts must do, and it is a fact that some Jews resisted, while the great majority did not. The actual number of resisters is not available because where religion did not matter, many thousands of Jews fought as Yugoslavs, Frenchmen, or Russians rather than in separate Jewish battalions.

SHEEP OR WOLVES?

Some historical events speak so clearly that they need no interpretation, others evolve into controversial expositions. The problem of Jewish militancy belongs to the latter category. Some scholars, notably Raoul Hilberg and Hannah Arendt, stated that the Jews were almost totally passive and that the *Judenraete* rendered valuable aid to the Nazis. The death toll, in their view, would have been smaller without the cooperation of the victims. Opposing this concept are, among others, Yehuda Bauer and Schmuel Krakowski. Their research led them to the conclusion that when and where it was possible, Jews fought back.

It is undeniable that six million were killed and that the lines leading to the gas chambers moved quietly. Most slave workers followed instructions in the mistaken hope that work would give them life. Jewish elders nearly always urged compliance for fear of retaliation. In the Vilna ghetto, for example, after a group of Jewish resisters escaped and joined partisans in the forest, their families were killed by the Germans. The head of the *Judenrat*, Jacob Gens, was not alone when he called the fighters traitors who endangered all the Jews.

Compliance, however, was not the complete picture. There is evidence of Jewish militancy. Revolts were carried out in several Polish ghettos and death camps. Jews, when permitted to join, participated in the quasi-military exploits of partisans. A viable Jewish resistance developed although it was constrained by a variety of obstacles. Jews rarely owned weapons and found it nearly impossible to acquire any. In order to fight the Germans from hidden enclaves, a supportive native population was essential. Polish Jewry, which suffered the greatest losses, could not count on much help from Christians. The Gestapo held all Jews collectively responsible for defiance by a single man or woman. This left the possible resister with a terrible choice: was it morally right to endanger the many in order to kill a few Germans? Most Jews could not believe that regardless of their resistance or compliance, the Nazis intended to kill them all.

It is valid to conclude that most Jews were acquiescent; but it should also be acknowledged that some Jews fought against the Nazis. As has been indicated earlier, Jewish leadership was unable to accept the unprecedented reality of total Jewish destruction. Time-honored survival methods of riding out the storm of anti-Semitic violence, of saving the remnant and rebuilding did not work, as entire communities were obliterated. Obedience to the SS masters, even usefulness to their war economy, did not bring about the expected remission of the killing process. It must be remembered that the reports of an ongoing genocide were received with skepticism everywhere. The reputation of Germans as civilized and educated Europeans concealed the truth for months, even years.

EVASION

Although it would be conjecture to estimate how many Jews might have been saved if resistance by flight had been more widespread, it is not unreasonable to presume that the number would have been considerable. If rabbis and community leaders had urged the Jews of Poland to flee for their lives, hide in woods, make their way south and east, the survival rate would have been greater. We know this by comparing the lives saved among the Jews who fled to Russia versus those killed who stayed behind. Another case in point is Holland. The Dutch Jews who ignored the call of their elders to accommodate German demands and assemble in designated areas for "resettlement" had a much better survival rate than those who did not hide. Evasion of roundups, passing as Gentiles, disappearing or joining underground fighting units were better choices than obedience to the Germans and the Jewish councils. The likelihood that Jews would outlive the years of German occupation was largely dependent on the attitude of native populations. In countries like Denmark where anti-Semitism was moderate or absent, where cooperation with the Gestapo was rare, where aid was willingly given, Jews had a realistic chance for survival. In the Ukraine, on the other hand, hunting escaped Jews for extortion, or betrayal to the Germans was an acknowledged danger to fugitives.

No other people encountered greater obstacles in organizing resistance during the years of Nazi terror than the Jews. All underground movements shared certain problems: There were informers in their ranks; obtaining weapons was difficult and dangerous; they lacked funds; they needed radios and vehicles to receive and pass information; false identity papers and ration books required secret printing presses; and rivalry between partisan groups was not uncommon. But only Jews lived under an automatic death sentence. Without engaging in any suspicious activity, without breaking any law, Jews were guilty of capital crimes simply by being alive.

THE WARSAW GHETTO

Every year, in the middle of April, Jews solemnize the anniversary of the Holocaust through religious and secular gatherings on a memorial day called Yom Hashoah. The April date was selected because it commemorates the beginning of the most extensive Jewish revolt, the Warsaw ghetto uprising. Although it was not the only such rebellion, the final weeks of the largest Polish ghetto mark a milestone in the history of Jewish resistance. Not until Christian Poles rose up in Warsaw in 1944 did any other European city fight the Nazis, nor did the millions of brutally treated Soviet prisoners of war rise up against their captors until the war was nearly over.

The brick wall enclosing the Warsaw ghetto had been erected during the summer of 1940. Its completion resulted in a drastic increase in the death toll by starvation until the numbers climbed to daily losses of three hundred to four hundred people. But such numbers were deemed insufficient once the Nazis had decided that the "Final Solution of the Jewish question" was total destruction. On July, 22, 1942, deportations to the death camp of Treblinka began and within two months the ghetto population was reduced by a staggering 300,000. The *Judenrat* was compelled to deliver 6,000 victims per day and it was no longer possible to deny the truth: Deportation was equivalent to death. At this point, with 120,000 Jews remaining, the authority of the council of elders was no longer accepted. Their acquiescence to German demands had proven to be a dismal failure. The emerging leaders were of an entirely different breed. They were mostly young and committed to resistance, not by hiding, but by fighting.

Political organizations had continued to function as best they could even in the ghetto. From the ranks of several such groups, mainly Zionists and Socialists, arose the planners and executors of the revolt. Six days after the expulsions to Treblinka began, political differences were set aside in order to present a united front to the community and to the Germans. The members of the newly created ZOB (Zydowska Organizacja Bojowa, Jewish Combat Organization), headed by Mordekhai Anielewicz, had no illusions. They knew that their choices were not between life and death but between death in combat or death in Treblinka. Grief for the many loved ones already lost was transformed into passion for revenge, and impotence became raw courage. Their combined strength approximated seven hundred to one thousand men and women, and for the most part they had the cooperation and support of the remaining ghetto population.

Anielewicz combined the attributes of the idealist with the activism of a realist. He came from a working-class family and was attracted to Zionism as a youth. In the ghetto, he published an underground newspaper, *Against the Stream,* wherein he called for Jewish armed resistance. Other young men and women were drawn to him and to his commitment to make a stand. During the last months of the Warsaw ghetto's existence, he was not only its military commander, but its virtual administrative head as well.

The first order of business was the procurement of arms. In this effort the ZOB was never very successful. Contact with the Polish Home Army, the major Polish underground militia, resulted in a few guns and some explosives. The Poles were at first not convinced that the ghetto fighters would actually fire these precious few weapons against the Germans. But on January 18, 1943, it became clear that the Jews were willing to fight. On that day, as a large group of deportees was escorted out of the ghetto, Mordekhai Anielewicz and a small contingent attacked the Nazis. During this skirmish, stunned Germans experienced losses at the hands of ghetto Jews for the first time. At the same time, a second ZOB cadre assaulted Nazis in a building and the myth of Jewish cowardice was broken. The Polish partisans were impressed and expanded the ghetto's allotment of arms. By April, when the major battles took place, the ZOB arsenal included many revolvers, grenades, homemade bombs, and one machine gun. Although pitifully inadequate, by means of resourceful deployment the little army snatched from the Germans their ability to do as they pleased within the ghetto. In the ensuing battle, an estimated fifty Germans were killed, but the ghetto fighters too had heavy losses. Nevertheless, the attack bolstered the spirit of the ZOB and increased the confidence of the ghetto population.

THE REVOLT

The ZOB could not stand up against the Germans in open battles where the enemy's superior weapons would annihilate them. It was clear that effective military action was contingent upon the Jews' ability to attack from entrenched positions, to retreat quickly, regroup, and fight from yet another bunker. With marvelous ingenuity, the ghetto army supervised and participated in the building of connecting strongholds and escape routes. At various points, they cached reserves of food, water, and ammunition. Some of the bunkers had electric current and radios. Tunnels were dug which bridged cellars, rooftops, attics, apartments, and sewage pipes until they formed a maze of hundreds of concealed hide-outs and combat positions. Their design always assumed that the fighters must not become targets in the streets but must be able to move rapidly and secretly from one command post to another.

While this feverish activity was taking place, the Nazis knew that many Jews were hiding and attempted to bring them out with lures and lies: there would be no further expulsions from the city; food, employment, and amnesty awaited those Jews willing to come forward because German employers needed workers in their factories. The ZOB presses countered these promises with the truth and urged the people to stand firm and evade the Germans by any means. When the deportation *Aktions* were halted shortly after the first skirmish, the ghetto dwellers mistakenly believed that ZOB counterattacks were responsible. It was then not known that the delay was due to the preparation of different tactics by the enemy.

The Germans realized that the destruction of the Jews in the Warsaw ghetto would require more than orders to the now-impotent *Judenrat*. On the first day of Passover, April 19, 1943, they were ready to attack. A new commander, SS Major-General Juergen Stroop was assigned to the task. Estimates on the number of his troops, which included SS men augmented by police as well as Polish and Baltic auxiliaries, range from two to five thousand. They expected to clear out the Jews in three days. Before dawn, they surrounded the ghetto to prevent escapes, and moved through the gates with an arsenal of hand-held weapons, armored vehicles, and tanks.

The ghetto army responded from its hiding places with a barrage of bullets, grenades, Molotov cocktails, and cross-fire from opposing attics. Because the ZOB fighters rushed from place to place, the Germans thought that the fighters were more numerous than they actually were. Again and again the Nazis withdrew to reorganize their assault. On the third day, they adopted a different tactic. German planes were called in to set fire to buildings, and listening devices were employed in order to locate the secret bunkers. Continued effective resistance had convinced Stroop that his best option was to raze the entire ghetto, burn it to the ground.

At least fifty thousand Jews were still in hiding, Jews that Himmler wanted in Treblinka. They refused to follow German orders even when SS guns attacked their hiding places. Only flame throwers or gas bombardments caused some of the trapped Jews to run into the open. They were killed on the spot or transported to death or concentration camps. German incendiary weapons created a veritable holocaust, a sea of flames. Stroop, with the approval of his superiors, burnt the ghetto, house by house, block by block. Six-hundred and thirty-one bunkers were destroyed. The beautiful main synagogue did not incinerate and was dynamited.

The number of defensive positions was shrinking. Eighteen days later, on May 7, the Nazis found the insurgents' headquarters on Mila Street. When all means of resistance were exhausted, the remaining fighters committed suicide or killed each other rather than fall into German hands. Among the dead was Mordekhai Anielewicz. He was twenty-four years old. Seventy-five of the surviving fighters escaped through the sewers to continue their resistance with partisans in the forest. Only a handful lived to see the end of the war. The ghetto lay in rubble. Nearly all its inhabitants were dead. On May 10, Stroop informed his superiors that the battle was over.

RESULTS AND MEANING

The rebellion ended and the Nazis claimed victory. Defeat of the Germans, however, had never been a realistic prospect for the ghetto fighters. When their aim was compared to their achievement, one cannot speak of defeat. They had hoped to prove to themselves and to the world that not all Jews were passive victims. That they did. Furthermore, the revolt inspired other terrorized subjects of the Nazis to resist. If a few hundred Jews could hold off the mighty Germans for nearly a month, other miracles were deemed possible. Prisoners in other ghettos, concentration and death camps, partisans in the forests, and underground fighters throughout the Allied world had a model to emulate. The stirring declarations of the rebels had been transmitted to the Polish government in exile in London, and were broadcast to the world. In several Polish cities, including Bialystok, young Jews refused to obey SS orders.

The estimates of German casualties in Warsaw range widely. Stroop admitted to only sixteen dead and eighty-five wounded; the Polish Home Army assessed that five hundred Germans were killed. No matter what the true number of casualties were, the symbolic importance of the ghetto revolt was never in question.

The Warsaw uprising was fought by Jews only. Appeals by the ZOB for assistance from the Polish partisan army were refused. While the ghetto fought without hope of victory, the Poles wanted to delay their armed struggle until there was a chance for victory. In the fall of 1944, as the Red Army advanced into Poland, and with Soviet encouragement, the Polish underground thought their time had come. It was a tragic irony of fate that the Home Army was left to fight and die alone, without Russian assistance. The Germans crushed the Warsaw uprising of Gentile Poles and some two hundred thousand members of Polish partisan battalions died in battle. Only after the Nazis had smashed the Polish insurgents did the Red Army march toward Warsaw. The establishment of a pro-Soviet regime in Poland was facilitated by the losses of the resistance army.

CAMP REVOLTS: AN OVERVIEW

Conditions in the ghettos made armed resistance extremely difficult, but organizing a revolt in the camps seemed totally impossible. Only in the death camps and only near the end of the war did prisoners in Treblinka, Sobibor, and Auschwitz-Birkenau attempt to resist their killers. The plotters hoped that an uprising would result in a break-out and some of the prisoners might escape. Even that limited goal was far-fetched. An abbreviated account of their overwhelming obstacles included the following:

1. The isolation of prisoners in death camps was nearly total. Not only was there no contact with the outside world, but within the camps various work battalions were prevented from communicating with one another. Organizing and planning any coordinated resistance required ingenious and dangerous circumvention of Nazi orders.
2. The prisoners lived under inhumane and debilitating conditions. Everything they had valued in their former lives was gone and the temptation to let go and end their suffering was inescapable. Suicides were common. Arriving prisoners required some time to orient themselves to the camp before it was possible to organize a circle of co-conspirators. However, the longer an inmate was in the camp, the greater the loss of his physical and mental stamina.
3. The opportunity to buy weapons was almost nil. Slave laborers who worked with the belongings of murdered Jews managed to hoard some valuables, but to exchange jewels for arms was deadly business. Some members of the Ukrain-ian and other auxiliary troops were willing to risk their own lives for the right pay-ment, but such arrangements were infrequent. Most of the arms used by the camp rebels were stolen from German armories or were made from parts filched from workshops. The number of weapons accumulated was pitifully small; clubs and shovels had to do for most of the fighters.
4. The prevailing anti-Semitic attitude among Polish people required that the ini-tial miracle of a successful breakout would have to be doubled, and redoubled. Survival on the other side of the barbed wire was unlikely for inmates in prison garb trying to blend into unfamiliar surroundings, amid people who generally dis-liked Jews and feared German retribution. The Nazis reacted with fierceness to any act of Jewish resistance and they were very successful in hunting down the escapees one by one.

Revolts in three of the death camps confirmed the desperation underlying this unequal struggle. As symbolic actions, these efforts merit respect, as battles to save Jew-ish lives they failed. The resistance group at Treblinka revolted in August 1943, two months before the official closing of the camp. There were 700 Jews working in the facility, mainly sorting the goods of dead victims or disposing of corpses. Upon a given signal, a group of conspirators rushed to recover their few hidden guns and grenades. They forced an entry into the SS arsenal. Two hundred men helped themselves to arms, the others used whatever would serve as a weapon. The crematoria was torched as well as several other buildings. The Germans responded with expected rage and called in supporting troops. Most of the rebels were killed within the compound. Between 150 and 200 men made their escape, but only 12 survived the intensive German manhunt. At the end of the rout, the gas chambers were still functional and their operation was resumed.

The Sobibor uprising broke out in October of 1943. This death factory, located near the Bug River, was enclosed by three circles of barbed wire, a minefield, and a ditch. An adjoining dense forest improved chances for a successful escape. The leader of the resistance was a Jewish Soviet prisoner of war whose military background contributed to the partial success of the breakout. In the workshops, Jews had been employed to make clothing and boots for the Nazis. On October 14, the tailors and shoemakers arranged staggered appointments for fittings for their "clients." When the SS men stepped into the workrooms, waiting rebels killed them. By the time the general attack began in the evening, nineteen officers, including the camp commander, were dead. The resulting confusion enabled some four hundred of the six hundred prisoners to escape. Of these, many died when they stepped on mines, some were killed in the manhunt organized by the Germans, others joined partisan groups in the woods. Only forty of the men survived to see the end of the war. But they had the satisfaction of knowing that as a result of their attack, the gas chambers at Sobibor were permanently closed down. Himmler ordered that the camp be leveled two days after the uprising.

At Auschwitz-Birkenau, an international resistance movement had been secretly organized. Although the members of the *Sonderkommando* who worked with the corpses in the death factories were kept apart from other inmates, a tenuous line of communication was established. Plans to stage a revolt involving both groups were developed but never completed. The men of the *Sonderkommando* knew their days were numbered when Eichmann's trains with Hungarian victims arrived less frequently. Unable to convince the underground leadership in the main camp to coordinate an uprising, the men working at the crematoria revolted on October 7, 1944.

The conspirators had no weapons. Over a period of months they had hoarded a small store of explosives which had been smuggled to them through the heroic efforts of several women prisoners who worked in an arms factory. The rebels killed several SS guards and blew up one of the four crematoria. About six hundred of them were able to break out through the barriers, but their freedom was short-lived. Several hundred SS troops went into immediate pursuit and it is believed that all the prisoners were killed. An investigation by the Gestapo revealed the involvement of Rosa Robota as the leader of the dynamite smugglers. Rosa was tortured but never betrayed the names of her friends. Nonetheless, she and three other girls were publicly hanged. These events took place when the war was drawing to its inevitable conclusion, when one might have expected the SS to be too preoccupied with the coverup of their crimes rather than the fate of a few hundred Jews. On January 18, when those inmates able to walk were marched westward, they were guarded by men still loyal to Himmler and Hitler.

WITH THE PARTISANS

The degree of harshness of Nazi rule differed widely from nation to nation. Nazi racial theories played a major role in their posture toward the conquered peoples, but military necessities and the need for food and oil also compromised the realization of

Himmler's Aryan fantasy. The treatment of Frenchmen, Danes, or Norwegians, for example, was quite dissimilar to the conduct of the conquerors toward the eastern Slavs. The great majority of all the subjugated people responded to the German presence with emotions ranging from dislike to hatred, and every nationality had its anti-Nazi heroes as well as its eager collaborators.

Between 1942 and 1943 secret anti-Nazi organizations began to develop in German-occupied nations. Romanticized in countless movies and novels, freedom fighters performed daring exploits despite hated Gestapo agents and their use of terror and torture. Actually, groups rather than individuals carried out the most successful missions. With the exception of Yugoslavia and sections of Russia, underground organizations were unable to engage the German army in battles and resorted to hit-run-hide guerrilla tactics. They became experts in sabotage, derailed trains, rescued imprisoned comrades, printed counterfeit identity papers, committed theft and robbery to finance their operations, and killed selected enemies. In the western occupied nations they often attempted and sometimes succeeded in saving Jews from arrest and shipment to the death camps. Whether urban cells or forest guerrillas, the object was the same: hasten the day of liberation by fighting the invader. In contrast with the uprisings in the ghettos and death camps, these resisters had reasonable expectations of surviving the war.

Many underground organizations were formed from the remnants of outlawed political parties; long-standing affiliations and old friendships promoted unity and trust. This was particularly true in the case of young Communists, Socialists, and Zionists. Excepting Tito's Yugoslav guerrilla forces, no other single national fighting organization emerged. In fact, rivalry and antipathy plagued the factions throughout their existence and often hampered their best efforts. Among the many causes for friction among Poles was the willingness or unwillingness of a brigade to accept Jews into their ranks. In the sparsely wooded area of central Poland, Jewish chances for admission and thus survival were minimal. Traditions of anti-Semitism were not shaken by the calamity which had befallen their Jewish countrymen.

When partisans had become effective fighters in 1943 and thereafter, the destruction of the Jews was almost completed. The leaders of some of the ghettos which faced liquidation urged their young people to escape into the countryside to join or create partisan units. The obligation to God to preserve a remnant that might someday rebuild Jewish life continued to motivate Jews, even as it tore families apart.

Escape from the ghetto was emotionally harrowing because the most fit had to abandon their helpless relatives. Nevertheless, the number of eastern Jews who fled was believed to reach tens of thousands. Their survival rate, however, was very poor. Many Polish, Ukrainian, and Baltic anti-Semites denounced them to the Germans or killed them; they froze and starved, singly and in small groups. Hope lay in acceptance by a partisan organization hidden in the dense forests of the Baltic states, eastern Poland, and the western Soviet Union. Jews eager to fight were generally admitted into Polish Home Army units only if they had weapons, that meant very few qualified. Brigades commanded by Russians and/or Polish Communists were more liberal in permitting Jews to join them. Considering the intensity of hatred that Jews harbored for Germans, the policy of refusing them an opportunity for revenge was self-defeating.

A number of family camps, a mixture of old and young, able-bodied and dependent Jews, were established in the woods. These groups were particularly vulnerable. Unless the local farmers gave or sold them food, they starved. When, in desperation, they tried to steal from the fields, they were hunted like animals. Family camps were a burden for the partisans. Food was the prime problem, but the inability to pick up and move to another location at a moment's notice restricted the vital mobility of guerrillas. The fact that several such groups were maintained in hiding throughout the war was a tribute to the endurance of its members as well as to the humanity of the Jewish and non-Jewish resistance fighters who provided for their needs.

Brigades which included complements of Jews were most numerous in eastern Poland and western Russia. In these regions some units were organized and commanded by Soviet soldiers who had been parachuted for this purpose. These officers (some were Jewish) enrolled all who were willing and able to fight. Several such squads accepted the obligation to safeguard family camps. In the forests near Vilna, a Lithuanian Jewish brigade operated; in White Russia and the vicinity of Minsk, Jewish guerrillas formed effective combat battalions. If the estimate that twenty thousand Jews survived in the eastern wilderness is correct, much of the credit must go to the Soviets.

In the western occupied nations, Jews had no difficulty in joining the resistance movements. In France and the Low Countries they played prominent roles among the underground soldiers. French Jewry, 1 percent of the population, was represented by 15 to 20 percent in the resistance. There was a Jewish Maquis, founded by Robert Ganmzon, who reputedly killed more than a thousand Nazis and committed many hundreds of acts of sabotage. Other distinctly Jewish battalions smuggled Jewish children into neutral safe havens. In the Balkans and in Greece, young Jewish men and women were active in their national liberation movements. Some two thousand Jews fought with Tito's army. In Italy, a Jewish unit was formed which later merged with other freedom fighters. It operated in Piedmont and in the Italian Alps. In Slovakia, Jews were among the original organizers of the resistance.

Clearly, history and the medals for courage awarded many Jewish fighters, often posthumously, contradict the presumption that during the Holocaust all Jews were passive. Where circumstances permitted, Jews fought with distinction. The military history of Israel could not have been written by a people unwilling or unable to defend itself.

RESCUE: TOO LITTLE, TOO LATE

Very little was done to rescue Jews during the Holocaust, that is a fact. It would be convenient, even satisfying to condemn the world for its lack of compassionate action, to oversimplify complicated issues by claiming that anti-Semitism was the root of all evil. Such a wide brush stroke, however, is not acceptable; it discounts the unsung heroes and martyrs who aided Jews at their own peril and ignores the efforts of some public institutions. Although the psychological motivations that underlie benevolent and malevolent behavior were relevant, they are not central in this history. The questions to be raised here concern the responses of governments, organizations, and individuals to the plight of the Jews. Specifically, it must be asked: what was known, what was believed, what was done, what might have been done? The answers, however, must not be influenced by the improved vision of hindsight. Fairness demands the re-creation of the appropriate context of time, place, and circumstance during a period awash with anxiety. The Western world endured twelve years of emotional, political, and economic shocks which influenced decisions on every level.

When the concentration camps were liberated and the Jewish survivors counted, their number approached forty thousand. There is no dearth of rationalization, breast-beating, or excuses to account for the failure of powerful nations and institutions which allowed the Nazis to kill six million. In fact, several successful rescue efforts, such as in Denmark and belatedly in Hungary, demonstrated that much more might have been done. As the leader of the free world during the war, the burden of inactivity falls heavily upon the United States. Great Britain, because of its policy of restricting immigration to Palestine, must share the guilt. No doubt, the failure of the refugee commissions of the League of Nations, the International Red Cross, and the international conferences in Evian and Bermuda, as well as the lack of activism by the great churches contributed to the genocide. Would the losses have been smaller if American Jewry had adopted a less diffident attitude toward Roosevelt? How destructive was the prevailing attitude that only the perpetrators of genocide were damnable while the mute bystanders were blameless? Accusations now will serve no purpose, but if future genocides are to be averted, then understanding the past is an absolute obligation.

ORDINARY PEOPLE

The challenges of rescue were more readily accepted by individuals than by institutions. Thus, nuns in convents saved Jewish children, while the papacy was silent; consuls representing governments as diverse as Japan and Switzerland defied their official instructions and helped Jews. In the occupied nations, gallant men and women from every walk of life, young and old, devout Christians and atheists, educated and unschooled, ignored dire warnings not to aid the persecuted. Perhaps someday we will understand the underlying rock of morality which motivated their goodness.

In Jerusalem, the Israeli government's Authority of Heroes and Martyrs at Yad Vashem designates deserving individuals as Righteous Gentiles. The title is bestowed on rescuers who derived no personal gain from their selflessness. The list contains about six thousand names at present. The search for others continues. It includes men and women from every European and some non-Western nations. While political leaders, from Vichy France to the United States, saw only the difficulties and possible negative consequences of saving Jews, ordinary people—dock workers, shopkeepers, farmers, and school teachers—opened their doors to the hunted. They hid children in attics, shared their food rations, and carried out their human waste. Often alone, sometimes in conjunction with other rescuers or partisan groups, they battled to deceive the Gestapo, to appear normal in the eyes of neighbors, and to prevent their children from revealing the secret guests in their basements or attics. The Nazis treated their altruism with efficient brutality; they were executed or sent to concentration camps. To discourage the protection of Jews, the SS was known to penalize uninvolved family members with equal harshness. Nonetheless, despite the danger, once the commitment was made, the righteous of all nations did not abandon their charges. After the war ended, when they were asked why they were willing to take such risks—often for people they did not know—the most common response was: "But what else could I do?"

Fleeing Jews passed along the names and addresses of safe houses, which in turn increased the danger to the hosts. Whenever possible, the persecuted were spirited across borders into neutral territory. Spain, Switzerland, England, and Palestine were their sometimes legal, often illegal, destinations. As has been noted earlier, the implementation of the Final Solution never moderated, even when invasion threatened the German heartland. That meant that in Poland and Czechoslovakia some Jews were hidden and supported for as long as six years. The memoirs of survivors express the physical and emotional strain experienced by both Jews and Gentiles who shared lives of unrelenting anxiety.

QUESTIONS OF OPPORTUNITIES

The ability to save Jews was affected by the type of control the Germans established in a region. Where Nazi authority reached into every sphere of human activity, such as in Germany and Poland, rescue attempts were most perilous. Where puppet governments had been installed, such as in Vichy France and Norway, the possibility for covert defiance of the regime was greater. The level of assimilation of the Jewish population also had an impact. For example, many of Italy's well-integrated Jews could disappear from German eyes by moving to a new location; on the other hand, a Latvian Orthodox Jew whose mastery of the native language was poor could not vanish among the local factory or farm workers. Every nationality, including Germans, can point to examples of righteous people among its citizens. The entrepreneur of *Schindler's List*, made famous in the motion picture, was Czech. Notable among the champions of Christian ethics in action were the villagers of Le Chambon sur Lignon in Vichy France. Under the leadership of their Huguenot pastor, they created a safety zone for Jews. Hundreds of men, women, and children colluded to save thousands of Jewish children and adults. Some Jews were given respite until the Maquis could guide them into Switzerland, others remained in the village until liberation. *The Diary of Anne Frank* is so well-known that the compassion, generosity, and courage of some Dutch people needs no further amplification. From the Pyrenees to the Urals, during a time when only might made right, possibly 5 percent of the population stayed faithful to their immutable concepts of decency, humanity, and courage.

WHAT WAS KNOWN?

Hitler had the advantage of doing the unthinkable, the unbelievable. For years, his ranting speeches, the threats in *Mein Kampf*, and the anti-Jewish legislation were viewed as appeals to German ultra-nationalism which would run its course in due time. Within Germany and in the occupied nations, no hint of the genocide was permitted to reach the public. News of the mass murders and the establishment of death camps were whispered in some circles but lacked verification. Then, in August, 1942, indisputable evidence reached the desk of Gerhart Riegner, an observer for the World Jewish Congress in Switzerland. A German industrialist, unnamed even now, contacted Riegner when he learned of the Wannsee decision. He hoped Riegner's contacts in America would find a way to stop the progression of the Final Solution. Riegner was stunned but wanted confirmation. He did not have to wait long before other sources corroborated the truth. As per arrangement, he passed this information through U.S. State Department channels to be forwarded to Rabbi Stephen S. Wise, the major spokesman for American Jewry. The State Department sought its own verification before contacting Rabbi Wise. It requested confirmation from the Vatican whose international sources were still intact. But the papacy would not or could not confirm the ongoing massacres. Unable to understand the lack of American reaction, Riegner alerted the British. Now the U.S. government had no choice but to notify Rabbi Wise. Eleven weeks had passed since the receipt of the first cable.

Though the alarm had been sounded, it did not cause a furious uproar in the Gentile world. With some notable exceptions, the Jews were alone in their distress. The general public and the Roosevelt administration reacted with moderate concern which was not translated into action. On December 17, 1942, the U.S. joined the other Allies in a general condemnation of German atrocities. That was all. Some of the rationale for the phlegmatic response will be discussed below; for the moment it should be noted that the world outside of Hitler's European fortress had been apprised of the fate of the Jews when the majority of them were still alive.

The authenticity of the ongoing atrocities was no longer in doubt. The Polish government in exile supplied much of the documentation, escaped prisoners told their horror stories, even photographs taken secretly at great risk were available. But the focus of the Gentile world was elsewhere. Except in the Jewish press, newspaper reports on such events as the destruction of the Warsaw ghetto were on the inside pages. There was a war on, and Hitler's war against the Jewish people was not fought in the main arena.

THE PROBLEM WITH NUMBERS

The statistics representing the national percentages of Jews murdered during the Holocaust do not reflect several factors which influenced the possibility of internal rescue. As mentioned above, the specific forms of Nazi rule and the degree of Jewish assimilation into the native mainstream affected the chances for sheltering Jews. Other variables must also be considered. Certainly, the length of German domination had a direct bearing. For example, in the case of Austria, a Gentile might have to look after a hidden Jew for seven years, in Hungary, the Nazis were in direct control for one year.

Topography, too, mattered. In the flat and almost woodless terrain of Holland, concealment was very difficult, while the mountains and forests of western Russia could swallow up thousands of refugees. The type and amount of aid dropped by Allied planes or smuggled across borders to support underground fighters varied considerably from place to place. Difficult to assess but surely significant was the quality of political and religious leadership. Thus, the Metropolitan of the Holy Synod of Bulgaria set an

example which strengthened the resolve in that country to withstand German pressure to transfer its Jews into Nazi hands. By contrast, Premier Lavalle of Vichy France tried to ingratiate himself with the SS with eager enactment of anti-Jewish legislation. Obviously, the lack or prevalence of anti-Semitic tradition related directly to Christians' willingness or reluctance to aid Jews. Some righteous Poles were hesitant to disclose their altruism even after the war was over, because they feared that their neighbors would not understand.

Finally, some weight must be given to the capability and/or inability of the Jews to act on their own behalf. The Jews of Budapest were saved largely as a result of the work of American Jews and the U.S. government, while the rescue of Danish Jewry was an entirely Christian effort. Within each of the countries implicated in the Holocaust, some residue of autonomy lingered. The Germans simply did not have sufficient manpower to manage every phase of the genocide. Puppet regimes received anti-Jewish directives and local police or militia were commonly used to round up Jews for deportation. The native authorities could obey Nazi instructions without protest or they could try to resist the abandonment of the Jews. Until the moment the trains to the death camps were sealed, some choices were still possible in the occupied areas: Give blind obedience to a superior force or take a grave risk and try to protect your innocent countrymen. The percentages listed below make their own eloquent statements concerning the prevalence of the former.

Approximate Percentages of Surviving Jews

Austria	33%
Baltic States (Lithuania, Latvia, Estonia)	10%
Belgium	55%
Czechoslovakia	17%
Denmark	99%
Greater Bulgaria	80%
France	70%
Greece	20%
Germany	20%
Holland	25%
Hungary	50%
Italy	85%
Poland	15%
Rumania	50%
USSR (occupied territories)	29%
Yugoslavia	27%

DELAY AND OBSTRUCTION IN THE U.S.

Half a century has passed since the death of Franklin Delano Roosevelt but his name and his policies continue to arouse passions of love and hate. When elected for the first time, his inauguration and that of Adolf Hitler took place only a few weeks apart. Some of the problems each was called upon to solve were comparable; severe unemployment, disillusionment with government, pressure from the radical right and left to use drastic measures, and disappointment with the outcome of World War I. The general misery set into motion a search for scapegoats; Jews and communists were often held to be conveniently responsible for everything from strikes to taxes. But in Germany the remedy was infinitely worse than the problems, whereas in America constitutional government survived.

Some historians pronounced harsh judgment upon FDR for his lack of action on behalf of European Jewry although no responsible researcher accused him of anti-Semitism. In fact, nearly all American Jews admired him, voted for him, and were grateful to him. Roosevelt made no religious distinction in his personal relationships or in his political appointments. His directives opened many more civil service jobs to the merit system and many bright young Jewish college graduates found employment in government agencies. It must be remembered that in the 1930s few hospitals, law firms, banks, universities, or large industrial and manufacturing companies hired Jews regardless of their qualifications. When Roosevelt broadened the civil service system, nominated Jews to his cabinet and to the Supreme Court, he never again needed to be concerned about the Jewish vote. A much larger constituency, however, was angered by this as well as his other New Deal efforts.

When the news of the ongoing genocide reached the United States, Jewish leaders believed that the president would share their deep distress and provide a haven for the persecuted. Perhaps Roosevelt did care, but not to the extent of jeopardizing the delicate balance of party politics. Congress had severely restricted immigration between 1924 and 1929, especially from eastern Europe. The legislature showed no inclination to lift these limitations in the 1930s when the number of jobless at home was still high and anti-Jewish feeling was significant. The incident involving the ship *Saint Louis* was a tragic case in point. Nine hundred Jews had been told by the Germans that their Cuban entry visas were valid even though that was not true. Upon reaching Havana, the Cuban government refused to permit the passengers to disembark. Urgent appeals to allow them into Miami, so clearly visible from the deck of the ship, were denied even though the American Jewish community was willing to defray the cost of their maintenance. The ship was forced to return to Hamburg and most of the men, women, and children became victims of the Nazis.

After 1942, the Germans no longer permitted Jews to leave, however, there were still possibilities for rescue. If the United States had provided energetic leadership, several of the neutral nations would have done more to provide for escaping victims of the Holocaust; England might have been more willing to ignore the illegal immigration to Palestine, and more visas might have been offered by non-European nations. Opportunities to save hundreds of children were frittered away by long bureaucratic delays in the State Department. Temporary reception centers could have been set up in neutral areas. American bombing missions could easily have inflicted damage on the perimeters of the death camps and the rail lines leading there. Several State Department officials, such as Breckenridge Long who controlled the immigration desk, were actively involved in preventing "these people" from entering the United States. Members of Congress counted the votes from the folks back home and decided that no action was their best action. It must be remembered that during the

early 1940s the United States was going through a national trauma. Most of the fleet had been sunk at Pearl Harbor, the war in the Pacific was going badly, England was hanging by a thread, and Hitler was at the gates of Moscow. The country exerted its supreme and total effort toward winning the war. To the cries for help for Europe's Jews, the administration responded again and again with assurances that winning the war was the first priority; the sooner Germany was defeated, the sooner Hitler's victims would be freed. How few Jews would remain alive to benefit from future assistance was as yet unimagined.

AMERICAN JEWRY

America's Jews were not passive in the face of the genocide. They organized rallies, circulated petitions, lobbied members of Congress, and collected money. Even though their voices were joined by some prominent Christians, they never received a resounding chorus. Today, after Martin Luther King, Jr. and others have instructed protesters in the art of civil disobedience, the activities of the Jews seem modest. They feared that too much pressure would backfire, first by increasing American anti-Semitism and second, by enraging the Nazis, causing them to commit greater atrocities. The division among Zionists and anti-Zionists further weakened the advocacy for immediate rescue attempts. It seemed to many American Jews that support of a Jewish homeland might be viewed as unpatriotic, likely to create the impression that their allegiance was divided. The Jewish conservative establishment was dismayed when the radical Committee for a Jewish Army ran an advertisement: "For Sale, 70,000 Jews; guaranteed to be human beings; at $50.00 a piece," in response to a Romanian initiative to "sell" its Jews. This, as well as many other suggestions, was negated by the State Department.

At the eleventh hour, the administration was finally energized. Secretary of the Treasury Henry Morgenthau provided the impetus. He had become aware of the inertia, even obstructionism, in the State Department. At his behest, a brief was prepared which exposed the tactics of the immigration officials who prevented the entry of Jews even within the established limits of the law. Morgenthau handed the president this exposé, provocatively entitled "On the Acquiescence of the Government on the Murder of the Jews." Roosevelt was shocked. He immediately initiated the War Refugee Board. Its purpose was rescue, its partner was the World Jewish Congress.

THE WAR REFUGEE BOARD

In January 1944, the greatest number of Jews in immediate danger of annihilation were the 144,000 assembled in Budapest. Eichmann was there, loading trains to Auschwitz. The resettlement myth was no longer believed and there was no doubt regarding the actual fate of the deported Jews. The Nazis were not without opposition in the destruction of this last of the major Jewish population centers. Efforts to save Jews had been mounted by the Hungarian Zionist Youth, by the International Red Cross, by the papal nuncio who issued false baptismal papers, and by the Swiss consular staff. The

Swiss embassy, flying its neutral flag, had become a haven for hundreds of Jews whom Eichmann could not claim. Nonetheless, the death trains were filled every day with terrified victims. This was the state of affairs when the American War Refugee Board went into action.

When the Board asked a young Swedish diplomat, Raoul Wallenberg, to undertake the mission to save Jews in Hungary, they made a brilliant choice. Wallenberg was daring, ingenious, and his pockets were lined with American money. His arrival in Budapest marked the beginning of a new intensity in rescue activities. Officially a member of the Swedish legation, he issued passports and safe-conduct passes, and bought houses in the name of Sweden. The protection of the neutral flag afforded safety to thousands. He organized a squad of four hundred operatives, young Jews, who imitated his bluff and bravado as they pulled prisoners out of transports, claiming they were under Swedish protection. The thousands thus saved required housing, food, medicine, and assurance, all of which the remarkable Wallenberg provided. His greatest exploit was executed as the Soviet Army approached the city. The SS commander had been ordered to murder all the remaining seventy thousand Jews before pulling out. Wallenberg, with a combination of threats and persuasion, convinced the general not to undertake such a horrendous massacre. It is tragic that the righteous Swede disappeared on the very day the Russians entered Budapest. Nothing was ever admitted, but it is probable that he was arrested by the Soviets who mistakenly believed him to be an American anti-Communist agent. Despite intensive inquiries, the exact nature of his fate remains unknown.

THE DANES

Hollywood could not have invented higher drama than the history of every nation which contravened the Nazi demand to cast out its Jews. It is not possible to detail here the many and varied responses to German pressure. There was Finland, uneasy ally of Germany in the war against the USSR, which simply said "no" to Himmler and kept its Jewish community of two thousand intact. Franco of Spain, the fascist dictator who had accepted German aid to attain power, remained neutral during the war. He turned a deaf ear to the complaint of the SS that he was frustrating Hitler's intent to obliterate Jewish existence. Franco's policies were responsible for saving forty thousand Jews, mostly refugees who were permitted to pass through Spain toward its harbors and overseas passage. Furthermore, Franco declared that Sephardic Jews, whose ancestors had been expelled by Ferdinand and Isabella in 1492, were de facto Spanish citizens, thus entitled to asylum in Spanish embassies. In Italy, even when Mussolini was in power, Jews who had fled from Greece, France, and Yugoslavia found protection. Only after Germany had occupied Italy did the trains begin to roll toward Auschwitz. The majority of Italian Jews lived through that traumatic final year of the war because the Italian people and their institutions were supportive.

A book on the history of the Holocaust cannot close without some detailed reference to Denmark. The number of Jewish survivors in that small occupied nation was a remarkable 99 percent. How and why was such an extraordinary rescue achieved? The pertinent play of events can be divided into three acts: first, a setting of the scene; second, the plot against the Jews; third, the rescue operation.

SETTING THE SCENE

The 6,500,000 Danes were swept into the German hegemony in a bloodless invasion during the spring of 1940. Since Danes were considered to be Aryans, and since cooperation was cheaper than force, the Germans opted for a lenient occupation policy. King Christian X, the parliament, (which included several Jewish members), the cabinet, and even Denmark's small army were left in place. Danish autonomy was, however, restricted in regard to its economic output and its foreign policy. As long as Danish food poured into the Reich, the German military presence under General Hermann von Hanecken and the diplomatic representative, Dr. Werner Best, were fairly unobtrusive.

Dr. Best, however, was an ambitious Nazi. What better way to ingratiate himself with his masters in Berlin than to institute anti-Jewish measures in Denmark? When Best approached Prime Minister Scavenius he was told the Danish cabinet would resign rather than pass such legislation. The king replied in the same manner, stating that there was no Jewish problem and all his subjects were equal.

That nearly eight thousand Danish Jews walked freely and unmarked on the streets of Copenhagen stuck like a bone in Werner Best's throat. Other problems were developing as well. The Danes had organized an effective anti-German underground which sabotaged goods going to Germany. German occupation soldiers complained that the Danes treated them with disdain and thus the hope of continued cooperation eroded. Best's situation became worrisome when Hitler berated him and warned him to do better. Empowered to teach the Danes the meaning of obedience, Best changed his approach. The executive and legislative branches of the Danish government were dissolved, the king became a virtual prisoner in his palace, and the army was forced to disband. This, predictably, increased the numbers and activities of the anti-German partisans. Best ordered the seizure of the records of the Jewish community; now he could identify nearly all the Jews in the kingdom. He inquired whether or not the Danish civil service would participate in any anti-Jewish action and the answer was a clear "no." Nonetheless, he decided that the time had come to execute a lightning strike against the Jews, surely it would restore him to Hitler's good graces.

THE PLOT

Best decided to arrest all Danish Jews on October 13, 1943, the eve of the Jewish New Year when most of them would be conveniently assembled in synagogues for religious services. In order to transport the intended prisoners as quickly as possible, he imported SS, German police, and railroad cars. Ships were readied in the harbor to ferry the sealed trains across the sea to Germany. General von Hanecken was opposed to the entire enterprise and had to be persuaded to allow fifty of his men to be made available in case of disturbances. The plan required the expertise of a maritime specialist. Best called in a German who was a long-time resident of Denmark, Georg F. Duckwitz. When apprised of the scheme, Duckwitz was appalled. At this juncture, Duckwitz made a decision which affected the lives of thousands; he followed the dictates of his conscience. He called on an old friend, a Dane, and revealed to him the fate awaiting the Jews of Denmark in just a few days.

A chain reaction was set into motion. The Danish underground was notified, neutral Sweden agreed to take in the escapees, the Jewish leadership had to be convinced that the threat was real, immediate provisional hiding places had to be found while long-range plans to smuggle out eight thousand people were formulated. The entire population of Denmark participated in an enormous conspiracy to save their Jews and defy the Nazis.

As word of the immediate danger spread throughout Copenhagen and to other Jewish communities, the intended victims simply disappeared. When the SS entered the main synagogue on Rosh Hashanah, it was empty. Hotels, hospitals, private homes in remote villages, Christian friends, churches, funeral parlors, taxis, ambulances and even the police became parties to the achievement of a single goal: Hide the Jews; do not by a word or a glance allow the Germans to find a single one. Amazingly, the secret was kept, the promise that the Jews of Denmark would not be abandoned was fulfilled.

THE ESCAPE

The few dozen Jews caught in the German net were people who did not believe or did not hear of the planned arrests. They were deported to the Teresienstadt concentration camp where nearly all survived due to the continued vigilance and food packages of the Danish Red Cross. The hidden Jews, meanwhile, had to be whisked out of the country as quickly as possible. Members of the underground found fishermen who were willing to risk Nazi vengeance and transport Jews to the Swedish shores. Throughout October there were daily departures. Danish doctors and nurses stood by every night to give injections to keep children asleep during the crossing. German ships patrolled these waters constantly and a crying child could endanger everyone on board. The Germans suspected that certain villages along the coast were used as departure points and tried to barricade the roads. In the skirmishes between the underground fighters and the SS, several Danes were killed. But, unlike the unfulfilled and wasted lives of so many millions, their deaths enabled others to live. The sea did not part on this exodus, instead, Danish fishermen conveyed the Jews across the waters of the Kattegat to safety.

Until the end of the war, that is, for nearly two years, the hospitality and generosity of the Swedish people and their government sustained the Danish Jews. When they returned home, they found their gardens had been tended by neighbors, their pets had been cared for, and their Torahs had been hidden in churches.

ACCOUNTING FOR THE DANISH ACHIEVEMENT

It is very tempting to use the Danish experience as an example of the possibilities of rescue which other peoples did not attempt. No doubt, a greater commitment would have saved lives, but it is a fallacy to believe the success of the Danes could easily have been duplicated elsewhere. Every European nation had distinct and unique problems during the Nazi era. Prevailing attitudes toward Jews differed widely, the determination of native leadership varied considerably, and diverse geographic factors affected the possibility of keeping Jews safe. The Danes saw an opportunity and went into action, that fact is forever to their credit.

The achievement was predicated on some, perhaps all, of the following prerequisites:

1. The Danes had a well-established humanitarian attitude toward their fellow men. Anti-Semitism had been outlawed since 1814!
2. The political leadership set the tone for ethical behavior.
3. The religious leadership was not intimidated and urged their parishioners to aid their imperiled countrymen.
4. When the Germans executed Danish saboteurs, they believed the population would be cowed, instead the opposite result was effected.
5. The willingness and closeness of neutral Sweden provided a necessary haven for the potential victims.
6. The underground movement was well organized and eager to prove its effectiveness.
7. The Jews were well integrated; their number was small, and except for their religion, they were highly assimilated into Danish society.

SOME CONCLUDING THOUGHTS

The Holocaust is a history of human failure. We cherish the exploits of a Wallenberg or the triumph of the Danes because they lit a candle in the darkness of savagery and irrationality. Hitler and Himmler represent the triumph of absolute evil. They were criminals who were totally indifferent to the human suffering caused by their criminality. German Nazis and their foreign collaborators camouflaged with patriotic slogans their inhumanity, their terrible ambitions and greed. It seems that depravity continues to have its disciples. The nightly news brings pictures of the suffering of the innocent into our living rooms nearly every day.

The Holocaust repudiated the concept that the teachings of Christ were practiced in the daily lives by most of those who professed to be believers. The onlookers who averted their eyes in order to keep their consciences untroubled also have much to answer for. Unless we become our brothers' keepers, a repetition of genocide in some part of the world is certain. We do not know the color, the nationality, the religion of either the next victims or the perpetrators. Sadly, events since 1945 bear out this dire prediction.

When, in 1948, the United Nations voted the state of Israel into legitimate existence, it discharged an act of international contrition. Perhaps a sense of guilt also motivates the unprecedented support by American Jews for that small, beleaguered nation. Israel is of extraordinary significance to the Jews of the world. It ended a sometimes hidden, sometimes overt sense of rootlessness and alienation experienced even by many Jews who were well integrated into their native countries. Israeli success in its struggle to survive against great odds is a legacy for all Jews. Pride has replaced the image of the powerless, submissive Jew; and the tragic lesson of the Holocaust can be summed up in two words: *never again.*

Glossary and Abbreviations

Abwehr: German military counterintelligence.

Appell: Roll call, often lasting hours.

Aktion: Nazi operation involving the deportation and/or killing of Jews.

Anschluss: German annexation of Austria, March 1938.

Bermuda Conference: Anglo-USA conference which failed to solve the refugee problem, April 1943.

Boycott: Nazi order to the German public to stop all economic dealings with Jews, April, 1933.

Bund: Anti-Zionist Jewish socialist party.

CV: *Centralverein deutscher Staatsbuerger juedisches Glaubens*: "union of Jewish citizens of Germany."

Der Stuermer: *The Attacker*; Julius Streicher's violently anti-Jewish weekly newspaper.

Displaced Persons: Europeans made homeless by the Nazis or as a result of World War II.

Einsatzgruppen: Mobile killing units of SS and SD members used mainly in Poland and Russia.

Endloesung: see Final Solution.

Evian Conference: International conference held in 1938 which failed to alleviate the refugee problem.

Final Solution: Nazi plan to solve Jewish problem by annihilation.

Gauleiter: Nazi administrative leader in a *Gau*, or district.

General Gouvernement: Western Polish territory conquered by Germany and administered by Hans Frank.

Genocide: The partial or total destruction of a racial, religious, or national group.

Gestapo: *Geheime Staatspolizei,* Nazi's secret state police.

Judenrat: Jewish council of elders, used by Germans in ghetto administration.

Judenrein: "cleansed of Jews," Nazi policy of removal of Jews.

Kapo: Prisoner in a concentration camp who was in charge of other inmates.

Kristallnacht: "Night of broken glass," pogrom carried out between November 8–9, 1938, in Greater Germany.

Lager: Camp, as in concentration or death camp.

Lebensborn: Kidnapping by SS of foreign children.

Lebensraum: "Room to live," Euphemism for German policy of expansion.

Madagascar Plan: Briefly considered notion by Germany to ship four million Jews to the island of Madagascar.

Maquis: French guerrilla fighting organization during Word War II.

Mischlinge: Nazi classification for people of Jewish-Christian parentage.

Mein Kampf: "My Struggle," book by Adolf Hitler which outlined his program of German totalitarianism.

Munich Agreement: Appeasement policy of England and France which permitted Hitler to take part of Czechoslovakia.

Musselman: Term denoting a concentration camp prisoner who had given up the struggle to stay alive.

NSDAP: *Nationalsozialistische Deutsche Arbeiterpartei*, "National Socialist German Workers' Party," the Nazi party.

Nuremberg Laws: German legislation which deprived Jews of citizenship rights, passed in 1938.

Protocols of the Elders of Zion: Anti-Semitic forgery claiming an international plot by Jews to attain world domination.

putsch: Attempted coup d'état.

Righteous of the Nations or Righteous Gentiles: Non-Jews who saved Jewish lives during the Holocaust.

RSHA: *Reichssicherheitshauptamt*, central German security department under the Nazis.

SA: *Sturmabteilung*, the Brownshirts; Nazi political storm troops.

SS: *Schutzstaffel*, the Blackshirts; elite of Nazi storm troopers.

Third Reich: Germany under the Nazis.

Umschlagplatz: Assembly place for deportees.

Wannsee Conference: 1942 meeting of Nazi leaders which decided on the implementation of the Final Solution.

War Refugee Board: U.S. government special agency to rescue and aid victims of Nazi persecution.

Wehrmacht: German armed forces.

World Jewish Congress: Represents a voluntary association of major Jewish organizations.

Yad Vashem: Israeli authority of commemoration and research on the Holocaust.

ZOB: *Zydowska Organizacja Bojowa,* Jewish fighting organization in Poland, active in Warsaw ghetto uprising.

Bibliography
and Selected Readings

The amount of material on the Holocaust is massive and the following books represent a small selection. The rationale for including a book while excluding hundreds of other excellent works was based on these factors: (1) Most students read English only, thus the research published in other languages is not useful. (2) Most books on Holocaust history contain further bibliographies; a long list here is likely to be redundant. (3) The books catalogued below are based on recommendations by students and the author. (4) The works listed should be easily available in university and public libraries.

ANTHOLOGIES AND ESSAY COLLECTIONS

Bettelheim, Bruno, *Surviving and Other Essays.* New York: Vintage Books, 1980.

Chartok, Roselle, and Jack Spencer, eds., *The Holocaust Years: Society on Trial.* New York: Bantam Books, 1978.

Friedlander, Albert H., *Out of the Whirlwind.* New York: Schocken Books, 1976.

Furet, Francois, *Unanswered Questions, Nazi Germany and the Genocide of the Jews.* New York: Schocken Books, 1989.

Laska, Vera, *Women in the Resistance and in the Holocaust, The Voices of Eyewitnesses.* Westport CT: Greenwood Press, 1983.

Niewyk, Donald, ed., *Problems in European Civilization, The Holocaust.* Lexington MA: D.C. Heath and Company, 1992.

Ritter, Carol, and Sondra Myers, *The Courage to Care, Rescuers of Jews during the Holocaust.* New York: New York University, 1986.

Roth, John K., and Michael Berenbaum, eds., *Holocaust Religious and Philosophical Implications*. New York: Paragon House, 1989.

ANTI-SEMITISM IN HISTORY

Abel, Ernest L., *The Roots of Anti-Semitism*. Cranbury NJ: Associated University Presses, 1975.

Hay, Malcolm, *Thy Brother's Blood. The Roots of Christian Anti-Semitism*. New York: Hart, 1965.

Katz, Jacob, *From Prejudice to Destruction, Anti-Semitism, 1700–1933*. Cambridge MA: Harvard University Press, 1980.

Rose, Paul Laurence, *German Question/Jewish Question, Revolutionary Antisemitism from Kant to Wagner*. Princeton: Princeton University Press, 1990.

DOCUMENTARY COLLECTIONS

Arad, Yitzhak, Yisrael Gutman, and Abraham Margialot, eds., *Documents on the Holocaust*. Jerusalem: Yad Vashem, 1981.

Hitler, Adolf, *Mein Kampf*. Trans. by Ralph Manheim. Boston: Houghton Miflin, 1943.

Mosse, George L., ed., *Nazi Culture*. New York: Schocken Books, 1981.

Noakes, J., and G. Pridham, eds., *Nazism: A History in Documents and Eyewitness Accounts*. Vols. 1–2. New York: Schocken Books, 1990.

Remack, Joachim, *The Nazi Years, A Documentary History*. Prospect Heights, ILL: Wavelength Press, Inc., 1990.

Snyder, Louis, ed., *Hitler's Third Reich, A Documentary History*. Chicago: Nelson Hall, 1981.

GENERAL HOLOCAUST HISTORIES

Bauer, Yehuda, *A History of the Holocaust*. New York: Franklin Watts, 1982.

Dawidovicz, Lucy S., *The War Against the Jews 1933–1945*. Philadelphia: Jewish Publication Society, 1975.

Hilberg, Raul, *The Destruction of the European Jews*. Vols. 1–3. New York and London: Holmes & Meier, 1985.

Poliakov, Leon, *Harvest of Hate, The Nazi Program for the Destruction of the Jews of Europe*. New York: Holocaust Library, 1979.

Yahil, Leni, *The Holocaust.* Trans. by Ina Friedman and Haya Galai. New York and Oxford: Oxford University Press, 1990.

MODERN GERMAN HISTORIES

Carr, William, *A History of Germany 1815–1990.* London: Edward Arnold, 1991.

Eyck, Eric, *A History of the Weimar Republic.* Vols. 1 and 2. Trans. by H.P. Hanson and R.G.L. Waite. New York: Atheneum, 1970.

Halperin, S. William, *Germany Tried Democracy.* New York: Thomas Y. Cromwell Co., 1946.

Shirer, William, *The Rise and Fall of the Third Reich.* New York: Simon & Schuster, 1960.

Spielvogel, Jackson J., *Hitler and Nazi Germany.* Englewood Cliffs NJ: Prentice Hall, 1992.

Valentin, Veit, *The German People.* New York: Alfred A. Knopf, 1946.

MONOGRAPHIC WORKS

Ainsztein, Ruben, *The Warsaw Ghetto Revolt.* New York: Holocaust Library, 1979.

Arad, Yitzhak, *Belzec, Sobibor, Treblinka, The Operation Reinhard Death Camps.* Bloomington IN: Indiana University Press, 1987.

Breitman, Richard, *The Architect of Genocide: Himmler and the Final Solution.* New York: Alfred A. Knopf, 1991.

Donat, Alexander, *The Holocaust Kingdom.* New York: Holocaust Library, 1978.

Gilbert, Martin, *Auschwitz and the Allies.* New York: Henry Holt and Company, 1981.

Gutman, Ysrael, *The Jews of Warsaw.* Bloomington IN: Indiana University Press, 1982.

Hoehne, Heinz, *The Order of the Death's Head.* Trans. by Martin Secker and Warburg Limited. Hamburg: Verlag der Spiegel, 1966.

Lifton, Jay, *The Nazi Doctors, Medical Killings and the Psychology of Genocide.* Scranton PA: Harper Collins Publishers, 1986.

Lipshitz, C.U., *Franco, Spain, the Jews and the Holocaust.* New York: KTAV Publishing House, Inc., 1984.

Marrus, Michael, and Robert O. Paxton, "The Nazis and the Jews in Western Occupied Europe 1940–1944." *Journal of Modern History.* 54, 1981.

Marrus, Michael. *Vichy France and the Jews.* New York: Basic Books, 1981.

Mueller, Ingo, *The Courts of the Third Reich.* Trans. by Deborah Lucas Schneider. Cambridge MA: Harvard University Press, 1993.

Novitch, Miriam, *Sobibor, Martyrdom and Revolt,* New York: Waldon Press, 1980.

Oliner, Samuel P., and Pearl M. Oliner, *The Altruistic Personality.* New York: The Free Press, 1988.

Steiner, Jean-Francois, *Treblinka.* New York: The New American Library, 1979.

Thalmann, Rita, and Emanuel Feinermann. *Crystal Night, 9–10 November, 1938.* Trans. by Gilles Cremonesi. New York: Holocaust Library, 1974.

Thomas, Gordon, and Max Morgan Witts, *Voyage of the Damned.* New York: Stein and Day, 1974.

Tusa, Ann, and John Tusa, *The Nuremberg Trial.* New York: Atheneum, 1986.

Waite, Robert L., *The Psychopathic God: Adolf Hitler.* New York: Basic Books, 1977.

Wyman, David S., *The Abandonment of the Jews, America and the Holocaust, 1941–1945.* New York: Random House, 1984.

Zuccotti, Susan, *The Italians and the Holocaust.* New York: Basic Books, 1987.

OTHER RELATED BOOKS

Allport, Gordon W., *The Nature of Prejudice.* Reading MA: Addison-Wesley, !986.

Arendt, Hannah, *The Origins of Totalitarianism.* New York: Harcourt Brace, 1958.

Engelmann, Bert, *In Hitler's Germany, Daily Life in the Third Reich.* Trans. by Krishna Winston. New York: Pantheon Books, 1986.

Howe, Irving, *World of Our Fathers.* New York: Harcourt Brace Janovich, 1976.

Patai, Raphael, *The Vanished World of Jewry.* New York: Macmillan Publishing Co. Inc., 1980.

Sachar, Abram Leon, *A History of the Jews.* New York: Alfred A. Knopf, 1958.

PERSONAL AND BIOGRAPHICAL WORKS

Astor, Gerald, *The Last Nazi, The Life and Times of Dr. Joseph Mengele.* New York: Donald I. Fine, Inc., 1985.

Borowski, Tadeus, *This Way for the Gas, Ladies and Gentlemen.* Trans. by Barbara Vedder. New York: Penguin Books, 1959.

Botwinick, Rita, *Winzig, Germany 1933–1946, The History of a Town Under the Third Reich.* Westport CT: Praeger, 1992.

Crome, Len, *Unbroken, Resistance and Survival in the Concentration Camps.* London: Lawrence and Wishart, 1988.

Des Pres, Terrence, *The Survivor: An Anatomy of Life in Death Camps.* New York: Oxford University Press, 1976.

Friedlaender, Saul, *When Memory Comes.* New York: Farrar and Straus, 1979.

Gross, Leonard, *The Last Jews of Berlin.* New York: Simon & Schuster, 1982.

Heck, Alphons, *A Child of Hitler.* Fredrick CO: Renaissance House, 1985.

Kershaw, Ian, *Profiles in Power—Hitler.* London: Longman Group, 1991.

Korczak, Janus, *Ghetto Diary.* New York: Holocaust Library, 1978.

Levi, Primo, *Survival in Auschwitz, The Nazi Assault on Humanity.* Trans. by Stuart Woolf. New York: Collier, 1966.

Meed, Vladka, *On Both Sides of the Wall.* New York: Summit Books, 1986.

Rubinstein, Erna F., *The Survivor in Us All, Four Young Sisters in the Holocaust.* Hamden CT: The Shoe String Press, 1983.

Wiesel, Eli, *Night.* Trans. by S. Rodway. New York: Bantam Books, 1960.

REFERENCE BOOKS

Encyclopedia Judaica. Jerusalem: Keter Publishing, 1973.

Gilbert, Martin, *Atlas of the Holocaust.* New York: Da Capo Press, Inc., 1982.

Marrus, Michael R., *The Holocaust in History.* Hanover, NH and London: University Press of New England, 1987.

Snyder, Louis L., ed., *Encyclopedia of the Third Reich.* New York: Paragon House, 1989.

RIGHTEOUS CHRISTIANS

Anger, Per, *With Raoul Wallenberg in Budapest.* Trans. by David Mel Paul, and Margarita Paul. New York: Holocaust Library, 1981.

Flenders, Harold, *Rescue in Denmark.* New York: Holocaust Library, 1963.

Hallie, Phillip, *Lest Innocent Blood be Shed, The Story of Le Chambon and how Goodness Happened There.* New York: Harper Torchbooks, 1979.

Tec, Nechama, *When Light Pierced the Darkness, Christian Rescue of Jews in Poland.* New York: Oxford University Press, 1986.

Index

Index